THE
FALLEN

GARDAÍ KILLED IN SERVICE
1922–49

COLM WALLACE

The
History
Press
Ireland

This book is dedicated to the Gardaí who gave their lives in the defence of Ireland and its people.

Tiomnaím an leabhar seo do na Gardaí a thug a mbeatha agus iad ag cosaint tír agus pobal na hÉireann.

First published 2017

The History Press Ireland
50 City Quay
Dublin 2
Ireland
www.thehistorypress.ie

The History Press Ireland is a member of Publishing Ireland,
the Irish book publishers' association.

British Library Cataloguing in Publication Data.
A catalogue record for this book is available from the British Library.

ISBN 978 0 7509 8376 1

Typesetting and origination by The History Press

CONTENTS

Acknowledgements 5

Introduction 7

1. Garda Henry Phelan 17
2. Sergeant James Woods 27
3. Garda Patrick O'Halloran 37
4. Detective Arthur Nolan 53
5. Sergeant Thomas Griffin & Garda John Murrin 61
6. Garda Thomas Dowling 73
7. Sergeant James Fitzsimons & Garda Hugh Ward 87
8. Detective Timothy O'Sullivan 103
9. Superintendent John Curtin 117
10. Detective Patrick McGeehan 127
11. Detective John Roche 141
12. Detective Richard Hyland & Detective Sergeant
    Patrick McKeown 155
13. Detective Sergeant Denis O'Brien 169
14. Detective Michael Walsh 185
15. Detective George Mordaunt 193
16. Garda Denis Harrington 205
17. Garda James Byrne 213
18. Chief Superintendent Seán Gantly 225

Afterword 235
Appendix 236
Notes 239
Further Reading 251
Index 253

ACKNOWLEDGEMENTS

This book has been a long time coming, but it was worth every second. I could not have finished, or even started, without the care and support of my family and friends. Whenever I have needed them, they have been there.

First and foremost, I would like to thank Rebecca for her unlimited patience in putting up with me while I was writing this book. I could not have undertaken this project without her endless support and belief that I could do it. A heartfelt thanks also to Kathleen, who kindly proofread this book several times, making it what it is today, with positivity and patience.

I am indebted to Tom Hurley, whose documentary, *A Boy of Good Character*, gave me a valuable insight into the story of Henry Phelan.

A special thank you to the staff of the National Archives, Military Archives, UCD Archives and National Library of Ireland who provided invaluable help with my research.

Finally, I would like to thank my mother and father for their unending love, support and encouragement. Without their selfless dedication to my education, I would not be writing these words.

INTRODUCTION

'You will have one great advantage over any previous police force in Ireland. You will be the people's guardians, not their oppressors; your authority will be derived from the people, not from their enemies.'

Michael Collins

'You are going out unarmed into a hostile area. You may be murdered, your barracks burned, your uniform taken off you, but you must carry on and bring peace to the people.'

Eoin O'Duffy, Garda Commissioner

Several systems of policing have existed in Ireland over the centuries with varying levels of success. The most sophisticated of these were the County Constabularies, in existence since the beginning of the nineteenth century. These were individual bodies responsible for maintaining law and order in their own local areas until 1836, when they were amalgamated with the Irish Constabulary. Belfast and Derry Police worked as separate entities until 1865 and 1870 respectively, when they too were subsumed into the umbrella organisation.[1] The Irish Constabulary was awarded the prefix 'Royal' in 1867 for their part in the suppression of the Fenian Rising of the same year. The Royal Irish Constabulary (RIC) was overseen from its headquarters in Dublin Castle, for seven centuries the ceremonial head of British rule in Ireland. John Morley, a British politician and supporter of Home Rule, would describe the British regime in Dublin as 'the best machine that has ever been invented for governing a country against its will'.[2] The police force was an integral part of implementing law and order on behalf of this regime.

By the end of the nineteenth century, the RIC was predominantly made up of Catholics and Irishmen. Despite this, it never managed to achieve the full support of the population. The force found itself as the main enforcers of tenant evictions during the Potato Famine and later the Land War, thus convincing many Irish citizens that the police were the enemy, rather than the protector, of the people. The RIC's association with the suppression of the Easter Rising and their relationship with the hated Black and Tans and Auxiliaries during the War of Independence did little to help their reputation in the country.

Éamon de Valera outlined republican policy succinctly in 1918 when he stated, 'Sinn Féiners have a definite policy and the people of Ireland are determined to make it a success; that is, to make English rule absolutely impossible in Ireland.'[3] In order to achieve this goal it was important to undermine the most fundamental of governmental duties: policing. Republicans knew that the RIC played a vital role in the day-to-day administration of the county and if the constabulary was to collapse then independence from Britain was sure to follow. In January 1919, on the same day that the first Dáil met in the Mansion House, two members of the RIC were killed. Their deaths are often cited as the first in the War of Independence. Patrick McDonnell and James O'Connell were shot dead by the IRA in an ambush in Soloheadbeg, County Tipperary. The two men were Irish Catholics. Over 400 more of their colleagues would suffer a similar fate before the end of the conflict.

The repeated ambushes throughout the 1919–1921 period resulted in hundreds of casualties and had a profound effect on the morale of the force. As the campaign intensified mass resignations followed. Some officers left their posts due to fear of the IRA while others resigned in sympathy with the republican cause. These resignations, along with the loss of RIC men killed in action and an unprecedented spate of suicides amongst serving policemen, left a shortage of officers. The decision was taken to withdraw the remaining members of the RIC from their vulnerable rural stations to larger towns where large numbers of constables were consolidated in fortified barracks, supplemented by British ex-soldiers in the form of the Black and Tans and Auxiliaries. This left large tracts of Irish countryside untouched by law and order. With no one to uphold the peace in many rural areas, petty crime became an issue, causing the IRA to step into the breach and found the Irish Republican Police, who oversaw policing in much of the country until the end of the War of Independence.

A treaty with Britain, ending the war, was signed in December 1921 and ratified by the Dáil the following month. It gave the Irish control of most of their own domestic affairs and also included provision for satisfying the Irish demand for disbandment of the RIC, who had been denounced by Eoin MacNeill of the first Dáil as a 'force of spies, a force of traitors and a force of perjurers'.[4] The formation of a replacement police force was thus one of the most pressing items on the agenda. Kevin O'Higgins described the unenviable situation the government found themselves in: 'We were simply eight young men in the City Hall standing in the ruins of one administration with the foundation of another not yet laid and with wild men screaming through the keyhole. No police force was functioning throughout the country and no system of justice was operating.'[5]

The first meeting to consider the prospective policing body was held on 9 February 1922 in the Gresham Hotel in Dublin. The government was represented by Minister for Defence, Richard Mulcahy and Éamonn Duggan, the Minister for Home Affairs. A committee was quickly set up under Duggan, the son of an RIC man himself, to decide on the fundamentals of the new constabulary. The committee also consisted of several former RIC officers. It was decided that the republican police that had served during the war were unsuitable due to a lack of training and discipline. A new force would therefore be necessary. Michael Staines, 1916 veteran and acting chief of the Republican Police, was appointed the first commissioner and he was responsible for many of the changes that made the Gardaí what it is today.[6] The RIC was in the process of disbandment, meaning Staines and his committee had just months to design, train and deploy an effective police force.

The committee proposed a non-political police force of 4,300 officers, broadly similar to the RIC, which would be directly account-able to the elected government and the Minister for Home Affairs. Unlike in England, where the police was divided into small sub-units, the Civic Guard would be centrally controlled but dispatched to 800 smaller stations throughout the country. The only exception was Dublin City, which would be policed by the Dublin Metropolitan Police (DMP). This was eventually amalgamated with the Garda Síochána in 1925. The badge was altered and the Civic Guard wore blue to distinguish them from the RIC, who had worn bottle-green uniforms. The changes amounted to far more than crests and cloth-ing, however.

Although the RIC had been predominantly Catholic, the upper echelons of the organisation had been mainly Protestant and union-ist. The new police force was primarily drawn from ex-members of the IRA, many of whom would have loathed the RIC and would never have contemplated joining the former policing authority. The initial criteria for membership were stringent: the applicant had to be an unmarried male, aged between 19 and 27 and was usually required to have fought in the War of Independence. He needed a written reference from a superior officer in the IRA, as well as a statement of good character from the local parish priest. The minimum height requirement was 5ft 9in, with a chest meas-urement of no less than 36in. The applicant had to be educated enough to have a good standard of reading, writing and arithmetic, a skill not universally possessed in 1920s Ireland. The new force was also strictly non-political and concerned itself only with civil and criminal matters. Furthermore, serving Civic Guards were dis-qualified from running in elections.

The government was mindful that large numbers of anti-Treaty republicans were determined to frustrate the new police at an early stage and the recruitment process was not widely announced. It was of paramount importance that the recruits could be relied upon to stay loyal to the pro-Treaty government, so their political affiliations were closely scrutinised. The first member of the Civic Guard, Sergeant McAvinney, was enrolled on 20 February, less than two weeks after the initial meeting. McAvinney and his colleagues faced a huge number of fundamental problems in the earliest days of the force. Shelter, perhaps the most basic requirement of all, was an immediate issue. As soon as the Crown forces evacuated a suitable building in 1922, the Irish Army moved in, using it as a training base in anticipation of the inevitable Civil War. For the first weeks of its existence, the Civic Guard could find no headquarters from which to conduct their operations.[7]

The first batch of recruits was eventually dispatched to the Society Showgrounds in Ballsbridge, a venue that was hopelessly inadequate for the education of a prospective police force. Much of the training and drilling of the new recruits was carried out by ex-members of the RIC, availing of the very same booklets and manuals that they had used prior to disbandment. It was probably common sense to have the training supervised by former policemen who had years of experience in maintaining law and order, but the appointment of ex-RIC men was a source of bitterness and anger amongst many former IRA volunteers who, up until months before, had viewed these men as their sworn enemy.[8] Even the men who had resigned from the RIC in sympathy with the republican cause during the war were viewed with deep suspicion by those who had secured Ireland's freedom. The deputy commissioner of the new force, Patrick Walsh, was also an ex-RIC man, a fact that was particularly unpalatable for rank-and-file officers.

George Lawlor, who was later to become a superintendent and founder of the Garda Technical Bureau, wrote of his time in the training camp and the tension that existed between former IRA soldiers and their RIC compatriots:

> My dislike for the police force remained with me and my training
> under ex-officers of the RIC did not soften my feelings towards the
> profession. The position of things did not make for the best form of
> police training. The knowledge obtained by men in law and general
> police duties was poor.[9]

Lawlor would not be the only Garda with reservations about the
training he received, and from whom he received it.

On 25 April 1922, the recruits were transferred to Kildare Military
Barracks. Shortly after arriving, a cohort of recruits, a minority of
whom were loyal to anti-Treaty republicans, mutinied. Angry and
disappointed by the presence of high-ranking former RIC officers in the new force, they refused to accept Staines' authority as
commissioner and took over the armaments and the running of
the camp. Staines was forced to leave the barracks under cover of
darkness and tender his resignation to the fledgling government.
A number of the rebels defected to the republican side, although the
vast majority would stay loyal to the pro-Treaty government. It was
arguably the biggest crisis in the history of An Garda Síochána but
proved to be mercifully short-lived. Michael Collins himself visited
the camp several times in its aftermath and came to a compromise
with the rebelling Gardaí whereby the RIC members would be reas-
signed as civilian advisers. The situation was quickly back under
control and former IRA commander and army chief of staff Eoin
O'Duffy was chosen as the new commissioner.

O'Duffy, who had served bravely in the War of Independence,
proved to be a tireless and energetic leader, although one who
courted controversy on occasion. The Monaghan native was a strict
disciplinarian who wanted the Civic Guard to be seen as an ordered
body of religious, nationalist and temperate men. He stood by his
recruits in almost every situation, regardless of the accusations lev-
elled against them. After a less than exemplary start, O'Duffy later
privately admitted that the early attitude to the Civic Guard was one
of distrust but under his stewardship it eventually began to mould
itself into a formidable and effective police force.

The new recruits were initially given firearms training but after the mutiny it was decided that the Civic Guard would be an unarmed force, a ruling that caused much surprise and debate throughout Ireland. The country found itself facing the frightening prospect of Civil War. The newly formed nation was also awash with guns and the timing of the announcement baffled many. The seeds of this radical policy had been sown after several tragic incidents in the early days of the Guards, however. Between April and September 1922, three trainee officers were accidentally shot dead by their colleagues, while two members of the force committed suicide using a gun. These tragedies, along with the mutiny, caused the provisional government to rethink their initial plan to issue a gun to each member of the Guards and an unarmed policy was adopted, one which has continued to this very day.[10] It was decided that any armed disturbances, especially political ones, would not be dealt with by members of the Civic Guard, instead being handled by the army of the state. Crucially, this limited the number of dealings that Guards had with the IRA in the troubled early years of the 1920s, helping to depoliticise the force and cement their reputation as honest brokers in political disputes.[11]

The Criminal Investigation Department (CID) was an example of what the Gardaí could have been. The CID was also in existence in Ireland for the duration of the Civil War and its officers were permitted to use arms in the discharge of their duty. Acting as a parallel plain-clothes police force, the CID was based mainly in the Dublin area, its headquarters being Oriel House. This armed policing unit was completely separate from the Civic Guard and soon became mired in controversy and criticised over their brutal methods. Despite being heavily armed, it suffered four deaths at the hands of the IRA in the course of its short existence. The unarmed Guards, often commended for their even-handedness during the Civil War, were more fortunate, suffering just one fatality. It would later be revealed that Liam Lynch, Chief of Staff of the IRA towards the end of the conflict, had forbidden the killing of the unarmed Guards, although he encouraged attacks on their barracks.[12]

Despite the lack of fatalities, the Guards were not popular amongst republicans. The government's claim that the force's only duty was to apprehend criminals and that they would take no part in politics was refuted by many on the republican side. Rory O'Connor openly said that the force was not needed as policing could be carried out by the Irish Republican Army. He also claimed, falsely, that the Civic Guard was largely made up of the hated Black and Tans.[13] The laws and court system of the British era remained largely unchanged and republicans were immediately hostile to the new force, which they saw as a continuation of the status quo.

On 28 March 1922, the subversives ordered that recruitment to the Civic Guard be halted and added that any man who insisted on joining the force was to be boycotted in much the same way as the RIC had been. Several warnings were posted in the first days of the Civic Guard, threatening what the Irregulars called 'the semi-military force' with serious repercussions if they did not vacate their posts.

They followed through with their threats. Instances of violence against potential recruits were common in the early days of the force, a number of trainees being intimidated, beaten and kidnapped. On 10 April 1922, a party of men called at a house in Skreen, a village situated near Dromore West, County Sligo. They asked for a young man named Barrett, who was known to have enlisted in the Civic Guard shortly before. When his father would not allow his son outside, they shot the elderly man in the head instead, before fleeing. Just days later, republicans occupied a number of important buildings in Dublin City, amongst them the Four Courts. From this base they sent peace terms to the government in a desperate attempt to avoid Civil War. Foremost among their demands was the disbandment of the new police force and the responsibility for the detection of criminals to be handed back to the IRA. These terms were rejected. The Civil War began at the end of June 1922, just before the police force was to be deployed. Without the support of a vocal minority of the country, there was a widespread sense of foreboding that the Civic Guard would get off to a violent start.[14]

The last RIC officers left their posts in August 1922. Meanwhile, regular incidences of crime, agrarian violence and attacks on landowners and unionists necessitated the swift deployment of the new recruits of the Civic Guard. By September much of the east of the country had been pacified and the first detachment of Gardaí was deployed to the parts of the twenty-six counties considered safe by the National Army. Tracts of the country, particularly Munster and Connaught, remained paralysed by violence, however, and were not considered safe for the new recruits. Even some of the areas regarded as peaceful faced spontaneous attacks; stations in Kilkee, County Clare, Wolfhill, County Laois and Blessington, County Wicklow, were all attacked and ransacked shortly after the Guards had been installed.[15] The IRA had broken the morale of the RIC during the War of Independence and they appeared to be following a similar path with the Civic Guard. It was widely speculated that the unarmed Guards were left vulnerable to attacks by members of the anti-Treaty IRA and between September 1922 and the summer of 1923 over 200 Garda stations were attacked, bombed or burned and 400 Guards were assaulted, stripped or robbed.[16]

Although the repeated attacks by republicans continued, the Guards attempted to stay above the political fray and stick to strictly criminal matters. In November 1922, Henry Phelan was shot dead in Mullinahone in an attack suspected to have been carried out by republicans. He was the first Garda killed in the line of duty. Surprisingly, no other Garda was killed during the conflict. The IRA had realised that the attacks were unpopular with the general public. The organisation released a further memorandum a month after his death that forbade violence against unarmed Guards.

The clashes with the IRA continued over the decades, however, and many Gardaí were killed in fire fights. Even more disturbingly, on occasion the IRA ambushed and killed policemen who they felt had been giving the organisation too much attention. Although the IRA remained the greatest threat, other dangers befell unsuspecting Gardaí. In the history of the Free State, Gardaí met their deaths at the hands of armed bank robbers, deranged lunatics and even colleagues and fellow members of the force.

In each case the Gardaí identified suspects almost immediately but obtaining convictions proved to be no easy task. Many of the attacks were carefully planned and the perpetrators were able to avoid detection or receive an acquittal in court. When the criminal was identified, tried and convicted, the penalty varied. One of the suspects was declared insane, another was sentenced to just twelve months in prison. In other cases, examples were made of those found to have murdered Gardaí. A number of prisoners were condemned to death and met their end in front of a firing squad or at the hand of Pierrepoint, the state hangman.

The Garda Síochána Temporary Provision Act of 1923 laid down the rules under which the new police force would operate. The government was well aware of the likelihood of Gardaí being killed in the line of duty and Section 7 of the Act allowed compensation to be paid to dependents of Gardaí 'killed in the execution of their duty or dead in consequence of wounds received in the execution of their duty'.[17] However, getting compensation from the government would prove to be no easy task.

The Irish Free State lasted until 1949 and in 1923 the Civic Guard were renamed An Garda Síochána (Guardians of the Peace). The Gardaí deserve a great deal of credit for helping to pacify a nation after the horrors of the Civil War. By the end of the 1920s, the force had a ratio of just 1.5 Gardaí to every 1,000 people in certain parts of the country, yet were able to oversee an increasingly law-abiding society.[18] This small number of men helped in no small way to get a fledgling nation onto its feet. It would come at a heavy cost, however. This book tells the story of the twenty-one policemen, members of both the Gardaí and the DMP, whose lives were cut short in the course of their duty during the lifetime of the Free State.

1

GARDA HENRY PHELAN

'You can take it from me, it was an accident.'

The Civic Guard was founded in February 1922 and was sent out amongst the people in the early part of September of the same year. The bitter Civil War was still ongoing at that stage and the deployment of thousands of government-backed Gardaí was certain to cause unrest, particularly in areas controlled by republicans. The assurance that the Gardaí was above politics and concerned themselves only with criminal matters cut little ice with the anti-Treaty IRA and their supporters. The potential difficulties became obvious in early October when a bomb was thrown over the wall into the barracks on Ship Street behind Dublin Castle. Dozens of barracks were attacked in the first months and it seemed only a matter of time before a young Garda would find himself on the wrong end of an IRA bullet. Henry Phelan would be the unfortunate victim in the wrong place at the wrong time. He was the first member of the force killed in the line of duty.

Henry Phelan was born on Christmas Day in 1899 in the townland of Rushin, just outside Mountrath, in what we now know as Laois but was then called Queen's County.[1] He was the youngest of a large Roman Catholic family of nine children. When he was a small baby his father had died, forcing his mother and siblings to run the farm alone. Despite this, Henry received a remarkably thorough education for the time, attending Paddock National School until the ripe age of 16, when he left to work on the farm.[2] As he grew older he became interested in nationalism, eventually following the well-worn path of many of his generation to serve in the IRA during the War of Independence. Although Laois had been relatively quiet during the period, Henry was described as 'an active member of the IRA flying column' in the Black and Tan War by no less than Eoin O'Duffy, Garda Commissioner. This was despite the fact that he had three older brothers who were officers in the RIC, one of the IRA's prime targets.

After the truce had been signed, Phelan continued working as a farmer but had designs on membership of the Civic Guard. He applied and was quickly accepted into the force, undergoing a short period of training in the Curragh. After he qualified, he was amongst the first detachment of twenty-six Gardaí sent to the old RIC barracks on Parliament Street in Kilkenny City on 27 September 1922. The force, described as a 'fine body of young Irishmen, athletic and intelligent', was greeted warmly and Phelan spent a month in the city.[3] At the end of October, along with twelve of his colleagues and a sergeant, Phelan was transferred to the rural town of Callan, where he was tasked with keeping the peace in south and west Kilkenny. The new force situated itself in a vacant house beside the Bank of Ireland and near the ruin of the RIC barracks, which had been burned down by the IRA the previous year.

Despite being the county that had produced such ardent nationalists as James Stephens, Kilkenny had been relatively quiet during the War of Independence, particularly in comparison to neighbouring Tipperary. The town of Callan was an exception, however, as the seventh battalion had based itself in the town and frequently linked up with South Tipperary brigade in attacks on British personnel during the conflict.[4] The new Gardaí could thus expect some republican resistance and this was borne out by an eventful first week, shots being fired on Bridge Street in the town near the barracks on one occasion, while separately a number of bicycles were commandeered by armed men. Worse was to follow for the inexperienced young Gardaí.

Just after 3 p.m. on Tuesday, 14 November 1922, Henry Phelan was with Garda Irwin and Garda Flood, both recruits from County Limerick. The men decided to seek an afternoon's leave from Sergeant Kilroy, their superior officer. Their request to leave the barracks and venture out to Tipperary was granted on the condition that they return promptly by 5 p.m. The Gardaí had by no means gained full acceptance in that early stage of their existence and the three men's choice of destination was a risky one.

They had decided to cycle the 5 miles south-west over the county border to the small village of Mullinahone. The trip was a recreational one and the Guards' intention was to buy a sliotar (a hurling ball) and hurleys for a new team that Guard Phelan was attempting to set up in the Callan district. Phelan was a keen sportsman and, being from the parish of Castletown in Laois, still known for its hurling prowess, it is little surprise that hurling was his first love. Mullinahone was a small village of less than 300 people but one with a vast republican legacy whose most famous son was Irish poet and revolutionary Charles Kickham. Like much of the county of Tipperary, Mullinahone was supposedly under the command of the government but realistically Irregulars, or the anti-Treaty IRA, held great power in the area in November 1922.

Just three months before, on 23 August, the IRA had sent out a message to backers of the government. On that day, a national soldier named Patrick Grace was on leave and visiting relatives in the village when he was shot in the head and killed by an Irregular named Patrick Egan. In a twist of fate, Egan would himself be shot dead by soldiers the following year.[5] Nevertheless, the three unarmed Gardaí felt safe enough to go to the area, entering the quiet village at 4 p.m. Its main street 'presented its usual atmosphere of peace'.[6] The conflict had now entered into a period of guerrilla warfare, however, and unexpected danger was liable to be around any corner in unsettled districts such as this.

Phelan and his colleagues succeeded in their mission of purchasing the sliotar and decided to go to Miss Mullally's licenced premises and general grocer's on Kickham Street in the village before they started off homewards. Gardaí were discouraged from drinking by their superiors, Commissioner Eoin O'Duffy being a vocal opponent of alcohol. The men followed their instructions to the letter, and chose to order lemonade. After entering, Irwin and Flood stood at the bar, while Henry Phelan sat sideways on a low stool at the counter, facing the door. After about seven minutes in the bar they ordered a second round of lemonade and were just finishing it when three armed men rushed into the premises. The first of the intruders produced a revolver, while the man directly behind him held a rifle level with his hip.[7] The first man fired a shot in the direction of the three men from a distance of about 3 or 4 yards. It hit Henry Phelan in the face and he fell heavily onto the pub's floor. The belated order was then given by the second man: 'Hands up'.[8]

The remaining two Gardaí were horrified but complied with the command. The shooter then asked the shocked policemen if they had any arms. They replied that they did not. The second raider, who was still pointing a rifle at Irwin and Flood, seemed just as surprised by the shooting as the two Gardaí and he asked his compatriot, 'What are you after doing? Why did you fire?' The first man muttered something inaudible and placed the revolver back in its holster. The third man was still standing at the door and said nothing during the altercation. Garda Thomas Flood begged the men to allow him come to the aid of the stricken Henry Phelan, who was still lying on his face and hands. They replied, 'You may.'

Guard Irwin, who still had his hands up, then asked the raiders if they would allow him go for a priest. They did not answer. Irwin bravely walked past them anyway, mounted his bicycle and made his way to Fr O'Meara's house. Flood knelt down beside Phelan and lifted his head, to find blood haemorrhaging quickly onto the stone floor. The two raiders nearest the door exited and the man who had taken the shot asked again if they had guns to which Flood replied angrily, 'No, and it is well ye ought to know we haven't'. The raider answered, 'You can take it from me, it was an accident.' He then walked out of the premises. Flood, on confirming that his colleague was dead, went to the door to see if Garda Irwin was returning. He could not see him, but did witness the three raiders walking slowly down the street.

Miss Mullally had rushed into the back kitchen in terror when the armed men entered the premises. After they left she returned with her daughter and a local nurse, and the three women attended to Phelan. Garda Irwin had managed to locate Fr O'Meara and Fr Kelly, two local priests. Both were quickly on the scene to administer the Last Rites to the mortally wounded guardsman. The local GP, Dr Conlon, also came swiftly but could not be of any assistance as the Garda was already dead. Henry Phelan had not spoken after the shot and had died almost instantly. Word spread quickly about the first member of the Civic Guard to be killed in the new state.

Newspaper reports of the time describe the feelings of the local population:

> There was indignation … that unarmed men, whose sole interest was the preservation of the peace, should have been set upon in such a manner [and that] the life of one of them was ruthlessly taken away without any cause whatever.[9]

Phelan's body was initially laid out in the pub but removed from Mullinahone to Callan by motor car that night. The locals were already aware of the senseless shooting and large crowds awaited the hearse. The Garda's remains lay in the barracks through Tuesday night and early Wednesday and 'they were visited by throngs of people and fervent prayers were offered up for the repose of his soul'.[10] A large crowd gathered to mourn at the Garda's funeral in Callan and all the businesses and houses closed and drew their blinds. Several other Gardaí carried the coffin while a contingent of National Army soldiers watched on before the cortege travelled the 42 miles onwards to Mountrath where the young man was buried in his home parish.

The inquest into Garda Phelan's death was held at midday on Thursday, 16 November. Dr Conlon explained to the court that the bullet had entered Henry Phelan's left jaw and exited through the back of his neck, thus severing his spinal cord, killing him instantly. A deeply affected Miss Mullally also appeared in the stand and outlined the events of the day. She was asked if she could identify the shooter in question, to which she replied, 'It is very hard.' She then replied that she could, although she would not like to say his name out loud. She consequently wrote the murderer's name on a piece of paper and handed it to the doctor, who in turn passed it to the jury. It was not read out loud.

Dr Crotty also spoke, describing the Gardaí as 'men of peace … with no interest or concern in political or army matters. Deceased was the first member of the Civic Guard who has met his death under such circumstances and I hope and pray he is the last.' This statement was met in the courtroom with cheers and cries of 'Hear, hear!' The doctor, and indeed the members of the court, were not to know that this earnest desire would not be fulfilled and that Henry Phelan would prove to be the first in a long line of members of the Gardaí murdered while carrying out their duty. After a lengthy deliberation, the jury came to a verdict: 'The deceased died from a gunshot wound wilfully and maliciously inflicted and that the person who fired the shot is guilty of murder.'

Condemnation of Phelan's death was swift. Garda Commissioner Eoin O'Duffy said of his slain colleague, 'Young Guard Phelan was foully murdered in broad daylight without getting time to say "the Lord have mercy on my soul" … He was guilty of no greater crime than going into Mullinahone to buy a hurley ball.' He added sarcastically, 'Two heroes armed with rifles held the door while the third put a revolver to his head and fired a bullet through his brain.' He then sympathised with Phelan's mother, remarking, 'She did not think that when her son survived the Black and Tan terror that there were still people in Ireland who could act so callously.'

The day after Phelan's death, with the manhunt for the suspects in full swing, the local Gardaí suffered another blow when twenty-five men escaped through a tunnel from Kilkenny Jail, which had been used to hold military prisoners.

It was at this point that the government took the gloves off in the Civil War against the IRA. Three days after Garda Phelan's death, four IRA volunteers became the first people to be executed by the Irish state after being found to have guns in their possession illegally. The executions would come thick and fast from then on. Eighty-one republicans were executed in the course of the Civil War, thirty-four in the month of January 1923 alone.

As for the actual shooting of Henry Phelan, it would be almost two years before anyone was detained. At 5 a.m. on the morning of 1 August 1924, local houses suffered surprise raids. Two local republicans were finally arrested by Gardaí and Military Police and charged with the Garda's killing. The first was James Daly, a labourer and ex-British soldier from Coolagh, 4 miles from Callan. The second man was named Philip Leahy and was a farmer's son and native of Poulacapple, just inside the County Tipperary border. Poulacapple is a small townland just outside Mullinahone that was well known for its republican sympathies. It had even hosted one of the last anti-Treaty IRA meetings before the end of the Civil War, six months after Phelan's death. Neither Daly nor Leahy were alleged to have fired the shot but both were described as 'aiders and abettors' to the crime.[11]

The prisoners, described as having a respectable appearance, stood before the District Court in Kilkenny three days later.[12] Neither man would participate in the trial, however. Both sat facing away from the judge and refused to take their hats off their heads or stand up, merely stating that they refused to recognise the court. This was in spite of the Garda present forcibly removing their headgear and admonishing them for not respecting the process. Superintendent Feore told the court that when arrested, the men had told Gardaí that they had nothing to do with the crime. It was also mentioned that neither man was accused of murder and that although the name of the man thought to have fired the shot was known, he was not before the court at that present time as the Gardaí were unable to locate him.

Garda Flood entered the witness box and reiterated his version of events of that fateful day. He would not conclusively identify the prisoners, however, telling the court that the raider with the rifle looked like Daly, while he could not definitively identify Leahy as one of the three men present at all. Garda Irwin disagreed. He believed that Leahy had carried the rifle but Daly was not one of the three men in question at all. The men were initially remanded on bail but the chances of a conviction on such contradictory evidence seemed slim.

So it proved. No conviction was forthcoming against either man, and the perpetrator was never brought to justice, in spite of the fact that Miss Mullally had been able to identify him. The Garda Commissioner, hinting that he knew the identity of the culprit, described how 'Guard Phelan was an active member of the Flying column in Mountrath during the Black and Tan terror and his assassin was fighting on the side of the British.'[13]

It was speculated in later years that Phelan, the only Garda killed during the Civil War, was mistaken for his brother, an RIC officer, or for another man who had served in the police who had the same name as his brother. Other accounts claim that local people were unaware that the Gardaí were unarmed, due to the lack of communication into the town in those troubled times, and that the raiders had gone in to procure arms before the gun had gone off accidentally.[14] Either way, the shooter had allegedly been spirited away to America in the aftermath of the crime, never to face justice for the act.[15]

During the War of Independence, an astonishing forty-six RIC policemen had been shot in County Tipperary. Henry Phelan would have believed that the new unarmed Civic Guard would be able to go about their business without the same safety concerns but tragically this was not the case. He was not the first policeman to be shot dead in the Premier County; neither would he be the last. The shooting of the young Garda was extremely unpopular, locally and nationally. He had been unarmed and posed no threat to the gunmen. Less than one month after his death, a general order by the IRA was circulated, instructing volunteers not to fire on unarmed Gardaí.[16]

Henry Phelan's comrade, Inspector Bergin, gave a touching tribute to his fallen colleague as he was lain to rest: 'May the holy soil of Erin's Isle, rest lightly on your breast, may your name be wrote in letters of gold, on the roll of Erin's best.'[17] As the first Garda killed in the line of duty, Henry Phelan's memory has lived on. A memorial was unveiled in his name in the Garda station in Mullinahone in 1997.

2

SERGEANT
JAMES WOODS

'I will make you talk.'

By December 1923, the Civil War had been officially over for some six months. However, sporadic skirmishes still occurred. The situation in County Kerry, part of the so-called 'Munster Republic', was particularly difficult to control. As the Civil War had continued, the republicans had retreated further south and west until eventually Kerry was their main base. The county had a huge republican contingent and the National Army struggled to gain popular support there, often having to bring in men from outside the area to maintain an uneasy peace. These transfers of troops often occurred by sea as the county was too dangerous to access by land. More than seventy state soldiers had been killed in County Kerry alone during the conflict. The army responded in kind, killing a number of republicans in controversial circumstances, the deliberate blowing-up of eight anti-Treaty prisoners in the Ballyseedy Massacre causing particular outrage. Incidents like these ensured that governmental officials were wildly unpopular amongst sections of the county's population.

This unpopularity extended to the Civic Guard. One newspaper remarked on 18 November 1922 that, 'With the possible exception of Kerry, the Civic Guard are today in every county of the twenty-six administered by the provisional government.'[1] However, by the beginning of December, the government deemed it safe enough to send a contingent to the county and by 17 January the Gardaí and court system were reported to be functioning well in Tralee, with three other Civic Guard outposts scattered throughout the rest of Kerry.[2] The Gardaí largely stayed out of the IRA's line of fire in its first months, apart from a few isolated incidents, such as in the spring of 1923 when officers were twice held up by an IRA leader named McCarthy, who deprived them of their bicycles. He was shot dead by Gardaí in Dingle shortly afterwards.[3] Garda Henry Phelan had been the only member of the force to meet his death during the Civil War but on 3 December 1923 this run of good fortune would come to a shocking end in Scartaglen with the shooting of a second officer. James Woods would be the first sergeant killed in the history of An Garda Síochána.

Scartaglen is a small village in the Sliabh Luachra area of East Kerry, which is renowned for its rich heritage in music and literature. Like most of that part of Kerry, the area was also well known as a strong republican heartland in the aftermath of the Civil War. In a confidential report to the Minister for Home Affairs in 1923, Garda Commissioner Eoin O'Duffy specifically named the village as a hotbed of Irregular activity. He described how armed men moved freely and he urged the army to 'make a special effort to catch them as their presence is having a very bad effect'.[4] The RIC had been attacked and expelled from the village at an early stage in the War of Independence and by the time the first Gardaí arrived in the area at the beginning of 1923 it had been without a functioning police force for a considerable period of time.[5] The first recruits were almost exclusively young, inexperienced men. They were faced with the difficult task of attempting to re-impose law and order on an area where they faced a good degree of opposition. The overwhelmingly anti-Treaty area would remain hostile to anyone working for the Free State government for a long time after the Civil War and Sergeant James Woods and his officers faced an unenviable assignment.

Woods was born in 1901 in Craggycorradan West, a townland situated between Doolin and Lisdoonvarna on the west coast of County Clare. His parents, James Snr and Margaret, were farmers and James was the second of nine children born to them.[6] He proved to be a good scholar and after reaching adulthood embarked on a career in teaching, spending a year training in Waterford. He had strong nationalist sympathies though, and after the year was complete he left this potentially comfortable existence to fight with the IRA in the War of Independence. When the Anglo-Irish Treaty was signed and the call came for young men to join the fledgling Civic Guard, Woods applied immediately. He came from a family steeped in the newly formed Garda force, having two brothers who achieved high ranks early in their careers. Powerfully built, over 6ft in height and academically gifted, James Woods seemed a perfect fit and was accepted into the force in November 1922. After a short period of training he was stationed briefly in Bantry, County Cork, before he was promoted to the rank of sergeant. Woods was just 22 years of age but O'Duffy's policy was to appoint men with some form of higher education to senior positions.[7] The young sergeant was then dispatched to the troubled village of Scartaglen.

The Garda force found themselves woefully under-resourced after their deployment. Many of the former RIC police barracks had been razed to the ground by the IRA in the previous years so the Gardaí had to put up with makeshift barracks, particularly in the more rural parts of the country. In Scartaglen they found themselves forced to use the house of local man Jerimiah Lyons as their temporary Garda station. The owner still occupied the house and it was clearly ill-equipped to serve as a police station as his family and the Gardaí living in the house were forced to share a kitchen. But desperate times called for desperate measures, and as the dwelling was reasonably comfortable and situated in the middle of the village the Gardaí chose it as their short-term headquarters under the stewardship of Sergeant Woods.

At around 8.30 p.m. on Monday 3 December, six armed and masked men arrived at the police barracks under the cover of darkness, brandishing weapons. Three of the men entered the kitchen while the others stayed on the porch. The crowded room contained Guard Patrick Spillane, Jerimiah Lyons and his wife and six children, two local brothers named James and Michael Kearney and two young local boys who were playing cards. The sergeant was in the guardroom while two other Gardaí from the station were out on patrol. One of the masked men announced his arrival by immediately hitting James Kearney in the face with the butt of his weapon, breaking the unfortunate man's nose on impact.[8] They next went straight for Guard Spillane, the station orderly, shouting 'Hands up', an order that was swiftly obeyed by the young Garda. They ordered him to get a light. Spillane lit a match but it extinguished again immediately. He was then struck on the side with a rifle. The men next dragged him to what the occupants called a stairs, but which was almost perpendicular to the ground floor and was more like a ladder. They ordered him to climb it, following on behind.[9]

When they reached the top floor they demanded that Spillane strip off his clothing. He refused, saying that he was prepared to die in defence of his Garda uniform. One of the men loaded a bullet in his rifle and threatened, 'If you do not strip it will be worse for yourself'. Spillane bravely stood his ground. Instead of shooting him, one of the raiders forced him onto the bed and ripped his uniform off him while a second man covered him with a rifle.[10] Spillane was stripped down to his shirt, which the raider ordered him to take off. The Guard refused, asking, 'Do you think I'm a Turk?' To which the answer was, 'No, I think you are a bastard.' The raiders eventually succeeded in taking the shirt and Spillane was then left completely naked. The men also took his watch and chain, as well as 30s that they had discovered in the pocket of his tunic.[11]

The armed men next burst open Spillane's wooden chest, which contained other personal items belonging to him. They removed more money and clothing and pocketed them, before forcibly opening the boxes of two other Gardaí and doing likewise. The boots and clothing were thrown down the ladder, where they were collected by other comrades who had by this point entered the house. Spillane was then put standing against the wall upstairs and asked where the sergeant was. When he did not answer immediately one of the men pulled back the bolt of his rifle and said, 'I will make you talk.' One of the men remained, covering Spillane with the rifle, while the second descended the stairs, looking for the sergeant.

He started asking loudly for Sergeant Woods as the other men spread throughout the house, ransacking various rooms. Woods had been in an adjoining room situated just off the kitchen and had heard the commotion by this stage. He arrived in the kitchen and one of the raiders quickly instructed him, 'Put them up and get up the stairs.'[12] The masked man followed him, all the while pointing his rifle in the sergeant's direction. As Woods was ascending the ladder, Spillane could see him from the room upstairs. Suddenly the raider butted the sergeant with the rifle between the shoulder blades, in what appeared to be an attempt to force him to hurry his progress. At that point a blast of a rifle was heard. A bullet struck the sergeant in the back of the head and he fell forward on his knees on the ladder. The raider behind him then gave him a sharp prod with the muzzle of the rifle as if to make him get up. He did not do so. Sergeant Woods was dead.

The gunman immediately shouted to his comrades to get down the stairs and leave the house. The rest of the men had already heard the shot and widespread panic was evident throughout the station. The party immediately left the building, the man who came downstairs having to jump over the sergeant's prostrate body as he made his hasty and premature exit. In the meantime, the other raiders had managed to steal items from the house, including several Garda uniforms, money and possessions. A number of these items were dropped or discarded on the way out, indicating the haste with which the masked men made their exit. Much of the loot was later discovered in the station and on the road outside, although a portion of the missing items could not be traced and appeared to have remained in the raiders' possession.

A panicked Guard Spillane went towards Castleisland for a priest as soon as he was dressed and it was safe to do so. From there he managed to wire the chief superintendent in Tralee, imparting the dreadful news. A young boy from the house was also dispatched to look for the Gardaí on patrol. He encountered them walking near the village and excitedly told them of Woods' death. They hurried back to find the station in disarray, their possessions ransacked and, worst of all, their superior officer lying dead on the floor. They placed a pillow under his head and waited for help.

The following evening an inquest into the death was held. The jury heard from Dr William Prederville of Castleisland that they would only give an identification and state the cause of death in order to allow the Gardaí more time to conduct their enquiries. The bullet had entered the sergeant's head at the back, around the base of the skull. The exit wound was at the top of the skull and the coroner commented that it was wide enough for him to put three fingers through. The brain protruded through the top wound and the coroner put his death down to laceration of the brain, adding that he had died instantly.

The local and national reaction to the death of another Garda was one of outrage and revulsion. The *Tralee Star* remarked:

> Why a peace force, which is a credit to our country, should be made the object of attack, is one of those things impossible to understand. The Civic Guards are drawn from the people. They are unarmed and rely on the good will of the people. Every decent and clean-minded man in Kerry condemns this crime.[13]

Sergeant Woods' Mass, which attracted an enormous congregation, was celebrated in the local church in Scartaglen.[14] He was then conveyed on his final journey to Killelagh Cemetery in Doolin, County Clare, for burial.

It was widely believed that the shot that night in Scartaglen had been discharged accidentally and that the sergeant's death had not been planned by the marauders. This did not deter the Gardaí and the National Army, however, who were determined to use all the resources at their disposal to catch the perpetrators. At 6 a.m. on the morning after Woods' shooting, a party of men went to the house of Mrs O'Connor in the adjoining townland of Dromultan. Con Horan, who was employed by the homeowner, was considered a suspect in Woods' death and was dragged out of his bed. A shot was fired at two women of the house when they attempted to intervene. Horan was then badly beaten and shot. Eventually he managed to escape from his captors by running through the fields. Horan maintained that he had no knowledge about the events of the previous night. Worse was to follow.

As the days went on with no apprehension of the culprits, larger numbers of troops converged on Scartaglen to root out the gunmen. Lieutenant Jerimiah Gaffney was placed in charge of one group of soldiers. He had previous experience of the village, having been stationed there during the Civil War when he was involved in a number of skirmishes with republicans. He also held a long-standing grudge against a family named the Brosnans. The feud concerned remarks the family had made about an affair he had been having with a woman in the village. On 6 December, three days after Sergeant Woods' death, Gaffney spent the day drinking with his men before ordering them into Brosnan's pub. Thomas Brosnan was brought outside and shot dead by the lieutenant and his fellow soldier, Denis Leen. Gaffney later claimed that this had been done because Brosnan had been one of the raiding party involved in Sergeant Woods' death, an accusation which was later found to be baseless; Woods and Brosnan had been good friends.

The brutal murder caused uproar and disgust throughout the country as Brosnan had little involvement in politics and was well liked locally. Gaffney was found guilty of the murder and hanged on 13 March 1924. His colleague Denis Leen was also sentenced to death but reprieved after Gaffney confessed at the last minute to having ordered the shooting.[15]

Commissioner Eoin O'Duffy came down to Kerry personally and sympathised with both Woods' colleagues and the Brosnan family

33

in Scartaglen. Newspaper reports carried the story that the two murders, although similar, had nothing to do with each other, a statement that was greeted with disbelief in the village.

The inquest into Sergeant Woods' death was eventually held jointly with Thomas Brosnan's on 2 January 1924. Jerimiah Lyons gave interesting evidence of the night in question, telling the jury that he was certain that Thomas Brosnan had not been one of the masked assailants in the house that night and that he had often come to the house to visit Woods. He also described how the raiders had asked only for Sergeant Woods and appeared to be aware that the other Gardaí from the station would be absent, indicating a great deal of local knowledge amongst the conspirators. Lyons also recounted how he had run to Woods after the raiders had fled but that the sergeant appeared to be already dead. The foreman announced that the jury believed that the sergeant had been murdered by a person or persons unknown, although he also remarked that the raid appeared to be for robbery and looting rather than for political reasons. Several of the jury members also refused to insert the word 'wilful', opining that the murder had been unplanned and committed accidentally in the course of a robbery.

The aftermath of the death of Sergeant Woods left the local population living in terror, it being reported that 'some people in Scartaglen have been afraid to sleep at home since the recent happenings there'.[16] Two murders in three days in the tiny village must have shaken the local population to its core. With Tom Brosnan's killer found and punished, the hunt for those who had shot Sergeant Woods continued for many months. Government Minister Kevin O'Higgins fumed that the perpetrators of the crime were 'well known to be hiding and to the knowledge of very many of the inhabitants'. A breakthrough did not come until June 1924 when several arrests were made locally. Amongst the men detained was Michael Healy, a native of Knocknagree, 12 miles from Scartaglen, over the county border in Cork. In Garda reports of late 1923, just weeks before Sergeant Woods' death, Knocknagree was described, along with its neighbouring villages, as 'by far the worst area in the state. The situation is so bad there that unless conditions improve it may become necessary to withdraw the Guards.' This proved a pertinent premonition. The authorities had been seeking Healy since the shooting but he had managed to evade them, often sleeping outdoors or in sympathetic neighbours' houses. He was finally caught at his own home at 6 a.m. on the morning of 28 June as he came up from the glen where he had slept the night before. He was swiftly arrested. When asked if he had anything to say to the charge, Healy replied, 'No, sir, but that I am innocent.'[17]

Surprisingly Michael Healy was not charged with the murder of Sergeant Woods, instead facing an accusation of armed robbery. His trial began in the Central Criminal Court in Dublin on 22 January 1925. Healy pleaded not guilty. Guard Spillane was the main witness against him, maintaining that he was able to recognise Healy on that night, despite the raiders wearing masks at the time. Spillane explained Healy's nose was protruding through the mask and he could see the lower part of his eyes. Guard Spillane further stated that Healy was the raider who seemed to be the leader and who had struck Kearney with his rifle, although he was not the man who had fired the fatal shot that killed Woods. Although Spillane had never seen the accused before the murder and only set eyes on him seven months afterwards in Tralee Garda Station, he insisted that he was in no doubt that the man in the dock was one of the masked gunmen who had robbed the station on that winter's night.

Healy's defence was that he had not been in Scartaglen on that evening at all. He had instead been at the house of Mrs Culloty, several miles away, where he had been playing cards. He added that he had numerous witnesses who could vouch for it and he had only been informed of Sergeant Woods' death the evening after the incident. Mr Carrigan, defending, added that, 'no one more condemned what took place than the prisoner, Michael Healy'. When Healy was cross-examined he admitted he had been in the anti-Treaty IRA and that he had owned a gun, but insisted he had given it up to the brigade quartermaster after an order to dump arms the previous May, following the Civil War. He also conceded that he had been evading the Civic Guard after Woods' shooting, although he knew they had been looking for him. These admissions did not amount to a crime, however. With the tenuous testimony of Spillane as the only evidence against him, it caused little surprise when Healy was found not guilty of the crime. The state kept him in custody in anticipation of other charges but Healy was eventually freed 'with reluctance' on 6 February 1925.

Sergeant Woods' mother Margaret was eventually awarded £80 for the death of her son, while his brother Thomas rose to the ranks of deputy commissioner of the force. Similar to the case of Henry Phelan, the Minister for Home Affairs (later Justice) Kevin O'Higgins was convinced that local people were shielding the killers of the unarmed Garda. In both cases the search for the killers continued, but each would remain unsolved. In 1995 a memorial was erected in Castleisland Garda Station in memory of James Woods, the first sergeant killed in the history of An Garda Síochána.

3

GARDA PATRICK O'HALLORAN

'Woman, come back or I will shoot you dead.'

Armed robberies were a popular tactic used by the IRA during the Civil War. Although risky, the raids often proved financially lucrative to an organisation in dire need of funds to finance the conflict. The number of robberies peaked in the early months of 1922, when hundreds of raids were carried out, mainly on banks and post offices. The Public Safety Bill of 1923 was initiated to counteract the robberies, introducing harsh punishments, including flogging, for arson and armed robbery.[1] Sure enough, by the beginning of 1924, the war had ended and instances of armed robbery had declined markedly. Nevertheless, on 28 January 1924, two towns suffered raids. Both banks in the small Waterford town of Cappoquin were held up, the three armed raiders getting away with more than £2,000. A bank was also targeted 100 miles north-east in Baltinglass, County Wicklow. On this occasion the armed assailants were not affiliated with the IRA and left empty-handed. They did, however, leave a trail of destruction and a dead Garda in their wake.

At about midday on Monday 28 January, the LSE Taxi Company received a phone call from a man calling himself 'Mr Doyle'. The caller requested that the company dispatch a taxi to pick up a man at the Ormond Hotel on the quays in Dublin City. James Smyth was the first driver in the queue so he was chosen to complete the job in his large blue touring car. When Smyth pulled up outside the hotel, a man came out carrying an attaché case. He entered the car, closely followed by a second man who had been standing on the footpath. The two passengers were wearing trench coats. One asked Smyth if he knew where Baltinglass was and how he would get there. Smyth replied that he did and that he would go through Blessington. The men seemed satisfied with this response and the car set off on the 50-mile journey.

The taxi driver later said that everything in the taxi seemed normal. The trip took close to two hours. The car finally reached its destination at 1.50 p.m. and the driver was directed to stop at the chapel in the centre of the town. One passenger got out and went into the church for a few seconds before returning to the car and asking the taxi driver to reverse in behind the post office. Smyth complied and the other man then left the car and entered the post office. He also did not stay inside long, exiting the building and walking into the nearby National Bank. He came out after a few seconds and arrived back at the taxi, explaining this mysterious behaviour with a claim that he was looking for a telephone. He added that there was none in the post office so he would have to make use of the one in the bank instead. At this point both men alighted the taxi, telling the driver that they would return in ten minutes.

Despite the men's unusual conduct, Smyth suspected nothing at that point. He saw the passengers walk back in the direction of the bank in the centre of the town. In reality they had been ascertaining that there was no telephone to report the crime that they were about to carry out. When the first passenger had entered the bank he had asked if there was a telephone present, but was told by bank manager Maurice Wolfe that the nearest phone was almost 10 miles away in the village of Dunlavin. The bank manager helpfully suggested that a telegram could be sent from the nearby post office instead, an offer that was refused by the passenger.

At 2 p.m., when the man returned to the bank with his fellow passenger, there was just one customer, a local man who was chatting to Wolfe, at his private desk. The two were therefore greeted by teenage bank assistant Cecil Shade. Shade asked the men if they wanted any help but received no reply. He then enquired if they wished to see the manager. They replied that they did, so he showed them to Wolfe's private office and knocked on the door. The bank manager came face to face with the smaller of the two men, who pulled out a revolver and ordered him to put up his hands and hand over the keys to the bank's safe.

Mr Wolfe did not meekly accede to their request, however. He himself had a weapon, a small automatic, which he whipped out and pointed at the smaller man. He later said that he had the opportunity to fire a shot but found himself unable to do so, saying 'I could not shoot a man in cold blood'. The men facing him did not suffer from any such qualms. One of the raiders raised his pistol to shoot the bank manager in the breast. Cecil Shade jumped at him at the last moment, causing him to miss his target; the bullet hit Wolfe in his side. The manager fell screaming to the floor, managing to fire a shot as he fell, which embedded itself in the wall. A third member of staff, Mr Corcoran, was at this point making a desperate attempt to hide the money. The raiders could not have foreseen the incredible bravery and resistance they would encounter. Not to be deterred, they picked up Wolfe's revolver and demanded the keys. Wolfe did not have the safe's keys on his person at the time, but threw a different set on the ground. The smaller of the two men ordered Cecil Shade to pick up the keys, took him to the boardroom and ordered him to use the keys to open the safe. Shade fumbled with the keys, claiming they did not fit.[2]

Mrs Wolfe had heard the shot from upstairs and ran into the bank to be met by the horrifying sight of her husband lying wounded on the ground. She asked what was wrong. Shade told her that her husband had been shot and to go for a doctor.

She went towards the door but the taller of the two men threatened, 'Woman, come back or I will shoot you dead.'[3] Mrs Wolfe bravely ignored the ultimatum and ran screaming into the street. The taller man followed her to the door, but he did not make good on his threat to shoot, instead locking the door from the inside and coming back in.

Mrs Wolfe's cries were heard throughout the town. A local Garda, Patrick O'Halloran, was already on his way, having been informed by a local man that shots had been heard in the bank. A merchant from the town, Joseph Germaine, having been informed by his wife that something suspicious was happening at the bank, retrieved a fully loaded colt pistol and made his way to the bank, where he found the unarmed Garda O'Halloran kicking the door in an attempt to get in. Germaine handed him the small automatic pistol. O'Halloran continued banging at the door but, receiving no answer, loudly blew his policeman's whistle.

Alarmed at the turn of events, the raiders whispered to each other for a few seconds. As they were doing so, Cecil Shade managed to throw the ring of keys out the window. Despite not having stolen any money, the raiders made up their mind to escape and rushed out the back door, leaving an empty attaché case behind them. This took them up the alley and onto the street, past a shocked Garda O'Halloran.

The Garda shouted for them to stop but the thwarted bank robbers continued onto the bridge over the River Slaney, which bisects the town. O'Halloran gave chase, his pistol held aloft. Eyewitnesses would later state that the Garda 'did not fire but he looked as if he were trying to press the trigger but it would not work'.[4] The taller man, who appeared to have a limp, found himself just yards away from the policeman. He used his own pistol to fire backwards at the oncoming O'Halloran. The bullet struck the Garda in the abdomen and he stumbled and fell critically injured on the path. Another local man was also armed and giving chase. He fired a shot in the direction of the marauders. It missed and they succeeded in getting into the taxi.

However, the driver James Smyth was nowhere to be seen. He had been walking up and down the street and had then gone into Jackson's pub in the village, where he purchased a hot drink as the day was cold. When he went out to light a cigarette, he noticed that both doors of his taxi were open. Suspecting something amiss, he ran to the car to see who was interfering with it. He found the two passengers inside, one at the wheel, with the other trying to start the engine. The man at the engine jumped into the car and screamed at the driver to 'drive like hell' for Dublin. Smyth did so. As he was driving off, he glanced into the rear-view mirror and spotted the passenger in the back holding a revolver, which he quickly attempted to hide. The car sped off without encountering any further obstacle.

The passengers directed Smyth to stop at a pub in Templeogue, just past Tallaght. They all went inside and his passengers offered him a drink, which he accepted. As they were drinking, one of the men asked him his name. When he told them it was Smyth, the man wrote it down on the back of a postcard but said nothing else. They then left the pub and drove on as far as the village of Terenure. They again stopped the car, saying, 'We are finished here', despite still being several miles from the city. The driver demanded his fare of £5, but the men told him that they had no money and were unable to pay. They promised that they would send on their dues to the Ormond Hotel the following day under the name Doyle. An angry Smyth had little choice but to continue back to the depot. He was suspicious of the men's strange behaviour and he informed his supervisor, later telling the Gardaí about the bizarre journey.

It was some time after Garda O'Halloran's shooting that a phone call was made by the proprietor of the hotel in Baltinglass, informing Gardaí that a robbery had occurred and that a Garda had been shot. The caller added that the perpetrators had fled in the direction of Dublin. The army from Carlow Town and members of the DMP flying squad gave chase but to no avail. The army camp at Tallaght was also notified and the army was quick to set up checkpoints on all the major roads into Dublin but the bandits did not appear. It seemed the army had just missed their quarry, a blue taxi having been spotted going through Tallaght between three and four o'clock in the direction of Dublin. The robbers had picked their location well. Baltinglass was the closest town with a bank to Dublin at that time that could not avail of a telephone in case of an emergency. If a telephone had been available in the town, the stations around Tallaght and South Dublin would have been informed quickly and would have had ample time to set up a roadblock. The delay had bought the two robbers some extra time and allowed the two raiders, for now at least, to escape the clutches of the Gardaí.

The attack itself had been planned well in advance. The two men had spent a night in Baltinglass on the night of 15 December, apparently in an attempt to scope out the town and ascertain whether it would be feasible to rob the bank, while satisfying themselves that there was no telephone. It would probably have proven a lucrative exercise had it not been for the extraordinary bravery shown by Mr and Mrs Wolfe, Cecil Shade, Mr Corcoran, Joseph Germaine and Garda O'Halloran, all of whom went to incredible lengths to thwart the robbers. Unfortunately for the two raiders, the manager of the hotel in which they stayed the month previously had also been on the street as the fire fight took place and he was able to identify both men, as well as the number of the taxi.

Meanwhile Garda Patrick O'Halloran was conveyed to the Curragh Military Hospital, arriving at 5.30 p.m. He was in a critical condition, having been shot in the abdomen, with the exit wound being in the right buttock. The bullet had pierced both his small intestine and his bladder and he was suffering from profound shock. Although there was an initial improvement after the operation on the night of the shooting, his condition deteriorated thereafter and an appeal was made to other Gardaí to donate blood so that a blood transfusion could be attempted. There was a huge response but sadly there was to be no recovery. Garda Patrick O'Halloran died at 3.50 p.m. on 29 January.

The deceased Garda was a native of the town of Gort in County Galway and was the second youngest of an Irish-speaking family with six children.[5] The republican heartland of South Galway had seen its share of tragedies at the hands of the Black and Tans and it is no surprise that O'Halloran was a volunteer in the IRA. He was a veteran of the Rising of 1916 and had taken an active part in the War of Independence. He had also been employed as a signalman in the railway station before joining the Gardaí in March 1922.[6] Like most young Gardaí in those days, O'Halloran was a single man. He had served in Skerries and Swords in County Dublin before being moved to Baltinglass in November 1922. He was a popular man locally, described as 'efficient, brave and temperate'.[7] A year before his death, on 13 January 1923, O'Halloran had shown an example of this bravery.

Although Wicklow was one of the quieter counties throughout the troubled early 1920s, the IRA still made several raids in the county during the Civil War. One of these was on Baltinglass Civic Guard Station. At that point, O'Halloran had been stationed in the town for less than two months. He was asleep in the station when a large party of men broke down the door with hammers and crowbars. Far from being cowed, the unarmed Gardaí jeered the intruders. O'Halloran apparently took out a picture of a former IRA commander and told the raiders that he had fought with him until he was murdered by curs like them. He then said, 'What do we care for you, a lot of contemptible robbers? I often looked down a rifle barrel.' The men burned the Garda uniforms before making an attempt to set the station alight. They may have succeeded were it not for the efforts of O'Halloran and his colleagues, who fiercely resisted the attack, despite being outgunned and outnumbered. O'Halloran had once again exhibited supreme courage when chasing the bank robbers. Unfortunately, he would pay the ultimate price for his devotion to duty.

The inquest into the young Garda's death was held two days after the shooting. The jury found it to be a case of wilful murder, expressing abhorrence that the Garda had been shot down while doing his duty.

O'Halloran's funeral procession was met in his native Gort by a huge crowd, including many dignitaries.[8] The cortège travelled onwards to Shanaglish Cemetery, where he was laid to rest.

Garda O'Halloran was the second Garda killed in less than two months and his death led once again to widespread calls to arm the Gardaí. General O'Duffy responded that whether the Gardaí would be armed was up to the population, stating, 'It is the people that must decide to place arms in our hands.'[9] There were also complaints that the majority of Garda stations throughout the country in 1924, including in large towns like Tralee, Wexford and Sligo, were not equipped with telephones. Newspapers waxed lyrical about the unsettled state of the country and clamoured for the robbers to be apprehended. They did not have long to wait.

By 1 February, the manhunt for the two suspects had led the Gardaí, and the Dublin Metropolitan Police, all over the country. Checkpoints were mounted and trains and buses were boarded in the search for the fugitives. Six men were arrested the weekend following the shooting, and two men were brought forward for trial, although both vehemently denied the charge. The cases against them were dismissed due to a lack of evidence. Neither Garda Phelan nor Sergeant Woods' killers had been apprehended and it seemed important that the Gardaí secured a conviction in order to regain the confidence of the people.

The flying squad of the DMP swooped on Monaghan Town early on the morning of 13 February and made contact with the local Gardaí, informing them of their suspicion that one of the Baltinglass raiders was in the vicinity. The Garda inspector was initially reluctant to co-operate with the DMP, which constituted a different police force, but he eventually came on board. The joint operation scoured the town and conducted a three-and-a-half-hour search. At 5.30 a.m. the smaller of the two suspected culprits was found in a house in Dublin Street belonging to his sister. His name was Peter Jordan. The taxi driver quickly identified him as one of the passengers on that fateful day and Jordan had little choice but to confess to his part in the outrage.[10] The Gardaí then descended on Jordan's Dublin address in St Paul's Street, where they found the revolver taken from the bank manager during the raid in Baltinglass under a pillow. They also searched a house in Kimmage where they discovered trench coats, caps and guns, as well as a scrap of paper indicating that the other suspect, Felix McMullen, had made a hurried exit to Liverpool. The Liverpool Constabulary were informed and located the suspect within hours. The Gardaí crossed the Irish Sea and McMullen was escorted on the Holyhead afternoon mail boat to Dublin, where he was detained in Bridewell Garda Station.

Both suspects, described as 'respectably-dressed young men', seemed unlikely armed bank robbers.[11] Jordan was 26 years old and a former National School teacher. The native of Adamstown, County Wexford, had left the teaching profession to fight with the IRA. He had accepted the Treaty and proceeded to join the Special Infantry Corps of the National Army, serving mainly in his native county and achieving the rank of captain. McMullen was 29 years old and originally from Springtown, just north of the border village of Kinawley, County Fermanagh. The eldest of nine children from a Catholic farming background, McMullen had left farming and his Fermanagh home to serve in the British Army for three years during the First World War. He had then enlisted in the National Army after independence. McMullen would also achieve the rank of captain after a period stationed in Wexford and it was here that his path would cross with Jordan's. Both men found themselves with demobilisation orders at the end of 1923.

The National Army at one point had over 55,000 soldiers in its ranks to fight the anti-Treaty threat. Frank Aiken then gave orders for the IRA to dump arms in May 1923, leading to an uneasy peace and leaving the army wildly over-subscribed for peace time. The decision was taken to cut the number of soldiers down to fewer than 30,000 by early 1924. This decision was met with anger from many recruits. Most soldiers had been in the ranks under a year and were unprepared for their unceremonious demobilisation and the financial hardship that would surely follow. Many would desert, taking their ammunition with them, while a number would take part in the short-lived Army Mutiny. Others would embark on a life of crime to earn a living; a scarcely believable 60 per cent of murders in 1923 are believed to have been committed by soldiers of the National Army. Jordan and McMullen were amongst the number to be deemed surplus to requirements who chose a criminal path. Both men were demobilised on 11 December 1923. Just four days later, they checked into a hotel in Baltinglass in preparation for the robbery that would cost Garda O'Halloran his life.

Jordan was quick to make a statement outlining the events of the day. He described the trip down to Baltinglass, admitting that he had been armed with a .45 revolver but insisting that he had fired no shots. He had heard shots fired on the bridge but did not know who had fired them. The gun under his bed had been picked up after the bank manager had dropped it, he explained, and had never been fired by him. McMullen initially denied the charge completely. He was confronted with his accomplice's statement, however, and he agreed to co-operate. He identified several of the items from the house in Kimmage as his own and made a statement admitting to being in Baltinglass on 28 January. It stated that the bank robbery was Jordan's idea and that it was Jordan who rang the taxi from the hotel and who had gone into the post office. McMullen confessed going into the bank with his co-conspirator, who had told those assembled to put their hands up. Someone had then knocked against him and his gun had gone off, shooting Mr Wolfe. After they had absconded from the bank, he realised he was being chased and put the gun behind his back, firing a wild warning shot.[12] He insisted that it was only the next day that he had found out that the Garda had been struck by the bullet.

Nevertheless McMullen and Jordan were swiftly charged with murder, their joint trial beginning on 7 July 1924 in the Central Criminal Court on Green Street, Dublin. Both men pleaded not guilty, despite the substantial evidence against them. Wolfe and Corcoran were able to identify Jordan and McMullen as the robbers, while a local man named Edward Brophy also gave crucial evidence. Brophy told the court that he had been near the bridge when he saw McMullen turning backwards and facing the guard before firing his gun. This directly contradicted McMullen's claim that he had not looked where he was shooting.

McMullen was in particular danger. He had fired the shot that ended the policeman's life and a death sentence was a distinct possibility. Several character witnesses from his army days took the stand and described their former colleague as 'a strict teetotaller and a good Catholic … a first-class officer, sober and reliable'.[13] One army general opined that the Fermanagh native bore 'a high and irreproachable character. He was a man who was incapable of committing the crime of wilful murder.' McMullen's defence pleaded that although their client had been 'actuated by a spirit of foolish enterprise … there was a very great difference between robbing a bank and committing deliberate murder'. They added that he was otherwise a man of good character. They also implored the jury to believe that he was under the influence of Jordan, the real architect of the plan. McMullen did not take the stand in his own defence.

The prosecution made no distinction between the accused prisoners, reminding the court that if a man is killed in the course of a robbery, even accidentally, then the crime is one of murder. The judge, Justice O'Shaughnessy, agreed in his summing-up, remarking that, 'if one of them caused the death of a man, both were equally guilty and there is no alternative in this case'. The jury was sent to consider its verdict on the second day of the trial.

They returned after half an hour, enquiring as to whether they would be entitled to bring in a verdict of manslaughter. The judge refused their request, telling them that the men must be found guilty or not guilty of murder, the charge for which they were indicted. After further deliberation, the jury returned, the foreman telling Justice O'Shaughnessy that they were unable to come to a verdict. O'Shaughnessy answered angrily that he had already given them a detailed summing-up and that 'this is not a case in which a jury should not be able to find a verdict'. They were again asked to deliberate but after two and a half hours, an extraordinarily long time by the standards of the era, the judge sent for them. It was clear that he believed that the prisoners should be found guilty of murder and was irritated by the lack of a verdict. He discharged the jury, complaining that some of them had ignored his ruling and taken the law into their own hands, decrying it as a shameful occurrence in the capital of the country.

A new jury was empanelled and the re-trial began just two days later on 11 July. The defence complained that the charge should have been downgraded to manslaughter in light of the previous jury's misgivings, but this application was refused by the judge. After hearing the same evidence, this jury found Felix McMullen guilty of murder with a recommendation to mercy. The judge then sentenced him to death, adding that the verdict was never in doubt. He did not follow common practice of mentioning the jury's recommendation to mercy in his response. A pale-looking McMullen replied to the verdict, 'I am very sorry that the Guard was killed, but I never fired a shot with the intention of killing anyone.'

Peter Jordan's solicitor had disagreed during the trial that his client was the ringleader, asserting that Jordan was accused of 'being guilty of the actions of his companion'.[14] Although Jordan admitted that he had planned the robbery, he said that there had been no intention on his part to use his deadly weapon. Evidently he was believed as he was found not guilty of murder. He was found guilty of armed robbery, however, and was sentenced to ten years' penal servitude. He was also given twenty lashes, to occur prior to the imprisonment. Jordan would go on to serve just over two years in prison.

McMullen submitted an appeal to the newly founded Court of Criminal Appeal. He was unable to pay for a transcript of the stenographer's case notes, which were not automatically given to condemned prisoners at the time. The defence submitted that the judge had no right to tell the jury that they could not come to a verdict of manslaughter, nor to discharge them and reconvene the trial. They pleaded that McMullen had 'told the truth about every circumstance of the case, knowing that he had been caught red-handed'.[15] He had fired the shot aimlessly while fleeing from justice, and this was thus a case of manslaughter. The three judges of the court eventually dismissed the appeal, stating that the facts had been established satisfactorily and they were unable to change the verdict. They reminded counsel that McMullen had already shown his willingness to shoot a man in the bank and by shooting at the Garda and killing him it was murder, whether murder had been his intention or not. Justice must run its course.

Several petitions were entered to the Governor-General for the reprieve of the prisoner, including large numbers from his home parish of Kinawley, County Fermanagh. The IRA brigades in the border region requested mercy for McMullen, as did many members of the clergy.[16] Juries from both of McMullen's trials also entered petitions, begging the government to spare the ex-soldier's life. The government dismissed these appeals, saying that as the trial had concluded their petitions were now treated as those 'of any twelve ordinary citizens'.[17] Mr Wolfe, who had recovered well from being shot, also showed extreme generosity by petitioning on behalf of the condemned man. All of these appeals fell on deaf ears. McMullen was visited by his parents on the day before the hanging and was said to have been 'perfectly resigned to his fate'.[18]

On the morning of his execution, at 4.30 a.m., with a little over three hours until he mounted the scaffold, McMullen wrote a letter to the deputy governor of the prison, Seán Kavanagh. The heading was: 'Condemned Cell, 4:30 a.m., 1st August 1924.' It read:

> I feel I must thank you for your great kindness to me under sentence of death. The thoughts of the first night I came in I could never forget. I hope that the Sacred Heart of Jesus will protect you and your wife and you will live long and happy lives. Thank God I am as happy as if I were in Heaven, where I shall be before night … Sacred Heart of Jesus I trust in Thee. Pray for me and I shall always pray for you. To Seán Kavanagh from Felix McMullen.[19]

The morning of 1 August 'broke in unpleasant rain and continued wet all through the morning'.[20] After the prison bell at 7 a.m.,

McMullen attended Mass and was deep in prayer. At 8 a.m. he was brought to the scaffold and hanged by Thomas Pierrepoint of the infamous English dynasty of hangmen. He was said to have met his death bravely. In scenes repeated at many executions, a large group of people gathered outside the prison, including a number of women reciting the rosary. When the notice of death was produced, several of them broke down in tears, one of them exclaiming, 'He's gone now.'

An inquest was held into the execution at midday, where it was concluded that death had been by hanging, which had caused the vertebrae to fracture. Felix McMullen (29) was then buried in an unmarked grave within the walls of the prison.

In a bitterly ironic twist, it would later emerge that McMullen himself, like many of the demobilised soldiers, had been seeking a position in the Civic Guard. He had even secured references from several high-ranking soldiers. What drove the ambitious young ex-soldier to commit an armed robbery with lethal consequences will never be known. The juries concerned seemed to believe that McMullen had not meant to kill anyone, despite shooting two men. A recommendation to mercy had been added and a reprieve discussed. The death sentence went ahead nonetheless. The government of the day may well have felt the pressure of the two previous unsolved Garda killings and so it was McMullen who paid the ultimate price. The government did learn something from the Baltinglass Bank Raid, however. Over the next eighteen months, telephones were installed in over 200 Garda stations throughout the country. This would help to ensure that a fatal raid could not happen again as easily. The lack of co-operation between the DMP and the Gardaí also paved the way for the amalgamation of the two forces the year after Garda O'Halloran's death.

The incoming Irish administration after independence had planned initially to abolish the death penalty, a hated relic of British rule. The impending Civil War changed minds, however, and the deterrent was kept on the statute books in order to counter the republican threat. Ironically, the first man hanged by the state was not a republican but a National Army soldier named William Downes. Like Felix McMullen, Downes was also demobilised and decided to embark on a crime spree. He shot and killed Thomas Fitzgerald, a CID policeman, in a botched factory robbery in Ashtown, County Dublin, in October 1923. He was hanged within five weeks, a few months before McMullen's execution.

4

DETECTIVE
ARTHUR NOLAN

'I have got you at last.'

It was decided in 1922 that the Gardaí would be responsible for policing the whole of the twenty-six counties of the Free State, unlike in England where the police had different branches throughout the country. The one exception to this rule was Dublin, which was instead placed under the stewardship of the Dublin Metropolitan Police. The DMP had a long history in the city and was generally better liked pre-independence than the RIC, partially due to the fact that it had been largely unarmed and thus less of a legitimate target for the IRA, although a number of its members were still killed in the conflict, including its assistant commissioner. Nevertheless, the DMP continued to oversee law and order in Dublin after independence and avoided the fate of the disbanded RIC. Their initial survival after the War of Independence would be but a brief stay of execution, however; the DMP was subsumed into the Gardaí in 1925, after eighty-eight years of active service.

In its three years of existence in the Free State, the metropolitan force saw its share of violence, overseeing the transition from war to peace in Dublin City. The crime rate declined, the instances of armed attacks going from a high of 205 in 1922 down to just ten three years later. Instances of murder in the capital also plummeted, from fifty-one in 1922 down to just one in 1925.[1] The DMP's dealings with wanton criminality still divided opinion, however. One senator described DMP officers as being 'as rare as a white blackbird', at a crime scene while others dismissed them as an embarrassment and an irrelevance in the fight between the IRA and the Crown forces.[2] Kevin O'Higgins also favoured its amalgamation with the Gardaí, describing the concept of two police forces in the Free State as wasteful.[3] Others lamented the passing of the DMP: 'As a general rule the DMP man performed his duties in such a calm and dignified way that he seemed to many to be a friend not only to those in trouble but to those endeavouring to avoid it.'[4]

There was one man who harboured a burning resentment towards the DMP and its members and he had murderous intentions that no one could have foreseen. This man, described as a mentally deranged lunatic, had delusions of persecution which led him to try to kill as many officers as possible. He would succeed in killing one DMP officer, Arthur Nolan, the only member of that force murdered in the course of his duty in the history of the Irish state.

Arthur Nolan had taken a fairly typical career path for an Irish policeman of the 1920s. Born in Rathfarnham, County Dublin, on 9 January 1885, Nolan had worked as a coal dealer and bread-van driver but joined the Old IRA (Dublin Brigade) in July 1914, long before most men of his generation had considered rebellion. He took part in numerous attacks on the British Army in the conflict, and was wounded in one engagement in his home village. Nolan professed loyalty to the Free State after the Treaty and was immediately placed in the Criminal Investigation Department. The CID was an armed police force based in Dublin that worked separately from the DMP and Nolan was appointed an Assistant Inspector in the organisation's headquarters in Oriel House.

Arthur Nolan had an eventful time in the organisation, finding himself involved in several skirmishes with republicans. The first was the Battle of Ballinascorney in the Wicklow Hills.[5] He and a party of five CID men were searching for looted goods when they were surrounded by up to twenty-five members of the anti-Treaty IRA. After a fire fight lasting an hour and a half, Nolan managed to lead his men to safety without sustaining any casualties. On another occasion, he gave chase to armed raiders who robbed the offices of Johnston, Mooney and O'Brien in Ballsbridge.[6]

Even more excitingly, Nolan had himself been arrested in England in 1922 when on undercover CID work. He had been tasked with travelling to Britain and confiscating weapons from Irregular members of the IRA who had procured them there. He succeeded in tracing the irregulars in question and taking their weapons but was arrested on a train by British police. He had huge amounts of armaments in his possession. The British, understandably, believed that Nolan was an IRA man bringing weapons across the Irish Sea to wage war with the new Free State government. He was immediately locked up until the Irish authorities could assure their counterparts that he had been doing work on behalf of the state.[7] When the CID was disbanded in October 1923, Arthur Nolan was transferred to the less exciting but equally important division that was the DMP. By this stage, he was married with eight children and was one of the many officers stationed in Dublin City centre.

Nolan's police barracks was situated on Great Brunswick Street, or Pearse Street, as it is now known. On Friday, 29 February 1924, a large number of Gardaí were in the station. Some were working while those on reserve duty played cards in a room adjoining the front office. At about 8.45 p.m., a strongly built man of about 55 years walked in. His name was George Lane and he 'shuffled into the detective office, his hands buried deep in his coat pockets'.[8] He went directly into the front office. Lane, a homeless man who was originally from Waterford, was of stout built but was well groomed with a slight moustache and was dressed in a well-cut suit, an overcoat and a felt hat. He had the look of a man who was unhappy, however.

Sergeant William Gibney (32) was standing beside the fire when the visitor entered the premises. The sergeant was acquainted with Lane as he frequently came into the station to make complaints against the police. The sergeant asked, 'Well, Lane, what do you want now?' Lane appeared sober, but excited. He began to talk wildly and abuse the detective, making sweeping allegations against the local DMP. Gibney had dealt with these particular issues previously but on this occasion the complainant elaborated, protesting to the policeman, 'I am always in trouble with you. You have brought me up from Waterford again. You are always shadowing me and following me around and I wish you would keep your slimy hands off me.'[9]

Two other detectives who were present made as if to answer Lane's allegations, before Sergeant Gibney told them, 'Don't mind him boys, he is not all there.' Turning his attention to Lane, he said facetiously, 'You ought to give £5 to a solicitor and you could get a summons against all the police.' He also instructed him to write to the commissioner with his complaint. The sergeant did not pay much more attention to the agitated visitor and an angry Lane left the building a few minutes later. Gibney would later depose that Lane had looked 'wicked' and his parting words had been something to the effect of, 'I will stop that.'[10]

Gibney did not think any more about it, going into the general office where he sat on a high stool with his colleague, Sergeant Whelan. Detective Officer McGillan stood nearby. Over a dozen policemen were meanwhile reclining in the mess room. Arthur Nolan, who was on reserve duty, had been with them some minutes before but had gone to man the desk in the charge office. Just after 9 p.m. George Lane rushed back into the Garda station without warning. He was brandishing a hatchet with an 18in handle. Nolan had no time to react before Lane brought the weapon down ferociously on his head, shouting, 'I have got you at last', although he had never met or spoken to Nolan before this point. A badly injured Nolan fell against a nearby cupboard. Lane was not finished yet, however. Still wielding the bloody hatchet, 'a silent rush carried Lane into an inner office before anyone knew that anything unusual had happened'.[11]

In the general office he found Sergeant Gibney and Whelan sitting at opposite ends of a desk. Lane approached Gibney from behind. The officer, who was writing, heard nothing until Lane raised the bloodstained axe and hit him on the back of the head with the edge of the hatchet. He then shrieked, 'I have got you, Gibney.' A badly injured Gibney somehow managed to get up and stumble away from the madman and out into the front office of the station. Lane then turned his attention to McGillan, who had not been paying attention and 'only realised something was wrong when he saw the blood flowing over the book in which Gibney was making entries'. Lane swung the lethal weapon at him; McGillan ducked and narrowly avoided it.[12]

Lane's next target was Sergeant Whelan, whom he approached with his hatchet swinging. Whelan waited until Lane came around the table before throwing an office chair in his direction, aiming for his face. The sergeant could not say whether it hit him as he quickly turned and ran to the mess room, where the rest of the officers were present. Whelan screamed that Sergeant Gibney had been 'done in' and for his colleagues to get their guns from their lockers. The axe-wielding madman was in close pursuit. All the officers jumped to their feet. Driver Booth managed to pull out his revolver, but in the confusion he did not fire, afraid he would hit one of his colleagues in the chaotic frenzy.[13]

Detective Officer George Fennell, one of the men playing cards in the mess room, had heard the shout and was the first to race to his locker to retrieve his revolver. He found himself isolated in a corner with the onrushing Lane approaching him with the uplifted axe. Fennell attempted to defend himself with his hand but Lane managed to strike him in the temple with the weapon. Fennell said, 'Oh my God', putting his hand to his forehead. Lane attempted to hit the officer a second time. As he swung back the axe, Detective Officer Fagan caught his arm. He then bravely put his hand around Lane's throat and brought him crashing to the ground before disarming him. Lane fought furiously, lashing out with his arms and legs, but was eventually overpowered by several of the DMP men present. He was immediately arrested. He replied, 'I want to get hung, I'm sick of the lot of you.' After being asked why he had carried out the vicious attack, Lane merely reiterated, 'I want to get hanged.'

Gibney had, at this stage, managed to get outside where he saw Constable William Prendergast standing on the footpath. He shouted to him, 'Come out quickly; there is a madman inside after killing us all.' The constable entered the station and was horrified to find Arthur Nolan staggering around with blood oozing from his head. The critically injured officer was in the act of falling but Prendergast helped him outside and covered his head with a handkerchief. He was able to talk, although he seemed delirious.[14] Prendergast hailed a private motor car to take the wounded officers to nearby Jervis Street Hospital. Nolan's colleague, Sergeant Whelan, had also telephoned for two ambulances, which arrived at the scene quickly. Fennell was transported to Mercer's Hospital to receive medical aid. Although the heavy blow of the hatchet had fractured the bone in his forehead he was found to be in a stable condition and discharged after just over three weeks. Gibney also spent some time in hospital but he too was discharged in time to appear at the trial.

Prendergast held Arthur Nolan on a couch in the accident room as he was examined by the doctor. Despite the gaping wound on his forehead, Nolan managed to say, 'What did I do on that man that he should strike me with a hatchet?' He also told those present that he believed he was dying. The detective had sustained a devastating wound to his frontal bone and a laceration of the brain. Almost all of the muscles on the back of Nolan's neck were cut but no major arteries were severed. He was operated on and a large piece of bone that was projecting on his brain was removed. His condition seemed favourable for over a week, although he never fully regained consciousness. He eventually succumbed to his devastating injuries at 5 a.m. on the morning of 11 March 1924. He was the third policeman in Ireland to be killed in less than three months.

The inquest was held in the City Morgue the day after Nolan's demise, where his body was identified by his brother-in-law William Brien. The jury concluded that Nolan had been wilfully murdered by George Lane and that death had been due to laceration of the brain caused by wounds sustained during the frenzied attack. The DMP were now looking at a murder investigation. News of the attack caused widespread outrage and shock throughout the country.

Nolan's funeral was held in St Joseph's church, Terenure, on 13 March before his tricolour-laden coffin was buried in Glasnevin Cemetery. Large numbers of DMP and Gardaí were present. The inquest summed up the general feeling when it stated that 'Nolan's death was deplored by every member of the police force, of which he was a capable and efficient officer.'[15] Although Sergeant Gibney was unable to attend, the inquest had sufficient witnesses to find Lane guilty of wilful murder and refer him for trial to Green Street.

George Lane was eventually arraigned on a charge of attempted murder, as well as maiming, wounding and aggravated assault. His trial began in the Dublin Commission on Green Street in front of Justice Samuels on 4 April 1924. Lane did not appoint any form of a legal team for himself so one was chosen for him by the state. The accused was fortunate not to be facing a capital murder charge where the penalty at the time was almost certain to be a death sentence. The state had already put five people to death in the first two years of the state's existence, including National Army Lieutenant Jeremiah Gaffney the previous month, so the prospects for Lane could have been grim indeed.

Lane was described as a land surveyor, albeit one with no fixed place of residence. Despite this, at the time of his arrest he had on his person the princely sum of £26 as well as a gold chain and a silver watch. His accusation of shadowing was denied vehemently by the DMP but Lane clearly believed it. Shortly after being arrested, Lane told how he had bought the axe on Capel Street for 2s 9d 'to kill a few CID men. I bought the axe four months ago and I have been waiting my opportunity until I get one man alone in the front office.'[16] He added that he had arrived from Limerick on the 7.40 a.m. train the day before the murder with that very purpose in mind.

Lane appeared perfectly calm and collected on the stand, although his behaviour was bizarre, to say the least, and in court he disagreed with the testimony of the officers in the dock. Although he did not challenge the serious matter of him attacking several men with a hatchet and killing one of them, he was vehement in his denials of the words attributed to him, remarking, 'I do not remember uttering a single word from the time I went into the CID office until the time that I came out.' He did reveal before the trial that his motivation for murdering Nolan and attempting to murder his colleagues was their laughter when he had tried to make a complaint.[17]

The sanity of the defendant was the first question considered. Dr Hackett, of Mountjoy Prison, gave evidence about Lane's mental condition, which he had been observing since his arrest. The doctor had conducted daily interviews with the accused and he opined that Lane was suffering from 'Constant and persistent delusions of persecution'. He went on to say that, in his medical opinion, Lane was unable to put forward a coherent defence or even take an interest in proceedings. The jury thus had little choice but to return a verdict that George Lane was unfit to plead. The judge was therefore forced to direct that the prisoner be detained in an asylum 'until his majesty's pleasure', the British king at that point being the ceremonial head of state. Detective Arthur Nolan was desperately unlucky to find himself in the wrong place at the wrong time; had it not been for Driver Fagan's quick thinking and bravery, there may well have been other fatalities on that terrifying night in Pearse Street.

SERGEANT THOMAS GRIFFIN & GARDA JOHN MURRIN

'That poor fellow is dead.'

At 3.45 p.m. on the afternoon of 5 May 1924, Garda Joseph Collins was on bicycle patrol in Cregg. The townland is 2 miles north of Carrick-on-Suir and is situated in Tipperary, although it straddles the border with County Kilkenny. Collins spotted a man he did not recognise cycling on the footpath in the direction of Carrick-on-Suir. The Garda shouted to the man to get off the footpath but the cyclist did not obey the order, speeding off instead. About half an hour later, Collins again witnessed the man cycling, this time in the middle of the road and in the opposite direction. The Garda backed up against a wall so as to avoid being seen by the errant cyclist. When he got within 100 yards, Collins sprang out and approached him with his hand in the air, ordering him to stop and disembark the bicycle so his name and address could be taken down.

Events took a sinister turn at this point when the stranger produced an automatic .45 Colt revolver without warning from his pocket and used it to fire a bullet in the direction of the startled Garda 3 yards away. The shot missed its target narrowly and Collins decided, for his own safety, to desist from chasing his quarry further. He instead continued his duty, arriving back to the station in Carrick-on-Suir at 6.30 p.m., where he made a report to his sergeant, Thomas Griffin, of the bizarre and unprovoked attack.[1]

Griffin was born in April 1899 and spent his youth on St Patrick's Terrace in Greenmount in Cork City. Known as Tam, Griffin was from a comparatively small family at the time, having just two siblings. His father had been a soldier in the US Army for several years and his sister had even been born in New York.[2] The family had returned to Ireland and the young Thomas was also destined to become a soldier, but he took a different path to his father, instead joining the IRA and participating in the fight for Irish freedom. He had not enlisted in the National Army after the Treaty, however, instead being amongst the first recruits to the Gardaí in April 1922.

The youth of the new force meant that many of the superior officers would be young men and Griffin was no exception, being promoted to sergeant in August 1922. He was aged just 23. The new sergeant was posted to Kilkenny and in June 1923 to the south of County Tipperary, a district still largely considered hostile to the newly formed Garda force. Griffin was obviously held in high esteem and was 'chosen for Tipperary because it was an area that required great tact and ability to deal with'.[3] He was put in charge of the barracks in the large town of Carrick-on-Suir, which lies on the border of three counties, Tipperary, Kilkenny and Waterford.

On arrival, he promised that the Gardaí would 'protect the lives and property of the people and administer the law in a just manner'.[4] This would be no easy task, Carrick-on-Suir being a busy district that had seen much unrest. The prospective Garda barracks had been burned to the ground by a party of a hundred Irregulars during the Civil War. The conclusion of that conflict did not fully pacify the town either. Kevin O'Higgins remarked, 'It is only with great difficulty that Civic Guard Stations have been established in such important towns as Mallow, Carrick-on-Suir and Claremorris.'[5]

Shooting at Gardaí was an unexpected and unacceptable act however, even in a hostile town, and Sergeant Griffin was quick to initiate some enquiries. He went with Garda Rossiter to Cregg, where they received information that the cyclist was a man by the name of Michael 'Sonny' O'Dwyer. O'Dwyer was a native of Cregg and a notorious republican who was known to bear animosity towards the Gardaí and to be in constant possession of a firearm. Just hours after he had allegedly shot at Garda Collins he would also threaten the life of Sergeant Griffin. On that evening, O'Dwyer was outside the home of his neighbour, blacksmith John Harris (45) in Cregg. He beckoned to Harris and when Harris reached him, O'Dwyer shoved a gun through the garden gate, pointing it directly at his neighbour. O'Dwyer accused the blacksmith of stealing his guns when he had been arrested by the Free State Army some time before. Before Harris could answer, Sergeant Griffin and Guard Rossiter came into view. Harris remarked, 'There are the Guards.' O'Dwyer replied that he would shoot both Harris and the Gardaí. Harris replied, 'Shoot away.' O'Dwyer did not make good on his threat and left hurriedly, managing to avoid the attention of the Gardaí.

The Gardaí heard this strange tale from Harris and decided it was safer to wait until the next day to take action against the suspected gunman. On the afternoon of 6 May, Sergeant Griffin again went to Cregg to attempt to capture O'Dwyer. This time he enlisted the help of Garda Murrin in what had the potential to be a dangerous assignment. John Alphonsus Murrin came from the small townland of Aighan, not far from the village of Bruckless in the south of County Donegal. He was born in 1898 into a relatively wealthy family, his father being a successful merchant and member of the Donegal Board of Guardians. Their house contained over thirteen rooms and a roof of slate, something uncommon in that part of the world at that time.[6] The family also employed several servants. This comfortable background did not deter Murrin from doing his part for his country and enlisting in the Irish Volunteers during the War of Independence. He took the pro-Treaty side after the conflict and became a soldier in the National Army, before joining the Gardaí in April 1923. He was swiftly deployed to the district of Carrick-on-Suir, where he found himself on that summer day.

Most of their colleagues were stationed at that day's Clonmel Races when Griffin and Murrin left for Cregg; neither man was armed, despite the obvious danger of dealing with a man who had recklessly shot at a fellow officer the previous day. Murrin and Griffin arrived at O'Dwyer's farmhouse at around 4 p.m. The house was unoccupied and appeared to be empty. The two men entered cautiously, with Sergeant Griffin in the lead. When Griffin got to the back of the house, he saw a man, who pulled a revolver out of his pocket and held it behind his back. The sergeant continued to approach the stranger nonetheless. When he was about seven paces away, the man quickly pulled the revolver out and shot Griffin in the abdomen.[7] Garda Murrin, who was some distance behind, ran in on hearing the gunfire. He too was shot, receiving a bullet in the spine.

Mary Burke was also a resident of Cregg. She lived two fields away from the O'Dwyer house, or a quarter of a mile by road. Just before 4 p.m., she saw her neighbour Philip O'Dwyer crossing the river to his house. Minutes later she heard him calling to her from the bridge. She ran to him and found him breathless and shaking uncontrollably. Burke asked her neighbour several times what was wrong but he was unable to answer for a period, putting his hand on her shoulder and saying only, 'Jesus, Mary and Joseph, what will I do?' Eventually he continued, 'There were two or three guards shot over the way' and begged her to 'go over and stop with them and give them a drink,' while he went for a priest and a doctor. He then ran in the direction of Carrick-on-Suir.[8]

Mary Burke ran into the yard of the O'Dwyer house first, where she saw Murrin and Griffin lying on the ground yards from the house. There appeared to be no one else present. Murrin was conscious and lying high up in the garden while Griffin lay unresponsive at the end of the hay barn. Murrin gestured towards his colleague and remarked, 'That poor fellow is dead. Get me a glass of water.' Burke herself believed at the time that the sergeant appeared to be deceased.[9] Garda Murrin asked to be propped up and Mary Burke hurried back to her own house, retrieving two cushions out of a car to perform the task. It then began to rain and she went into the house, finding blankets and coats which she placed on the two men.

Griffin was lying underneath a spout and was getting covered with water so Burke and her young son decided to move him. It was at this point that Mrs Burke discovered that he was not dead when he gently squeezed her hand. The sergeant also managed to open his eyes and ask for a drink, which she gave to him. He then begged for a priest, and Burke comforted him, telling him that he would be all right. Griffin replied that it was no use and that he just wanted a priest.[10] Burke attempted to keep him talking and asked him who had shot them. He was able to answer lucidly, saying it was Sonny O'Dwyer. He added that if Sonny O'Dwyer's brother Philip had not come up with a load of lime the gunman would have shot them again and killed them both.

At 4.15 p.m., a clergyman rushed into Carrick-on-Suir barracks and breathlessly told Garda Thomas Smith that two of his men had been shot in Cregg. Smith immediately sent a motor car to the scene with two Gardaí in it, also wiring for the military in Clonmel to attend the crime scene. It was quickly apparent that the lives of the two Gardaí were in danger and Fr O'Byrne was summoned to administer to the critically injured men. He gave both the Last Rites. The local GP, Dr Stephenson, also arrived and attended to the Gardaí. It was very cold for that time of year and Stephenson was immediately worried about the men's condition.

Sergeant Griffin was by now unresponsive and lying in a pool of blood in the yard in a collapsed condition. Garda Murrin was also lying on the ground in front of the house. He was conscious and mentioned being very cold. He also complained of great pain, informing the doctor that he was unable to move his legs. The Garda car then arrived at the scene, driving back to the barracks with Garda Murrin in it. Sergeant Griffin arrived some minutes later in a different car. Both men were subsequently taken the 14 miles to Clonmel Hospital.

Dr Crean of Clonmel examined Griffin at 7 p.m. on the evening of 7 May. He found the sergeant to be in a state of collapse. The bullet had entered the lower part of his abdomen on the left side and passed downwards, piercing his hip and lodging in his right buttock. The doctor succeeded in removing the bullet but the abdominal cavity was full of blood and it was felt that he would not survive long, although he was relatively lucid for much of the two days following the shooting. It was thus decided to take a statement, which would later prove to amount to a dying deposition, where the victim described the confrontation in his own words. The statement left little doubt about the condition of the sergeant, beginning, 'I, Thomas Griffin, having fear of death before me, and without any hope of recovery, make the following statement'. It then outlined the events of the day:

> We crossed the bridge below Harris's and went into Dwyer's yard. We went into the house and I saw a riding breeches. There was no-one inside. We went out and I called Garda Murrin. I saw someone round the hay. Jack came round from the back. The fellow put out his head. I saw him put his hand into his pocket and pulling out a .45 Colt revolver. I advanced towards him and was speaking to him and when within about seven paces of him he cocked the revolver and fired three shots at me. I then fell and heard him firing shots at Murrin. I think the man who fired the shots is Sonny O'Dwyer. I don't remember any more.[11]

The statement concluded at 8.14 p.m. The sergeant would be dead just hours later, passing away at 3.50 a.m. The cause of death was shock and haemorrhage. Chief Superintendent Clinton described his deceased colleague as 'One of the pioneers of the Guards in Tipperary' and mentioned that he had fought hard against blackguardism and ruffianism in the county. He had been popular in the district and although he had been known to Sonny O'Dwyer, he had never had any confrontation with him before that fatal encounter.

On the evening of 8 May, the remains of Sergeant Griffin were removed by train to his native Cork City to be interred in St Joseph's Cemetery. 150 Gardaí silently mourned their colleague while thousands of people lined the route. The cortège wound its way to the graveyard where Garda Chief Commissioner Eoin O'Duffy spoke. He described how Griffin had been 'carrying out his duty courageously and manfully' before he was 'callously done to death by the hand of a cowardly assassin'. The commissioner urged the people to stand by the Gardaí for the good of their country before sympathising with Griffin's mother, remarking, 'It is better to be the mother of the slain than the mother of the slayer.'[12] There was widespread revulsion locally and nationally to the crime, but it was not universal. Just days after the shooting, a woman was arrested in the neighbouring town of Clonmel for causing a disturbance. She struck the arresting Garda in the face and shouted, 'You should have got what the chap in Carrick got.'[13]

Meanwhile, Garda Murrin was also seriously ill. He had received a bullet into the spine and paralysis was quick to set in. Just two days after the shooting, the newspapers were reporting that the Garda was 'so seriously wounded that little hope is entertained of his recovery'. On 9 May, the young Garda was removed by military ambulance to St Vincent's Hospital, Dublin. The doctor on duty described how the bullet had struck Murrin in the spine and lodged in his left shoulder. Murrin himself, when conscious, showed great fortitude and courage and continually asserted that he was going to live. By 21 May, the newspapers had altered their outlook for the better, reporting that Murrin's progress was satisfactory.

On 29 September 1924, John Murrin, now described as paralysed from the middle of the body down due to his spine being severed, was brought to the North Wall in Dublin. It was the first time he had left the hospital since he had been admitted four months before. He and about twenty others were to be transported to Lourdes in France as part of the Cardinal's Party. They would receive spiritual and medical attention at the holy shrine for about a fortnight. After his return, his condition had deteriorated and

Murrin himself told Gardaí that he believed he was going to die. At 1.50 p.m. on Saturday 18 October, Sergeant Edward Mangan, of the Garda Depot in the Phoenix Park, visited the hospital and asked Murrin if he wanted to make a statement. Murrin did not reply.

Eventually he agreed to the request. Before the interview, Murrin was shown a picture of Sonny O'Dwyer. He asserted that the man in the picture was the gunman guilty of shooting him and Sergeant Griffin. He began his statement in the same mournful fashion as his deceased fellow Garda:

I, John Murrin, having fear of death before me, and not hoping to recover, make the following statement. I distinctly remember seeing the man that shot Griffin and me at Dwyer's in Kilonerry [Cregg] on Tuesday 6 May 1924. I recognise in the photograph which I have signed the man who shot Sergeant Griffin – the only difference that he looks younger in that photo. That is the man who shot Sergeant Griffin and me. That is him.'

Murrin then signed both the statement and the photograph, as did his sister and doctor, who were also present during the interview.[14]

The day after he had given a statement, Garda Murrin died in the hospital. The cause of death was myelitis, or inflammation of the spinal cord, and heart failure brought on by septic absorption. The injuries were consistent with a gunshot wound. Murrin's body was removed by train from Dublin to Donegal. It was then conveyed onwards to the village of Bruckless, where Garda John Murrin, less than a year in An Garda Síochána, was greeted by a similarly large crowd as had awaited Sergeant Griffin. He was then laid to rest in his family plot in the local graveyard.

Much like that of his late colleague, the death of Garda Murrin was greeted with horror by the newspapers of the day. One editorial described the murders as 'a lamentable revelation of senseless savagery', but also remarked of the victims that 'their stubborn courage has done much not only to range popular sympathy on their side but to nerve civilians to stand up against the menace of the gun-man'. The newspaper went on to say that gun violence was sheer criminality and no longer acceptable as an act of war and that the criminals were no longer part of an organisation but acting as lone wolves. Unfortunately for the Gardaí, in this case the lone wolf was still at large, despite his identity being well known.[15]

The military arrested Philip O'Dwyer, along with his brother Edward, in Callan, County Kilkenny, under the Public Safety Act the day after the murder. Both men were listed as living in Kilonerry, just yards over the Kilkenny border from Cregg, and were brothers of Sonny, the suspected assassin. The men had expressed sorrow for the shooting allegedly committed by their brother. Mr Kearney, a solicitor representing Philip O'Dwyer, the owner of the house where the shooting occurred, did appear and addressed the court. He told those present that his client was ill on account of the horrific tragedy but had said that when he appeared he would supply any information he could to help in the apprehension of his fugitive brother. He also stated this his client wished Garda Murrin all the best with his recovery. A representative of the Gardaí would later castigate some of the local people of the district, fuming that the fugitive was still at large and would have been caught long before had he not been sheltered and protected by members of the local community. After the shootings, the Gardaí spent several weeks searching suspected safe houses in the locality, mainly in the early hours of the morning, but they had no success.

By 30 June, Sonny O'Dwyer was still on the run but his two brothers remained in custody, despite not being present when the fatal shots were fired. They were transferred to military custody at that point, where they were interned with twenty-two others under the Public Safety Act. The O'Dwyers' case was adjourned no less than four times and they were still under internment in Limerick Prison on Christmas Eve 1924. They refused to appeal their internment or plead for legal assistance even though they were entitled to do so.[16] Their conduct was described as very satisfactory and, with no charge forthcoming, the brothers were eventually released.

The manhunt for Sonny O'Dwyer continued. He was a man known to have murdered two members of the Gardaí in cold blood. In May 1925, an inquest was held into Griffin's death at Clonmel Union Boardroom, twelve months to the day after the sergeant had been buried in his native Cork. The coroner described it as a most remarkable case. Gardaí had been merely attempting to question a man for the trivial offence of cycling on a footpath, but the affair had ended in the death of two policemen. Mr O'Connor, addressing the jury, described O'Dwyer as a man who had become desperate without reason and was constantly in possession of a loaded revolver. He had threatened to shoot his neighbour John Harris and the two Gardaí, a threat he had followed through with the following day. The Gardaí had no chance to save themselves and O'Connor told the jury that he knew they 'were a body of very intelligent men, and I am sure you will have no difficulty coming to a verdict'. The jury did indeed come to a swift verdict of wilful murder against the absent Sonny O'Dwyer. But where was he? It was rumoured the suspect had been spotted in the district a week before the inquest.

Sergeant Griffin's sister, as his next of kin, was awarded £300 for her brother's death while his mother was granted £200. A few miles up the road, less than three years before, Garda Phelan had been shot down and his killers had not been implicated. Despite the fact that the gunman who had deliberately shot down Sergeant Griffin and Garda Murrin had been definitively identified, he would also never face justice for his crime. Local Superintendent Sheridan lamented that the gunman was 'being sheltered by people in adjoining districts; he would be in custody today only for the people who are sheltering him'. The search for Sonny O'Dwyer continued but he would never be discovered. Tragically the zealous attempts to apprehend O'Dwyer would lead to the death of an innocent man.

Denis Hayes was 22 years old and described as 'one of Tipperary's best fighters during the Black and Tan regime'. He was at a dance in a house at Casey's Cross, 3 miles from Nenagh, on 19 May 1924, some two weeks after the shooting of Murrin and Griffin. Two local Gardaí, along with a military party, raided the dance on that night on the lookout for a man who had committed a string of robberies locally. As they looked around the room, Garda McGuinness caught sight of Hayes. McGuinness whispered to his colleague Garda Geraghty, 'He is the dead image of Sonny Dwyer', having been shown a picture of the fugitive before. They approached Hayes, ordering him to halt. Hayes, a high-profile anti-Treaty republican, began to run. Shots were exchanged and a soldier fired a bullet in the direction of the IRA man, which struck vital organs in his abdomen, killing him instantly. The military inquest found that he had been shot in the course of the army shooting because he was thought to be a wanted man.[17] Denis Hayes died, but Sonny O'Dwyer was never caught.

6

GARDA THOMAS DOWLING

'We shot a man last night but
we don't give a damn anyway.'

Thomas Dowling was born in Ballyouskill, County Kilkenny, on 5 July 1896, but as a young boy moved to High Street in nearby Ballyragget. He was the only son of carpenter John Dowling and his wife Bridget. The couple also had two daughters.[1] Described as a man of fine physique, Dowling had served with distinction as a lieutenant in the IRA during the War of Independence. Unlike the neighbouring county of Tipperary, renowned for its opposition to the Treaty, Kilkenny had been predominantly in favour of the agreement and Thomas Dowling was no different. He joined the National Army in its early days, attesting in his local town of Castlecomer on 10 March 1922.

Although the Free State Army made rapid gains throughout the country, they also sustained many casualties. Dowling was badly injured in an ambush at Woodroofe, near Clonmel, after he and comrades had attacked an IRA brigade that had commandeered houses and weapons in the town.[2] He recovered and went on to reach the rank of lieutenant of the engineers. Dowling survived the Civil War and enlisted in An Garda Síochána in March 1924. He was posted to Fanore on 27 December of the same year. The new police force had succeeded for the most part in pacifying the country and the crime rate was dropping steadily after the horrors of the Civil War. However, on 28 December 1925, almost a year to the day after he had arrived, Garda Dowling was brutally shot dead.

Fanore is a quiet seaside village situated on the north coast of County Clare. It lies 30 miles from Ennis, the county town, and is surrounded by the harsh and sparsely populated beauty of the Burren. Despite the tranquil surroundings, the area was home to agrarian outrages in the early part of the twentieth century and there were major difficulties locally regarding the distribution of land. It was situated on Ireland's impoverished west coast and had lost over 10 per cent of its population between 1911 and 1926, mainly through emigration.[3] The illegal distillation and supply of poteen, or extremely potent homemade alcohol, was one sure way to earn money in the economically depressed area. It is an addictive drink that was frequently produced in unhygienic conditions and known on occasion to cause ill health or even death. Fanore is one of the closest points to Connemara and the Aran Islands by boat and the lucrative supply of illegally distilled poteen was widespread. The alcohol was frequently smuggled across Galway Bay to quiet beaches far from the long arm of the law.

Poteen was a major industry in the country at the time, particularly on the west coast. The homemade alcohol was popular as it was easy to obtain and far cheaper than the legal alternative. During the War of Independence, there was often no policing to speak of, leaving rural dwellers free to produce as much of the potent alcohol as they wished. This meant that by 1925 there were also 13,000 public houses in Ireland, an average of one pub to every 230 people in Ireland. The newly formed Irish government had several members who were appalled by the drinking culture in Ireland, Kevin O'Higgins foremost amongst them. He stated, perhaps facetiously, that as a result of the poteen trade in the west of Ireland 'children going to and coming from school are reeling round the road drunk'.[4] It was decided to clamp down on the nation's enduring love for alcohol, although legislation stopped short of prohibition, which was being implemented in the United States at the time. Instead draconian new legislation was introduced in the form of the Intoxicating Liquor Act (1924). Its aim was to limit the availability of the substance, prohibiting pubs from opening after 10 p.m. Alcohol was also made illegal to those under the age of eighteen. Meanwhile, a 'holy hour' was inaugurated, which banned the sale of the substance to anyone at specified hours during the day. St Patrick's Day was also off limits for drinkers. Eoin O'Duffy believed that alcohol was a scourge on the nation and actively discouraged all members of the Gardaí from drinking, even going as far as issuing an intemperance order in the early days of the force.[5]

Unfortunately, the laws clamping down on pubs also served to increase the demand for poteen. As a result of this, ordinary Gardaí found that one of their most unpopular duties was the suppression of the trade of the illegal alcohol. Their interference often caused serious aggravation amongst the poteen makers; in one case in December 1922, a Garda station was burned to the ground in Gweedore, County Donegal. This act was believed to have been carried out by distillers of the illegal alcohol.[6] The Fanore Gardaí were particularly vigilant in their attempt to stamp out the trade of the substance and Garda Dowling would pay dearly for this devotion to duty.

Fanore was Thomas Dowling's first post after his training in the depot. The inexperienced young Garda was considered to be of quiet and retiring disposition and would have found the village, where both English and Irish were spoken, a difficult community in which to keep order.[7] He shared the three-room rural station, situated in the townland of Murroogh and converted from a labourer's cottage, with three other colleagues and a sergeant. The officers had to deal with agrarian problems on a daily basis. Cattle-driving, intimidation and the knocking of stone walls were particularly widespread occurrences in the district. As late as November 1923, Garda reports stated that the north-west Clare area was 'overrun by armed criminals'.[8] A type of local soviet was said to exist, local businesses having been taken over by force several times throughout the 1920s. Litigation amongst neighbours was also common and the deeply unsettled area was an unpleasant posting for a young Guard.[9]

Clare was one of the most troubled parts of the country in the early part of the twentieth century. The IRA had been strong in the area during the Anglo-Irish War and at one point locals were considered so dangerous that any Clare resident required a special licence to travel outside the county. In the aftermath of independence, the county consistently voted for anti-Treaty candidates in general elections, with republican leader Éamon de Valera regularly topping the poll. The government and its representatives were thus met with suspicion by many Clare denizens. The local Gardaí also struggled to obtain co-operation in criminal matters and by 1925 had taken to patrolling the Fanore district nightly on bicycles in an attempt to snare local law-breakers. One newspaper described these efforts as 'almost useless in preventing the operation of the lawless band' and claimed that 'respectable people in the district contend that if the Guards were armed on night patrol these outrages would cease'.[10]

Monday 28 December was another mild day in what had been an agreeable winter. At 7 p.m., 29-year-old Garda Dowling left Fanore Garda Station as usual to circumnavigate the district, checking for criminal activity. He noted nothing untoward. Although he was rostered for several hours' patrol, he ended his duty prematurely and met with his colleague Garda John Cahill. The two men went to the house of Joe McNamara in the townland of Derreen, just outside Fanore, where they played cards until about 9.45 p.m.[11] After the game, they mounted their bicycles and headed back in the direction of the barracks, 2½ miles distant. It was a bright, dry, moonlit night. At around 10 p.m., the two men rounded the bend close to Craggagh Graveyard just outside the village.

Suddenly, from just a few feet away, a volley of bullets rang out. Dowling was closest to the assailants and a number of pellets hit him in the right side. He fell off his bicycle, inches from the grave-yard wall. A shocked Cahill asked, 'Are you all right?' There was no reply from Dowling.

Cahill continued cycling quickly, unaware of the condition of his colleague. He managed to escape, although he described hearing 'the click of a rifle bolt, and a bullet whizzing by my ear, followed by three gunshots'. He went about 30 or 40 yards before disembarking and turning around. He heard a moan and saw Garda Dowling lying prone on the ground and two men standing inside the graveyard's wall. One of them was middle-sized and wearing leggings. He also heard one of the men shout, 'Oh! He is gone.'[12] Another shot was then directed at Garda Cahill, who rapidly got back on his bicycle. Four bullets in all were fired after Cahill, who somehow managed to get back to Fanore unscathed. He reported the ghastly affair to his sergeant immediately. The station was not fitted with a telephone at that time, so Garda Cahill was forced to cycle on a further 6 miles to Ballyvaughan to impart the tragic news.

Sergeant Smyth led a party of Gardaí back to the scene some time later. They discovered the body of Dowling, although the assail-ants were nowhere to be seen. The Garda appeared to have died instantly, his bicycle having fallen across his body. His body was bent up and his face and head were covered in blood. It appeared that the ambush had been planned well in advance as it took place where the road was at its narrowest (just 14ft wide) and at a sharp bend. The bullets that had struck Dowling were not ordinary pel-lets; the cartridges had been emptied and refilled with pieces of a broken metal pot. There seemed little doubt that it was a targeted attack on members of the Gardaí and that the intention had been to cause serious injury or death.

An inquest was held on the body of Guard Dowling shortly after his death. Guard Cahill lied by telling those present that he had been at McNamara's house at seven o'clock while his colleague did not arrive until 9.30 p.m. He admitted later that the men had arrived together and that he had made up this statement in order to protect Dowling, who was supposed to be on patrol. When asked, 'You knew you were swearing what was false in a matter of life and death?' Cahill answered, 'I did.'[13] Regardless, the inquest found that Dowling had sustained two full charges into his right side. The pellets had smashed five of his ribs and penetrated his body with over ninety pellets in what the court described as the 'most atrocious murder that had occurred in Clare in years'. He had died of shock and haemorrhage, the jury determining that his death was one of wilful murder by persons unknown. They also called on the local population to aid the authorities in their efforts to capture the perpetrators.

Dowling's death was greeted with shock all over the country. Although he was single, he was due to be married in his home county the following year to a lady from the neighbouring parish of Castlecomer. It was reported in the media at the time that he had bought her a pendant just days before for Christmas. As one newspaper aptly remarked, 'Instead of his marriage a funeral is now taking place.' The funeral, held in Dowling's native Ballyragget, proved to be a well-attended affair with a large number of Gardaí and army officials present. The body was conveyed to Ballyouskill Cemetery, where he was laid to rest beside his mother, who had predeceased him.[14]

The Deputy Commissioner Éamon Coogan was from nearby Castlecomer and acquainted with Dowling. He led the oration at the graveside, telling the assembled mourners that:

> [Garda Dowling] was giving sterling service in Clare, and because he did his duty by the people who employed him, he was shot down by cowardly assassins. It was not so much they killed him, but the manner of the killing that pained us most. The cowardly assassins waited in a graveyard with murderous intent in their hearts because the guards did their duty to try and save the people from that mental depravity and demoralisation which years of poteen drinking has brought about.[15]

Commissioner O'Duffy also praised the fallen Garda and railed against the poteen culture in the west of Ireland.

The Gardaí had a poor record of apprehending those who had killed members of the force and they would spare no resources in their hunt for the assailants on this occasion. Lorry-loads of officers were dispatched to the area within days. Armed with machine guns, rifles and bayonets, they embarked on a desperate hunt for the party of raiders. The scene at Craggagh was immediately examined. It was discovered that the ambush party had arranged seats behind the wall to aid in their ghastly purpose. They had also left several items behind. Four empty cartridge cases, one of which had the word 'slugs' carved into it, were discovered, as were cases filled with slugs and an empty rifle cartridge case.

Gardaí had started conducting their first house searches on the residences of potential suspects by 1 a.m. on 29 December, just three hours after the killing. Every residence in the locality was visited. One man immediately wanted for questioning was John O'Connor (or Connors). He was known to Gardaí, having been questioned and searched days before in relation to poteen-making. O'Connor was found to be in bed with his brother, but two empty cartridge cases were discovered in a box. O'Connor was under suspicion immediately. This suspicion appeared to be confirmed when a local farmer named Denis Rabbitte came forward. Rabbitte claimed that at the late hour of midnight on 27 December he had been called out of bed by O'Connor, who was with a friend named Patrick Conway. The men first apologised for the lateness of the hour, before asking the farmer for the loan of his shotgun for two days. They allegedly claimed that they wanted it to shoot birds.[16] Rabbitte agreed and gave the men the gun, which was clean. The night-time visitors then left. They returned the shotgun the next night at 12.30 a.m., just hours after Dowling was shot, again rousing Rabbitte from his sleep. O'Connor handed him the firearm and said, 'I came back with your gun.' Rabbitte said that the gun was quite dirty and appeared to have been used in the meantime.[17]

By 26 January, three young local men were in custody for the murder of the Garda. O'Connor, Conway and another man named Augustus Linnane (all aged about 20) were charged with murder, with a further charge of conspiracy to murder also being added. Thomas Dowling had come across all the accused in his time, questioning and searching them for arms and poteen. All three denied the crime initially, O'Connor responding to the charge by saying, 'I am innocent of the charge brought against me. I know nothing about it and almighty God knows that.' The District Court decided that Conway and O'Connor had charges to answer, but could not agree regarding Linnane, who was released without charge.

The two remaining prisoners were then brought to Ennis District Court. A local publican, whose premises was just 150 yards from the ambush site in Craggagh, deposed that all three men had been in the pub an hour before the ambush, 'where they had a plentiful supply of drink'. Another witness, Corney Cullinane, corroborated that the three men were together on the night of the shooting and that they had asked him to join them for a drink. A handwriting expert would also testify that the word 'slugs' found at the scene had been written by the same hand as writing in a copybook in O'Connor's home.[18] More crucial evidence came from a firearms expert, who opined that three empty cartridges found at the scene had been fired from the gun lent to O'Connor the night before the shooting. Several other pieces of circumstantial evidence were given, including that of a local boy who heard O'Connor say, 'I will get my own back out of them fellows yet', after a Garda had searched his house for poteen on Christmas night, just three days before the shooting. It was also alleged that Conway and O'Connor had travelled together across the mountains to Lisdoonvarna the day after the murder, staying away until nightfall, behaviour considered suspicious by the prosecution.

There were several other witnesses lined up to give evidence for the prosecution, but they did not testify as expected. Lizzie Kenny, a local girl of 16, had earlier sworn that she had seen the three accused on the road at Craggagh near O'Donoghue's public house on the night in question. In court, however, she mentioned seeing two men creeping down towards the sea in the dark but refused to identify them. She would no longer swear that she had seen any of the accused, saying only in court that 'I thought it was them that was in it, but I'm not sure'. She was treated as a hostile witness. Another local man, James Howley, had previously sworn that O'Connor had said after being searched, 'The guards did not search much when the Black and Tans were out. We will have our own back.'[19] In court, Howley admitted accusing O'Connor of these words but insisted that he had only done so after the Gardaí took him in a motor car to the barracks and a detective struck him and tore the collar off his shirt. Howley also claimed to be in fear of the Gardaí as they had threatened that he would be executed for the crime. He (Howley) did concede in court that he would not be able to recognise the detective who had done such a thing, however.

Patrick Conway, a farmer's son from Derreen West just outside the village, had made numerous statements after being arrested. Crucially, in his second statement he had told the Gardaí that his neighbour John O'Connor had asked for help to kill Patrick McNamara, a neighbour of the men. McNamara was a Garda in the Dublin Metropolitan Division but was home on leave over that Christmas and due to depart the day after the shooting. Co-incidentally McNamara, the intended target of the fatal volley, was present in the barracks when Cahill had come back to break the news about Dowling's murder. He was also a brother of the men the Gardaí were playing cards with shortly before the shooting. Conway asserted that he had refused to help in this venture twice after O'Connor had asked him, 'Would you be game to do it?'[20] When Conway refused, his friend had replied that he 'will get two fellows that will do it', naming the men as Andy Connell and Tourna. Conway continued that O'Connor had told him at 5 p.m. on 28 December, 'I am going to commit murder tonight – I'll meet Guard McNamara or one of the Guards', and on the following day, 'We shot a man last night, whether it's a Guard or Mac but we don't give a damn anyway'.

In a further statement, Conway did admit that he was present at the killings, as he was coerced at gunpoint to go along 'by threats and fear'. He was advised to say his prayers for the following night if he did not help with the assassination. Conway eventually agreed and met O'Connor 'between the two little hills near his own house'.[21] He next went to O'Connor's house where two brothers named Connell were waiting for him. One of them, Andy, said, 'Ah, you had to come. Take this gun out of my hand.' Conway did so, but reiterated that he would not fire a shot. The party of men walked to Craggagh and waited in the darkness. At about 10 p.m., they heard the Guards cycling past and two of the men aimed and fired, hitting Guard Dowling. Conway said that O'Connor had said after the shooting, 'We have got the wrong man. The other bastard McNamara is gone. We have a man for our trouble anyway.'

This was enough to see him in court on a murder charge, the death penalty almost a certainty if he was convicted. John McNamara testified that he had seen three men at Craggagh graveyard earlier in the evening; Conway and O'Connor were amongst them. Augustus Linnane, who had initially been arrested with Conway and O'Connor, also gave evidence. Linnane claimed that at one point he was in the exercise yard with Conway in Galway Jail, when Conway turned to him and said, 'How are we to get out of this?' Linnane replied that it would be easy for an innocent man to get out of it. Conway answered, 'We ought to swear false on Connors and the two of us will get out of it.'[22] Linnane had refused. This cast doubt on the truth of Conway's initial statements.

Denis Rabbitte would thus be a crucial witness to determine the guilt of the accused. He repeated his story of the night-time visit but had a difficult time on the stand. Rabbitte denied at length that he had been forced by the local Gardaí to concoct the story of the gun being borrowed due to his position as head poteen-maker of a local gang. He admitted in court that he had formerly distilled poteen but insisted his story of the night-time visit was true. His wife was also called, but she maintained that she had not been woken up by her husband going to the door to answer the knock from Conway and

O'Connor, thus undermining the evidence of one of the prosecution's star witnesses.

Conway would not stand by either of his statements in court. He was now denying being anywhere near the murder, stating that he had been in bed before ten o'clock, a claim that was corroborated by his mother and brother. He also denied point-blank that he had borrowed Denis Rabbitte's gun. The accused refused to answer several questions during examination in court and he was lost for words when it was put to him that he had described the events of the murderous night very accurately for a man who had just made up the details. He pleaded not guilty, maintaining that the information he had given the Gardaí was false and that he had been induced by a Garda to make his statements through threats. Conway alleged that the Gardaí had threatened, 'Yourself and O'Connor are for the swing', leading him to make a false statement in an effort to save himself. When he told them he was willing to alter his statement to clear himself, he alleged that one Guard said, 'If you have any luck you will because O'Connor is hanging you.' The Gardaí denied these claims. Mr Justice Sullivan must have found the defendant's assertions credible, as he refused to admit the statements into evidence, declaring himself unhappy that either had been made voluntarily.[23]

Patrick Conway was tried on three occasions for the crime. Despite making several statements directly implicating himself, none of the juries would be able to agree on his guilt and he was discharged after the third trial, finding himself a free man.

John O'Connor was tried separately and also pleaded not guilty to the charge. The prosecution said that the motive for the crime was obvious as in that part of Clare 'a general feeling of resentment existed against any form of law … when a crime was committed little or no assistance was given to the representatives of the law'.[24] They went on to detail O'Connor's alleged lingering resentment towards Patrick McNamara, the intended victim of the crime. As a young National Army soldier, McNamara had allegedly arrested IRA man O'Connor during the Civil War.

O'Connor's brother entered the witness box and told the court that he had slept in bed with John and that his brother had retired at 9.40 p.m. that night, not leaving the house again. He also described a detective coming to his house, grabbing John and pointing a revolver in his direction before threatening to blow his brains out. His sister corroborated this account. The accused himself also took the stand, knowing that his life was on the line. He admitted to having been a member of the anti-Treaty IRA during the Civil War but denied any grudge against the Gardaí or McNamara. He stuck to his story and performed reasonably well under pressure.

Garda Cahill again gave his evidence of the night in question but the defence solicitor scoffed at his testimony, describing Cahill as 'a confessed perjurer' and saying that his evidence was no longer credible.[25] Apart from lying about the time Dowling had reached the house, he had also claimed it was a cloudy night at the inquest but had since changed his mind, saying it was bright. O'Connor's counsel added that terrorism existed amongst the Gardaí in Clare, whom they maintained had beaten a number of witnesses in order to get the information that they required to secure a conviction. Several witnesses withdrew their original statements against the accused, stating that they were in fear of the authorities. When the judge asked the rhetorical question, 'Surely nobody is afraid of the police down there?', he was answered with laughter from the assembled crowd.[26]

The state's case had all but collapsed and the jury needed just twenty minutes to find O'Connor not guilty of the charge of murder. Both suspects walked free.

In July 1926, Thomas Dowling's father had an award of £300 compensation disallowed by Clare County Council.[27] In lieu of this he was awarded a meagre £100 as a gratuity from the state to pay his legal bills and expenses incurred during his quest for compensation.[28] Dowling still struggled to pay the bills and pleaded that he had been 'reduced to penury' after his son's death. He sent a letter to the Minister for Justice begging that the costs incurred by bereaved parents of Gardaí be borne by the government from then on. Unfortunately for Dowling, the Free State was in dire straits financially, attempting to set up a system of governance for a new state with a reduced income while simultaneously paying reparations to Britain. Multitudes of unpopular cutbacks were made and great lengths would be gone to avoid paying compensation, even to the families of slain Gardaí. His request was refused by the minister.

In June 1926, Garda Cahill and a colleague witnessed a boat carrying three men coming ashore near Black Head at 4 a.m. The men were cousins named O'Malley from Lettermore in Connemara and they carried casks of poteen. The Gardaí called on them to stop but the smugglers picked up large rocks and hit their captors, seriously injuring Garda Cahill. The young Garda had an incredibly turbulent time in 1926 and it came as no surprise that he decided to resign his post in the Gardaí in July 1926. The party of men who had shot at him and killed his colleague were never officially identified. The illegal distillation of poteen became less common as the decades progressed and Fanore reverted to a tranquil rural village with little crime to speak of. It was so peaceful, in fact, that in 1962 the Garda station in the village was closed forever. Today the lonely stretch of road at Craggagh gives little indication that a Garda met his end on a winter's night here. However, if one looks closely, a single stone cross stands on the side of the road some metres past the graveyard towards Fanore. Erected by his fellow Gardaí, it prays for the repose of the soul of Thomas Dowling, 'who died on this spot'. The cross makes no reference to the brutal nature of the Garda's death, nor the ultimately fruitless attempts to bring his killers to justice.

SERGEANT JAMES FITZSIMONS & GARDA HUGH WARD

'After all his sacrifices for Ireland his reward was to be murdered.'

James Fitzsimons was born in 1903 on the Downpatrick Road in Strangford Lower, County Down, on the shores of Strangford Lough. He was the middle of three children born to Helena and James Snr. After he completed his schooling, James worked as an electrical engineer in Belfast. His father had been a member of the RIC but despite this the Fitzsimons were a staunchly nationalist family. James eventually decided to join the Irish Volunteers, spending eighteen months in the 3rd Northern Division during the War of Independence. Like many from that part of the island, however, he found himself faced with a difficult choice after the Anglo-Irish Treaty was signed. His home village was situated deep within the six counties and thus under British and unionist rule. Fitzsimons eventually decided, as many other northern nationalists did in those turbulent times, that his future lay south of the newly created border and in the territory of the twenty-six-county Free State.

After making this difficult decision, Fitzsimons enlisted in An Garda Síochána in November 1922. Following a short amount of training, the new Garda was sent out on the beat to oversee the law and order of the country, although he was barely in his twenties. On 1 September 1925, he was dispatched to Cork City where he served in a station on the Lower Road. The following July, he was transferred to the newly opened St Luke's barracks in the centre of the city, where he was promoted to the rank of sergeant and considered to be a 'most popular member of the Gardaí, held in high esteem by his comrades and the general public'.[1]

Cork was part of the 1st Southern Division of the IRA, which as late as April 1924 had nearly 3,000 volunteers, comfortably the strongest republican area in the country.[2] Sergeant Fitzsimons was active in the hunt for IRA activists and had been instrumental in the discovery of bombs and dumps throughout 1925 and 1926. He last executed a warrant for the discovery of an arms dump in September 1926 and subsequently told a colleague that he had information that would lead to the discovery of more arms. He even featured in the national newspapers on 9 November 1926 when he gave evidence against a man who had violently resisted arrest. His name would once again be in these papers less than a week later, but for much more tragic reasons.[3]

Hugh Ward was also a Garda. Born on 14 February 1897, Ward was raised in a family of eight children. The Wards lived on a farm in Cloughmacoo, a townland near the village of Nobber in County Meath. Ward took a similar path into An Garda Síochána as Fitzsimons, taking up with the Volunteers at an early age. He was extremely active during the War of Independence. As well as being a quartermaster of the Nobber Company of the IRA, Ward was a member of the Back to the Land association, which agitated for land reform.[4] He was arrested in 1919 for unlawful assembly and later caught by Black and Tans carrying an important IRA message and was 'almost kicked to death but still he refused to give the information they wanted'.[5] After this incident he was court-martialled in February 1921 and sentenced to two years' imprisonment for having a list of IRA members concealed in the lining of his hat. Ward was interned at the infamous Ballykinlar Camp. He spent his time detained in Compound Number 2, amongst thousands of other republicans, his brother replacing him in his role as quartermaster in Nobber.[6] He was not forgotten during his time in prison. The high esteem in which he was held locally was illustrated by the fact that the prisoner was co-opted onto the Nobber Electoral Division in 1921.

Hugh was released at the time of the general amnesty in December 1921. He and two of his brothers took the pro-Treaty side in the Civil War and served in the National Army before Hugh was transferred to the military police, apparently as a result of his fine physique.[7] This experience encouraged Ward to enlist in An Garda Síochána on 27 May 1924. After stints in counties Roscommon and Cork, the Meath native found himself stationed in the rural County Tipperary village of Hollyford, situated at the foot of the Slieve Felim Mountains, halfway between the towns of Nenagh and Tipperary. By this point he had just under three years' experience in the force.

Hugh Ward and James Fitzsimons were both unmarried young men with a similar background who had chosen to serve their country by enlisting in the Gardaí. Both were considered brave and capable officers who had fought for independence with distinction and now worked to keep the country safe and peaceful.

The newspapers of 15 November 1926 were full of the stories of the impending trial of Henry McCabe, who would be found guilty and hanged for the killing of six people in Malahide, County Dublin, in one of the worst mass murders in the history of the state. The McCabe trial would also be amongst the most closely followed trials in Irish history but would be pushed off the front pages by news of the series of co-ordinated raids the previous night that had been organised by the anti-Treaty IRA. By late 1926, the IRA appeared to be waning in influence and popularity. The subversive organisation had gone from a membership of 14,541 in 1924 to a historic low of just 5,042 two years later.[8] Nevertheless the group was still made up of committed republicans hell-bent on showing their ability to undermine the legitimacy of state institutions.

For Gardaí stationed in barracks throughout the land, 14 November would have seemed like a normal evening. They were not to know that the IRA planned multiple attacks with the express aim of seizing important government documents from twelve Garda stations, mostly remote outposts situated miles from the nearest town. The meticulously planned attacks occurred between 6 p.m. and 7.30 p.m. The fact that they occurred on a Sunday evening was not a coincidence; it was known that there would be very few Gardaí on duty at that time.[9] The plan targeted areas throughout the land, include Kilmessan, County Meath; Castleisland, County Kerry; Rathgormack, County Waterford, as well as Tallaght Military Camp in County Dublin. The raiders cut telegraph wires, felled trees and blocked roads to scupper the follow-up investigation. Whether shootings were planned is not known but many of the party were armed and varying degrees of violence occurred, causing injury and death to some of the Gardaí on duty.

That November night would see more incidents in Cork than any other county. Cork had grown accustomed to tensions between the pro- and anti-Treaty factions and sporadic troubles had continued after the conclusion of the Civil War. On this particular night, several cars were stolen from the town of Macroom, 24 miles west of the city, which were then used in armed ambushes on stations.

Blackrock was one of the first stations under attack. A large party of men, possibly up to twenty, approached the small barracks on foot, and succeeded in gaining admittance to the building. They then handcuffed the officers and locked their wives and children in the bedrooms before ransacking the station, breaking furniture and destroying documents. In Togher, 6 miles to the west, a similar situation was unfolding – in this case, however, shots had also been fired in the direction of one officer, although he was unharmed.

Money and property was stolen from the station. Similar outrages occurred in the villages of Rylane and Ballincurrig, although no shooting took place in either of these incidents. The ambush of St Luke's station in Cork City, one of the few urban stations targeted, was the most violent of all and had fatal and far-reaching consequences.

Just after 6 p.m., most of the Gardaí in St Luke's were sitting around the table having their tea. Their superior, Sergeant Fitzsimons, was present. He had been on plain-clothes duty, returning to the station at 5.40 p.m. Suddenly a loud knock was heard on the door. The barrack orderly, Garda Patrick Beirne, was in the day room. He arose and walked out to the hall. He asked, 'Who is there?' through the door, only to be answered by a male voice saying, 'It is all right.' Beirne was obviously placated and opened the door into the dark and cold evening where he came face to face with three masked men.[10]

The man nearest Beirne had the bottom half of his face covered with a handkerchief and a soft hat pulled down over his forehead. He sprang out of the darkness as soon as the door was opened. He was armed with a black revolver, which he pointed at the orderly, shouting, 'Hands up.' Far from complying, Beirne had the courage and presence of mind to strike the intruder on the wrist, knocking the firearm from his hand. Beirne then attempted to slam the door but the other raiders, who were also armed, forced it open and rushed into the station from the darkness. They pushed the Garda back and he turned and retreated through the mess room, where he saw Sergeant Fitzsimons eating at the table. Beirne continued running into the kitchen, slamming the door behind him. Several other Gardaí were already present. They could hear what sounded like a scuffle out in the hallway and dishes breaking. This was followed by the unmistakable sound of a gunshot.

Sergeant Fitzsimons, on hearing the commotion, had risen from the table, and rushed out into the narrow hallway where he stood face to face with the assailants. 'Hands up,' was again shouted by one of the men. Without giving the sergeant an opportunity to follow his order, the masked man fired once. From a range of just a few feet, he hit his target and Sergeant Fitzsimons slumped against the wall. The sergeant crumpled to the ground and blood began to seep out onto the cold stone floor.

The raiders, whose plan appeared to have been to seize papers from the station, wasted no time in turning tail and escaping out the door. They then scattered in different directions. It seems that it had not been their intention to commit violence and a sergeant lying fatally wounded on the floor was more than they had bargained for; the only other damage caused had been some broken plates and furniture. Sergeant Fitzsimon's colleagues, who had rushed out to the back yard, hurried back into the hallway on hearing the marauders leaving. They found their comrade lying on his back, with documents strewn all over the floor. He was alive, although unable to speak.[11] Meanwhile another Garda had escaped out the back to summon the help of the military; he saw three shadowy figures running from the barracks.

A local GP, Dr Mullane, was quickly summoned, arriving to find the sergeant lying on his back in deep shock. He had been hit in the upper abdomen and was haemorrhaging blood. The doctor was quickly joined by a priest; the fire brigade and ambulance arrived fifteen minutes later. The critically wounded man was then brought without delay to the North City Infirmary. He was in deep shock, his liver having been perforated. His condition was hopeless and life slipped away quickly. Sergeant Fitzsimons was pronounced dead on arrival at the hospital.[12] Panicked phone calls were rapidly made to stations all over Cork, imploring the Gardaí to stay inside and take precautions against further attack.

Meanwhile, some 60 miles north, in Hollyford, County Tipperary, Garda Hugh Ward and his colleague Garda Martin McTighe were settling in for the night. The station had four Gardaí under the command of Sergeant Cahill but one officer was not rostered for duty that evening. The sergeant and another Garda had gone on patrol at 6.30 p.m., leaving Ward and McTighe in charge of the barracks. Six years previously, a large contingent of IRA volunteers had attacked the RIC barracks in the village, led by the legendary rebel and local hero, Seán Treacy. On that occasion grenades and homemade bombs were thrown into the building and bullets were sprayed from every angle, reducing the station to a smoking ruin. By 1926 Garda Ward and McTighe, representing a truly Irish police force, could have realistic expectations of more peaceful times in the rural outpost.[13]

Garda Ward was at the door at around 7.15 p.m. when he saw two local girls named Nellie Shanaghan and Lena Allis. As they walked by, the Garda called to them, inviting them to come in to listen to the gramophone, a much-prized possession in rural Tipperary in 1926. The girls agreed, coming in and standing in the day room. After a few minutes they heard footsteps and through the window they could see three shadowy figures walking across the yard. Ward thus instructed the girls to exit through the back door. They did so, leaving Ward to answer a knock on the front door.[14]

The Garda was immediately confronted with the three visitors, who turned out to be armed men wearing overcoats. The first intruder had a partially blackened face and, without warning, he fired two shots in quick succession. One of the bullets penetrated the Garda's left cheek, while the other lodged in his neck. Ward fell to the ground. Meanwhile, Garda McTighe was reading a catalogue of gramophone records in the kitchen. He had earlier heard his colleague talking and laughing with some girls in the day room but was oblivious to the horror unfolding. Although he heard three loud reports in total, he did not go to investigate as he assumed it was shots from a carbide tin.[15]

His first indication of what had happened was when two men burst through the kitchen door. The first intruder had his face partially blackened; the second wore no disguise. The first man, who was carrying a 'Peter the Painter' rifle, asked McTighe if he had any arms or if there were any men upstairs. The Garda did not reply to either question. The raider then ordered McTighe to put his hands up. McTighe again stayed silent and did not follow the order. It was only when one of the raiders fired a shot past him that he wisely acceded to the demand. The other man then rifled through the Garda's pockets, repeating the question about whether he was armed. McTighe told him that he was not. The raider took his official notebook, some documents and about £30 sterling before fleeing with his co-conspirators. The Garda followed them but was met by the third raider, who told him to get back. McTighe complied, but as he was returning into the kitchen he heard one of them shout, 'One of your comrades is shot; look after him.'[16] They then disappeared, having been in the station less than five minutes.

McTighe had been unaware that anything had happened to his colleague until this point and immediately rushed into the hall to find him. He followed a trail of bloodstains out the front door, discovering that Ward had crawled outside, towards the neighbouring public house. He was critically injured and bleeding heavily. He was lucid, despite having been struck by two bullets, and was able to tell his colleague, 'I opened the door and was plugged immediately.' McTighe ran to the station phone, trying unsuccessfully to ring for an ambulance and reinforcements. He then realised that the telephone wires had been cut. This cost Garda Ward valuable minutes in his fight for life.

Two local farmers named Philip and Patrick Ryan had been in the village at the time of the outrage. They had seen the shadows of several people through the window of the barracks and had heard a number of shots, causing them to run and take cover in some nearby sheds. The men then saw three of four raiders, whom they could not identity due to the darkness of the night. They were running away from the station in the direction of Cappawhite, one of them turning and firing a final shot before he left.

The Ryans waited until the men were out of sight before walking over to Garda McTighe. After finding out about the shooting, Patrick went and summoned a doctor and a priest, while Philip helped bring the stricken Ward to O'Dwyer's public house. Ward had a shawl tied tightly around his head and was put sitting on a chair. The men talked to him in an effort to keep him conscious. Bizarrely, he was asked at one point if he forgave the men who had shot him, the Garda answering that he forgave them fully. The doctor then arrived, and discovered a serious wound to the neck and the left side of Ward's face.

Ward's condition improved and was not thought to be life-threatening. The day after the attack he was even able to walk unaided from the ambulance to the train in Tipperary Town as he was being conveyed to St Vincent's Hospital in Dublin. On the same day, the Garda was described positively as making 'satisfactory progress towards recovery'.[17] Other sources stated that he was 'not regarded as critical'.[18] However, within two days, his condition had worsened. On 16 November, a physician found him unable to talk. The Garda collapsed shortly afterwards and at 5 a.m. that morning Hugh Ward was pronounced dead, making him the second victim of the attacks of that Sunday.

Inquests into the deaths of the two policemen quickly followed. Fitzsimons' was held in the infirmary the day after his death. It was ascertained that he had been shot once in the abdomen with a dum-dum bullet, which was designed to cause the maximum amount of damage. The bullet had not exited his body, instead rupturing his internal organs. Witnesses were produced who had seen men running from the scene of the shooting; one was spotted making his way in the direction of Dillon's Cross while another fled towards St Luke's. It was believed that a motor car was waiting nearby and the men managed to get to it without attracting much attention.[19] Sergeant Fitzsimons had died an agonising death and the jury wasted little time in bringing in a case of wilful murder by persons unknown. The inquest into Hugh Ward's death found that it had been caused by shock and haemorrhage, consistent with a gunshot wound. In both cases, verdicts of wilful murder were returned. A third victim, soldier Thomas Moloney, had also been shot and injured after a raid on Tallaght Army Camp. He would be more fortunate and survive the shooting.[20]

The news of the deaths spread quickly throughout the country. Although Cork City and its surrounding areas were known as hotbeds of republican sympathisers, condemnation was swift from all sides. The Gardaí and the army were visible in the streets of the southern capital over the next few days and they interrogated a large number of people. They also conducted raids and checkpoints throughout Tipperary and arrested well-known IRA volunteers.[21] Outrage greeted the death of the two officers, with one local priest in Tipperary decrying the attack on Hugh Ward by remarking that, 'after all his sacrifices and exertions for the cause of Ireland his reward was to be murdered'. He went on to say that the men who had performed the attack were not locals, but were being shielded by people who knew the identity of the assailants. Both men were ordinary Gardaí who had served their community well. The Church and several county councils, as well as many other bodies locally and nationally, put on record their disgust at the deaths of Sergeant Fitzsimons and Garda Ward.

The men's joint state funeral took place on 17 November 1926, and was attended by an immense congregation. The bodies were then conveyed onwards to Kingsbridge Station (now Heuston) in Dublin, where a large crowd, including several TDs, had gathered. Fitzsimons' coffin was brought the short distance to Glasnevin Cemetery to the sound of Chopin's *Funeral March*. The Taoiseach himself, W.T. Cosgrave, gave the final oration at Fitzsimons' grave-side, stating that the slain Gardaí's joint funeral was the biggest seen in the capital since those of Michael Collins and Arthur Griffith four years previously. Cosgrave commended the bravery of the deceased men in the face of danger, describing them as 'the guardians of all, ready to protect the rights of every citizen of the State'. Hugh Ward was meanwhile buried in his home village of Nobber as the rain fell heavily. The coffin was carried three times around the graveyard, an old custom in the area, before being lowered into the ground.[22]

The government debated bringing in new legislation (The Emergency Powers Bill) to deter the anti-Treaty IRA from carrying out further acts of this nature. This draconian legislation was to 'provide for the preservation of the public safety and the protection of people and property during national emergencies', and featured laws not in use since the days of the Civil War.

It would permit Gardaí to arrest anyone about whom there was a reasonable suspicion. Cosgrave described the co-ordinated raids as 'an attempt to terrorise the people of this country'.[23] Three days after the attacks, the new legislation was introduced. However, the powers immediately become controversial and just weeks later were suspended after Gardaí were accused of assaulting suspects in County Waterford.[24]

In the days after the deaths of Ward and Fitzsimons, 110 men were arrested nationwide, including twenty-three in Cork City alone. The arrests included some well-known local men, most notably the chairman of the Cork GAA County Board, Seán McCarthy, and Seán MacSwiney, brother of former Lord Mayor Terence. Two TDs were also detained.[25] The first was Michael Kilroy, a member of the newly formed Fianna Fáil party and a native of Mayo. Dr John Madden, a Sinn Féin TD from the same county, was also arrested, despite having at one time been the doctor for the Civic Guard. A journalist from the *Kerry News*, Con Casey, and the all-Ireland-winning captain of the same county's football team, John Joe Sheehy, were also detained under the Act. A number of the arrested men saw fit to write a letter to various local and national newspapers, denying culpability in the attack on the barracks in St Luke's, an unprecedented act by IRA members. All of the prisoners were released without charge within three weeks. The unrest continued; another Garda was shot in the wrist at Crumlin Barracks in Dublin just a week after the killings.

Shortly after the raids, the Gardaí conducted a raid on the offices of the republican newspaper *An Phoblacht*, and destroyed its printing presses in retaliation for its defence of the killings. The IRA later issued a statement regarding the raids through the same organ: 'The object of these raids has been misrepresented and misunderstood. The unfortunate deaths of two Civic Guards have been exploited by the government for the purpose of instituting a campaign of terrorism against their political opponents.'[26] The statement went on to explain that the raids were carried out in order to take documents containing intelligence on IRA members and that the Gardaí had only been shot because they had resisted, contrary to eyewitness accounts. The organisation did not express regret for the shootings, although it admitted they were unplanned, and it insisted that any money missing had been accidentally taken in bundles of documents and would be returned.[27]

Edward O'Reilly was eventually charged with the murder of Garda Ward in Hollyford.[28] O'Reilly was a native of nearby Goold's Cross in Clonoulty and had fought in the War of Independence. He was a committed republican who was known for his anti-Treaty sympathies. O'Reilly flatly denied the charge against him, stating on his arrest, 'All I have to say is that I was at Fr Moloney's last night.' However, his brother-in-law gave evidence that O'Reilly had arrived at his house at 10 p.m. on the night of the 14 November with another man, James Ryan (Dalton), placing them in the vicinity of the crime. McTighe confirmed the identification of the two men as members of the raiding party and O'Reilly was dispatched to Mountjoy Prison to await his trial. He would languish in a prison cell for over a year as authorities sought his co-conspirator, a matter that was even raised in the Dáil. A dozen other republicans were also arrested but none were brought in front of the court. Gardaí had visited James Ryan's house just hours after the raid and on more than a dozen occasions after that, although he was never home. Finally, in November 1927, English police swooped on a hotel in Penrith in Cumbria and arrested the 26-year-old labourer. Protesting his innocence, Goold's Cross native Ryan was extradited to face the same charge as O'Reilly.[29] It was asserted that, in league with others not yet in custody, the pair unlawfully raided and attacked Hollyford Barracks and caused the death of Garda Ward.

In the end it would come to nothing. The defence solicitor reminded the jury that on that dark night the only light in the Garda station was a single lamp hanging upon the wall. McTighe had vowed that Ryan was the undisguised raider and that his eyes were brown; this would prove to be incorrect. The solicitor implored the court to believe that McTighe was in a state of agitation with the gun pointed at him, and was now making a mistake in his identification of the two men. In the identity parade, he added, McTighe had failed to pick out Ryan on the first occasion. Ryan had witnesses to say he was 12 miles away on the night of the occurrence; O'Reilly's story of being at the priest's house was also corroborated. Finally, the solicitor admitted that the two men had not produced themselves for questioning after the shooting. They had been on the run but he explained that this was down to a legitimate fear of the retribution from the Gardaí and that all republicans in the district had done likewise. The jury evidently believed their story and they discharged the pair without hearing evidence for the prosecution. Despite being identified by Garda McTighe as the raiders, the two men were acquitted due to lack of evidence.

Some of the only convictions arising from the incidents around the country were against members of the Gardaí themselves. The day after the deaths of Garda Ward and Sergeant Fitzsimons, three republican prisoners were found to have been repeatedly assaulted in Rathgormack station while in custody. The men in question were awarded damages of between £3 and £30. Justice Minister Kevin O'Higgins wanted to dismiss the Gardaí involved in beating the suspects for bringing the force into disrepute but Eoin O'Duffy refused to countenance the action. There was a lengthy stand-off between the two men, both renowned for their stubborn personalities. Eventually the Gardaí in question were fined but kept their jobs.

A member of the Kilmessan raiding party, when told that the Gardaí there had no arms, remarked, 'We hear a lot about the unarmed Civic Guard but when we meet them they are generally armed.'[30] It was commonly felt amongst republicans that there were more guns in the ranks of the Gardaí than was revealed publicly. However, neither of the Gardaí shot dead on the 14 November had arms and they were shot dead without any warning. The botched raids of that winter's night had needlessly ended the lives of two Gardaí and were wildly unpopular nationally and disastrous for the IRA.[31] Several members of the IRA publicly expressed their disgust at the shootings and dissent within the ranks ensued, as well as a merciless clampdown on the organisation by the authorities.

In the aftermath of the attacks on Garda stations, Eoin O'Duffy heaped praise upon the Gardaí while directing scathing criticism at the IRA. He described them as a 'semi-secret organisation, led by the most extreme and fanatical. There is also a younger generation who are aggrieved that they missed the fun [during the War of Independence]. Reared in an atmosphere where citizenship is unknown, these youngsters have never learned anything of the sacredness of life.'[32] The commissioner added that the attacks had been planned to break the monotonous routine of drilling and training and allow the organisation's new recruits to experience physical force. Although O'Duffy was a former advocate of the unarmed policy of the force, he had grown increasingly authoritarian as the 1920s progressed. Shortly after the attacks, he wrote a letter to Kevin O'Higgins in which he reminded the cabinet that no armed member of the detective branch had been murdered but several unarmed Gardaí had. He now suggested that Irish people had been so long at war with authority that they lacked discipline. He further insisted that the time was right for Gardaí to be given firearms due to the perilous nature of their work, arguing that officers needed to have such resources at their disposal to respond to those who were willing to do them harm.

The government replied curtly:

> For the past five years the Garda has functioned successfully as an unarmed force. During that period the risk of armed attack was much greater than it is likely to be in the future, yet it can scarcely be contended that the Garda would have functioned more successfully had it been an armed force.

Unsurprisingly, the request was denied.[33]

A week after the shootings, Kevin O'Higgins discussed the subversive organisation in a letter he wrote to a colleague. He derided the co-ordinated raids, in spite of their fatal consequences, as 'unfortunate, of course, but just a kind of stunt flash in the pan; foolish young boys who believe they are heroes and patriots'.[34]

O'Higgins also lamented the Anglophobia that he believed was standing in the way of a united Ireland, as well as the high percentage of fools in the Irish population who prevented the reunification of the country. The minister pronounced himself certain that the IRA was not to be taken seriously by that point, but would himself be assassinated by the group on his way to Mass in Booterstown in July 1927 in an act that shocked the nation. The act was widely condemned as an attack on democracy, even by Éamon de Valera and Fianna Fáil. Despite O'Higgins' occasional spats with the force, the Justice Minister was also held in high esteem by many officers and hundreds of Gardaí were present to line the route of his funeral cortège. The Gardaí even dedicated the August issue of their official organ, the *Garda Review*, to the deceased minister after his death. In it, they described the minister as 'the creator of this great force' and one of Ireland's bravest and truest sons.[35] No one would ever be convicted for O'Higgins' murder, nor for the shooting of Ward and Fitzsimons.[36]

After a torturous spell attempting to get compensation, the Fitzsimons wrote to the government in disgust, complaining, 'It seems too bad that the parents of a man who laid down his life in the service of his country should be treated as we have been treated.'[37] After being offered just £50, the Fitzsimons family complained bitterly that Bridget Mary O'Higgins, the wife of Kevin O'Higgins, was awarded £20,000 for her loss. The Ward family received £80 in compensation for the loss of their son. Both James Fitzsimons' and Hugh Ward's names are in the Garda Roll of Honour for those killed in the line of duty. In 2014 it came to light that Garda Hugh Ward had been lying in an unmarked grave in Nobber since 1926. He was finally given a commemoration and a proper marker eighty-eight years after he died in the service of the state.[38]

DETECTIVE TIMOTHY O'SULLIVAN

*'I do not want to get into trouble
with people around here.'*

The murder rate in Ireland had steadily decreased after the Civil War and by 1929 it was down to just eight in the course of the year. The government, satisfied that the state of the nation had improved greatly, began to reduce the number of Gardaí nationally until it stood at 6,900, with just thirty-seven new Gardaí recruited in that year. The RIC, by contrast, had 9,300 policemen throughout the island in 1913.[1] No Garda had been killed for two and a half years by June 1929 and the government anticipated safer times ahead for the force. In that month, however, Detective Timothy O'Sullivan became the ninth in his profession murdered in the line of duty in just under seven years. A nation, already weary of years of violence, would once again mourn the killing of a policeman. Worse, the death had come about as a result of a plot that was deliberately designed to end the life of a serving Garda.[2]

Timothy (Tadhg) O'Sullivan was born to baker Daniel O'Sullivan and his wife Mary in November 1896. He was one of six children. The family resided in a five-bedroom house on 98 Street in the West Cork town of Skibbereen. As a young man, Timothy spent several years in the IRA, becoming the first captain of the Skibbereen Company, founded in 1917. He later rose to the rank of captain of the 'A' Company in the 4th Battalion of the 3rd Cork Brigade, made famous by its ruthless commander Tom Barry. O'Sullivan was an active volunteer, taking part in an attempt to capture the heavily armed RIC barracks in the town of Rosscarbery in the War of Independence. He was instrumental in leading attacks on loyalist homes in the area, also taking part in the fatal shooting of a British intelligence officer in the town. Like many of his colleagues, he had spent time on the run and been imprisoned by the British on two occasions.[3]

After the truce, O'Sullivan secured employment as a magistrate in the Parish Court in Skibbereen, which shows the high esteem in which he was held. He was also appointed Superintendent of Home Assistance in the area. When the Civil War began, he enlisted in the National Army, quickly rising to the rank of captain. He was instrumental in recapturing his home town from the anti-Treaty IRA in August 1922 and soldiered on with distinction for a further two and a half years. In March 1925 the Cork native was chosen for the Detective Division of An Garda Síochána, although he was at the relatively advanced age of 29 for a prospective Garda. On joining the force, O'Sullivan was stationed in the County Kerry towns of Tralee and Kilgarvan. He saw his fair share of action in these districts, even proving pivotal in the detection of armed bank robbers in Killarney at one point.

At the age of 33, the unmarried O'Sullivan was informed that he was to be moved north to County Clare. The detective spent a short time in Ennis but in December 1928 he was transferred to Kilmihil, a small village 10 miles to the north-east of Kilrush in West Clare. Although Kilmihil lies in an idyllic rural district, the village and surrounding parishes had seen their fair share of outrages throughout the troubled 1920s. The IRA played a part in various instances of land agitation and the area was generally considered to be one of the most unsettled in the country. Timothy O'Sullivan was amongst a number of extra detectives drafted throughout rural parts of the district to maintain the peace. They faced a difficult task in attempting to place order on the land-hungry aggressors in the area.

O'Sullivan was an officer of the Special Branch. The Branch had begun its days in 1924 as an extension of the DMP's detective division before it eventually assumed responsibility for the apprehension of subversion and political crime from the army. These included republican activities and, for the first time, Gardaí were given an official role in the detection of wrongdoing by members of the IRA. The Special Branch was considered by many IRA men to be little more than a reincarnation of the hated Oriel House CID from the Civil War era.[4]

Republicans in the South Clare district had formed themselves into a well-organised secret society which still refused point-blank to co-operate with government agencies and the increased Garda presence was bitterly resented. Shortly after O'Sullivan's arrival, posters were erected locally warning people not to give evidence to members of the CID. This did not deter O'Sullivan, who went about his task with gusto in the weeks and months after his transfer. He was particularly active in questioning people he suspected of involvement in the anti-government conspiracy in the locality. The detective's strenuous efforts to root out the trouble unsurprisingly proved unpopular amongst local republicans.[5]

The small village of Knock lies 7 miles from Kilmihil on the south coast of County Clare and suffered similar problems as its neighbouring parish. John O'Driscoll (27) was one of the detectives in Knock. A native of Sherkin Island off the coast of Cork, O'Driscoll found himself dealing with a cohort of republicans in the area violently opposed to the government. O'Driscoll later stated that his main duty throughout 1928 and early 1929 was searching suspects for arms and papers that would indicate that they held anti-government feeling. Like O'Sullivan he did his job rigorously and was therefore unpopular in certain local quarters.

On 15 February 1929, Gardaí descended on a house in the Kilmurray McMahon district where an IRA court martial was due to take place. Several of the occupants were arrested. Local IRA men later swore affidavits that the Gardaí had roughed them up in the course of their arrests. Clare County Council, backboned by Fianna Fáil councillors, quickly passed a resolution calling for an enquiry into what were described as the 'Black and Tan methods' being employed by the Gardaí.[6] The matter was even brought up in the Dáil by TDs, Garda O'Driscoll being mentioned amongst the names of the aggressors. However, there were no convictions meted out to any of the Gardaí, a fact that infuriated local republicans.

Suspicion was also growing as to who had given information to the Gardaí on the upcoming court martial and the IRA became convinced that they had an informer in their ranks. On 20 May, a 22-year-old tailor and section commander named Patrick Murray went missing in the Kilmihil district after leaving his home at 9.30 p.m. He was never found and it was widely speculated that he had been murdered by the IRA on suspicion of passing information to the Gardaí after being given a 'monetary inducement'.[7] There was also burning resentment towards the Detective Branch, which had been putting severe pressure on the organisation for some time. It was decided within the IRA that drastic action was needed.

On the morning of Tuesday, 11 June, the local postman delivered a letter to Knock station addressed to Detective O'Driscoll. He was out on duty in the sub-station in nearby Labasheeda for the day and did not arrive back to his base until 8 p.m. that night. It was only at that point that he opened the envelope, which contained a handwritten letter. It read as follows:

Dear Sir,

I found a box of ammunition and papers in a butt of hay in the haggard. The times are so dangerous I was afraid to keep it near the place.

I threw it inside the ditch at Lahiff Cross in Ardel's meadow yesterday. I want you to take it away as quick as you can. I do not want to get into trouble with people around here. Burn this letter.

Farmer

O'Driscoll knew Lahiff's Cross, which was situated just north of Knock.[8] Despite the lateness of the hour, O'Driscoll felt the issue warranted immediate consideration and he left the barracks at ten o'clock. The detective made his way out to the field and after some searching eventually discovered the cashbox, measuring 15in by 6in, which was left as described. He later reported that it was well made out of wood that was half an inch thick. O'Driscoll also observed that the box was fastened by a hasp and after some examination decided against opening it, perhaps mindful of the fact that bombs had been used by the IRA against Gardaí in the past. In July 1926 in Douglas, County Cork, a door into an upstairs room in an abandoned house had been fitted with a detonator. When it was opened, it exploded, injuring five Gardaí in the vicinity.

Detective O'Driscoll found that the box weighed only about 4 pounds, so he picked it up and put it under his overcoat, resolving to return to the barracks to seek further guidance.[9] He changed his mind as he cycled, however, and decided to head for the townland of Tullycrine instead. He was aware that a fellow Garda would be present in the area as a hut was situated on contested land. The farm was permanently manned by Gardaí, who were tasked with protecting its livestock due to a poisonous land feud. The issue was related to a National Army soldier, James Daly, who had served in the military for several years throughout the 1920s and let the land go into disuse. On his return, he discovered that his field was being used by other people in the area, many of whom had taken the republican side in the Civil War. He began to farm it again but found his cattle driven off the land numerous times, allegedly by Irregulars. He also received several threatening letters ordering him to leave the district. He refused, but was then shot and seriously wounded on Christmas Eve 1928. The Gardaí eventually agreed to deploy protection to the farm. O'Driscoll knew that a Garda would be stationed in the area so he decided to take the wooden box there as it was nearer than his own station. He travelled the mile and a half there and met Garda Cusack. As the men spoke, the unopened box was placed on the roadside.

As they were discussing the mysterious box, Detective Timothy O'Sullivan also happened to arrive at the scene. O'Sullivan had departed from his station in Kilmihil earlier that day and cycled the 9 miles to Kilrush, where he was needed to perform some policing duties. He found himself cycling home through Tullycrine, where he met Cusack and O'Driscoll. The three men stood at the roadside, discussing their options. O'Driscoll then re-read the letter. In it, 'Farmer' had described examining the contents of the box and finding ammunition and papers, implying that it could be opened safely and without fear. O'Sullivan brazenly suggested, 'We had better open it and see what is inside.' The other men agreed. The Gardaí still had their suspicions though. They walked in behind a gate near the Garda hut and laid the box on the ground, deciding that they would open it using a rough test in an attempt to retrieve the so-called 'treasonous documents', without actually standing directly beside the box.

The men removed 5 yards of strong barbed wire from a fence, which they attached to the hasp that held the box closed. They put a large stone against the box and retreated. From some distance away, and behind the partial safety of the mud hut, they then attempted to manoeuvre the wire to open the hasp. They tried repeatedly in the hope of either setting off the trap or opening the box but succeeded only in knocking it over onto its side several times. The men realised that this mechanism would not work and O'Sullivan was reportedly assuaged by the fact that a bomb had not gone off, despite the rough handling of the box. Combined with the contents of the letter, he came to the conclusion that he could now safely open the box. Described in newspaper accounts as 'A man without fear', O'Sullivan at this point uttered the immortal line, 'There could not be much in it.' O'Driscoll and Cusack came out from behind the hut while O'Sullivan approached the box before going down on his right knee and using both his hands to force open the clasp. 'A large explosion followed which flung his body yards away, to fall a dead mass of human flesh.'[10]

A dense cloud of acrid smoke hung over the field after the explosion, which had reputedly been heard several miles away. Although both Garda Cusack and O'Driscoll had been standing further away from the device and survived the impact, they were rendered unconscious by the blast. After several minutes, the men came to, only to find their colleague Detective O'Sullivan blown to pieces. The two men struggled to the road, Detective O'Driscoll light-headed from loss of blood. Neither man was able to move further but some time later they managed to stop a motorist with an empty car, requesting that he take them and their dead comrade to the hospital in Kilrush. The motorist refused, allegedly telling the injured men that he did not want his car to become covered in bloodstains.[11] Eventually Dr Thomas Daly of Kilmihil arrived on the scene and brought the dead and wounded to Kilrush. Garda Cusack was suffering from minor shock after the incident but would have no long-lasting repercussions. Detective O'Driscoll was more seriously injured, having sustained deep gashes to his throat and chest. He was said to be in a critical condition and was taken directly to St Joseph's Hospital in Kilrush.

The inquest into Garda O'Sullivan's death was held on the Friday, less than seventy-two hours after the incident. Mr Thomas Lillis, the coroner from West Clare, described the circumstances of O'Sullivan's murder as 'the worst case I have ever come across in my long experience'. Like Garda Dowling in the same county three years before, the death had been the result of a pre-arranged and carefully laid plot. Yet again, the intended target escaped death while an unlucky third party paid with their life. A live bomb had been placed in a box, which had been designed to go off as soon as it was opened.

For some time afterwards, a 10ft hole marked the spot where the explosive had detonated, indicating the strength of the explosion. The impact on Detective O'Sullivan's body had been devastating, completely blowing off both of the deceased's arms and part of his left leg. His boots and clothes had been blown clean off and his body had been mutilated beyond recognition. A newspaper in his pocket had been converted to dust while a watch he was wearing was never discovered. The blast had even embedded some of his shattered bones into the nearby mud hut.

Two weeks later, the evidence of the two injured Gardaí was heard. O'Driscoll had sustained deep wounds to his chest, neck and thigh while Cusack suffered superficial wounds, as well as severe shock. Both men described how O'Sullivan's body partially shielded them from the enormous impact of the blast. The box itself was not recovered, much of it splintering into O'Sullivan's body on impact. The lack of a box made it difficult for the Gardaí to ascertain what explosive had been used in the attack, although it was speculated that a potent mix of cheddite and gelignite had caused the immense devastation.

The coroner described O'Sullivan as a 'lovable comrade'. He went on to state that 'it was sad to think that such a worthy Irish life had been cut off in such a dastardly manner'. He also referred to the perpetrator of the crime as 'a low coward' who 'sheltered himself behind a letter to murder the deceased, whose only interest was to keep the district peaceful and quiet'. The jury returned with a murder verdict, and added that the bomb had been placed there for the purpose of 'the murder of him or others by some person or persons unknown'.[12]

Much of County Clare was distraught at the second Garda killing in the county in just three years and the County Council, the Ennis district judge and local bishops strongly condemned the act. It was felt that the reputation of the county had suffered greatly. It was also lamented by locals that when Clare played Tipperary in a hurling match the week after the detective's death, each time a Clare player got near the sliotar he was instructed by shouts from the crowd to 'pull on the bomb'. This was ironic due to Tipperary's justified record as the most dangerous place for Gardaí in the early decades of the state, but no less distressing for the Clare contingent. O'Sullivan's killing caused national outrage and a bout of soul-searching, both inside and outside the Banner County.

Timothy O'Sullivan's remains were removed from the church in Kilrush to the cathedral in his native Skibbereen on Thursday 13 June. It was thought prudent to use a closed coffin due to the extent of the injuries. A large crowd of mourners gathered to witness the detective making his final journey to the graveyard in nearby Creagh, the 'funeral cortege being well over a mile in length'.[13] As with the other Gardaí who had tragically lost their lives in the 1920s, the procession saw dozens of uniformed Garda, as well as numerous government representatives, standing under the tricolours flying throughout the town. The Gaelic games enthusiast, who had just played the previous Sunday in the Clare Senior Football Championship for the Clare Garda team and previously won a Cork County title with Skibbereen, was spoken of fondly throughout the ceremony and the graveside oration was given by Eoin O'Duffy.[14] The commissioner stated that this was the eighth time that the public had assembled to pay tribute to a murdered Garda. O'Duffy mentioned knowing O'Sullivan personally, having worked with him in the General Headquarters. He described his colleague as leading 'an exemplary life at all times ardently devoted to duty'.[15]

The death was the subject of much debate in the Dáil, with the pro-Treaty Cumann na nGaedheal party calling it 'one of the most cold-blooded murders in its calculation that has ever been perpetrated in this country committed by desperate, hateful-minded assassins'.[16] The opposition Fianna Fáil party remarked that there was nothing to say that it was not an accident, although their newspaper, *The Nation*, in an unprecedented denunciation, called the killing 'an act of utter cowardice'.[17] The party also expressed sorrow at the Garda's death, but referenced several complaints made against detectives throughout the country, particularly in Clare, where the force had reputedly harassed and attacked innocent civilians. They added that all these allegations had been

ignored by the government.[18] The Dáil nevertheless pressed on
with a new piece of legislation, the Juries Protection Act, designed
to act against the IRA. They namechecked the deceased detective
in the run-up to the vote, as well as Albert Armstrong, a Dublin
man shot dead as he parked his car at his home shortly after giving
evidence against republicans who had torn down a British flag
from the building of his insurance company. The Act was eventually passed by sixty-eight votes to fifty-eight. It introduced severe
penalties for anyone found to be intimidating jurors in criminal
trials and removed the necessity to have juries in certain criminal
trials. It also made it an offence to refuse to recognise a court of
law, a common tactic used by the IRA.[19]

Despite the proximity to the land dispute in Tullycrine, the
government believed that the bomb had nothing to do with the
issue. Instead they were convinced that it was related to a group
of Irregulars with a long-standing grudge against the police.[20]
The killing was rumoured to have been carried out by several local
members of the IRA who had been continually questioned, arrested
and reportedly beaten by the Gardaí. It appears that the men did not
get official sanction from IRA headquarters to plant the bomb, the
killing of Gardaí being against the IRA playbook owing to the outrage it would be sure to cause amongst the general public. The letter
had been marked with a stamp from Tullycrine post office and was
believed to have been sent by a local man.[21]

Gardaí made a number of house searches in the days after the
explosion. The republicans used their popular weekly newspaper,
An Phoblacht, to publicise the claim that several local volunteers
were beaten and harassed during the investigation. A carpenter
named Michael Hurley was apparently repeatedly interrogated as
to whether he had made a wooden box for anyone in the preceding weeks, while several men who were arrested were reportedly
threatened with punishment if they did not sign a confession.[22]

One local man, T.J. Ryan, came in for particular attention. Ryan
was an IRA commander from nearby Cranny and an important
figure nationally within the movement. He was strongly sus-

pected by Gardaí of involvement in the plot to kill the detective and was shadowed permanently in the month after O'Sullivan's death. At one point Ryan was returning home from Bodenstown, where he had been at a Wolfe Tone commemoration, when he was stopped at four separate Garda checkpoints.[23] On the fourth occasion, at Clarecastle, the officers ordered him to get out of his car before he was stripped, searched and beaten by numerous detectives. He alleged that they threatened to murder him. He further insisted that they assaulted him several times at the house he shared with his mother. Ryan claimed that they had broken into his house and at one stage they had beaten him into unconsciousness in an attempt to force him to admit planting the bomb. He did not do so. The Gardaí would later deny the claims, stating that in the presence of an officer Ryan had been kicked in the face by a cow he was milking. It was this incident, they insisted, that had caused his injuries. It is also alleged that at one point members of the force had a plan to kill the republican leader in retaliation for the death of their colleague. They hired a boat, planning to kidnap Ryan and drown him. When David Neligan, head of the Special Branch, found out about their plan he ordered that it be immediately aborted.[24]

Éamon de Valera himself went to visit Ryan, who gave him an account of the treatment to which he had been subjected. De Valera wrote a letter to W.T. Cosgrave, describing his visit to Ryan's house. In it he recounts being accosted by several detectives outside the house before he was eventually allowed in, only to be met by a visibly injured Ryan. De Valera wrote that he believed these injuries were inflicted by the Gardaí but the government rebuffed these claims. Minister for Justice, James Fitzgerald-Kenney, told the Dáil that he accepted the Gardaí's version of events.[25] Ryan was eventually arrested but after a brief period of imprisonment he was released due to lack of evidence.

De Valera had stated that the conduct of the Gardaí in West Clare had been called into question on numerous occasions. The relationship between the force and republicans in the south-west Clare area had indeed been fractious and would remain bitter long after

Detective O'Sullivan's death, with sporadic clashes continuing to occur between the opposing groups.

T.J. Ryan was involved in another altercation with Gardaí in August 1932 when the men with whom he was walking allegedly shouted, 'Hello cows' and 'Beware of the little black box' at Gardaí on the street in Kilrush. This was an apparent reference to Detective O'Sullivan's death and the groups began jeering and jostling each other. This soon turned into violent clashes, culminating in Ryan, along with a high-profile republican colleague George Gilmore, being shot and injured by Gardaí.[26] Incredibly, Ryan and Gilmore were initially charged with attempted murder, despite having been shot themselves, but the charges against them were dropped. The two Special Branch detectives were eventually dismissed, although they would again come in for media scrutiny later in the decade after accepting prominent roles within the Blueshirt movement.

In the aftermath of his colleague's death, John O'Driscoll claimed £1,000 compensation for his injuries, ultimately being awarded just over £400. The bill was footed by the six electoral districts in south County Clare where the subversive anti-government organisations operated. The O'Sullivan family claimed £8,000 from the County Council after the loss of their son, plus £250 for the education of Timothy's younger brother William, to whose education he had been contributing.[27] The request was denied by Judge McElligott in Ennis Circuit Court, six months after their son's death. He expressed regret, admitting that there was an anti-government conspiracy in the areas around Tullycrine, Knock and Kilmihil and that their son was doing his duty in trying to suppress it. Despite this, he would not award compensation as the letter had not been addressed to their son 'but it was only by chance O'Sullivan happened to be in O'Driscoll's company when the box intended to kill O'Driscoll was opened ... there was no malice against O'Sullivan'. The grieving parents were also refused costs. Depositions were made to W.T. Cosgrave himself by the Minister for Agriculture, describing the circumstances of the crime and begging him to reconsider the offer of compensation for the family who were 'very poor'. The O'Sullivans were eventually awarded a gratuity of £500.[28]

Although the Gardaí had strong suspicions about the identities of the conspirators, no one was ever prosecuted for the crime. What would have occurred had Detective O'Driscoll not cycled to Tullycrine and encountered his two fellow Gardaí on that summer's night? The usual procedure would have been to return to the barracks in Knock where the fatal parcel would have been dealt with by O'Driscoll and his colleagues. O'Sullivan would certainly not have met his end in a rural field in that eventuality, but significant loss of life would still more than likely have occurred. A memorial to Garda Timothy 'Tadhg' O'Sullivan is now in Kilrush Garda Station.

9

SUPERINTENDENT JOHN CURTIN

'A crime that was a disgrace not only to Ireland, but to civilisation.'

John Curtin was born in 1902 into a large farming family in Meengorman, a townland just outside the village of Meelin on Cork's north-western edge. Although he was only a teenager during the conflict, Curtin was said to have been a committed republican soldier during the Black and Tan War.[1] He took no part in the Civil War, however, instead being amongst the first recruits to the Civic Guard in April 1922. Curtin was quickly promoted to sergeant, a role filled almost exclusively by young former volunteers. The role of inspector followed not long afterwards and in July 1926 John Curtin was appointed superintendent. He had made incredible progress in under four years, showing the high regard in which the young Cork man was held in the force. After working for spells in Killarney, Longford and Leitrim, the superintendent had proven his worth, the recovery of £301 from a bank raid in Killarney amongst his finest policing achievements.[2]

In 1930, the 28-year-old pioneer held the rank of second-grade superintendent and was advancing rapidly towards the first grade. In May that year he was dispatched to Tipperary Town, a troubled part of a county that had remained a fractious spot since the Civil War and had already seen four Gardaí killed in just eight years. This particular district was described as 'disturbed' and organised armed crime by the IRA was commonplace.[3]

Curtin married Maureen O'Connor in Killarney Cathedral a month after his transfer. The marriage featured in several newspapers, both locally and nationally, further proof of the young superintendent's high profile. The 7ft wedding cake present was also widely lauded.[4] The newlyweds temporarily resided in a hotel in the village of Limerick Junction after their wedding. Shortly afterwards the Curtins decided to move in with Maureen's sister Irene and the trio relocated to a large residence, Friarsfield House, which was situated 2 miles outside Tipperary Town, off the main road to the village of Dundrum. The substantial house, which was attached to the well-known Ballykisteen stud farm, was situated in pleasant woods and approached by a shaded avenue about 150 yards long.[5]

Although by this point the superintendent had been stationed in Tipperary for less than 12 months, he had investigated several high-profile crimes. He was initially in the local headlines due to his involvement in enquiries about a lucrative mail robbery and shortly afterwards assisted in the arrest of four Tipperary County Councillors on bribery charges. Curtin was also responsible for the investigation of subversive activity. South Tipperary had been one of the most active areas in the whole country during the War of Independence, even firing the first shots of the conflict at nearby Soloheadbeg. Forty-six RIC policemen were killed in three short years and the Gardaí found that they were not universally welcomed as the arbitrators of law and order by certain sections of the community. The IRA still believed that they were the true army of the republic and they would tolerate the Gardaí only if they left them to their own devices. The superintendent, however, was keen to clamp down on what he saw as anti-social behaviour in the community by members of the organisation. A confrontation soon became inevitable.

The IRA first showed their displeasure at Curtin's methods in November 1930 when they sent him a threatening letter. The letter, which was signed by the organisation, warned the superintendent to desist from his campaign against them or face the consequences. He did not heed the malicious correspondence and continued in his attempts to investigate people that he felt were a threat to the community. He also refused to carry a gun for protection, although he was entitled to do so as a senior Garda.[6]

In 1931, legislation introduced by the Cumann na nGaedheal government made membership of the IRA illegal. Curtin interrogated several local men that he believed belonged to the organisation after receiving the letter. Four individuals were eventually arrested for the offence after a party of Gardaí, led by Superintendent Curtin, surprised them during an organised drill in a field. The prisoners were accused of illegal ownership of firearms and membership of a proscribed organisation. At the initial hearing, Curtin strongly argued against allowing bail for the four accused and the men were remanded in custody. The trial finally began on 18 March in Clonmel. Curtin lined up several witnesses who made statements implicating the accused men and giving evidence of their links with the IRA. At first glance the case against the accused men looked cast-iron.

However, almost all of the witnesses retracted their earlier statements in court, claiming that they had been beaten and threatened into signing them. One man, James Ryan, even accused local detectives of taking him to his uncle's barn and threatening to shoot him if he did not implicate the accused men. Another local resident, Michael Coffey, maintained that Superintendent Curtin had forced his statement out of him at gunpoint. The accused men's defence teams claimed that the prisoners had merely been playing hurling and that the guns had been planted by Gardaí during the raid. Evidence against the defendants was given by several detectives but just one local man, John Ryan, was willing to testify. The defendants were thus acquitted.

Curtin would later write to the head of the Special Branch, voicing his bitter disappointment at the outcome of the trial and decrying the fact that it was 'useless to have anything in the nature of a political case ever again tried in this South Riding of Tipperary. As far as the Gardaí was concerned all possible was done at every stage'.[7] The difficulty in securing a conviction against the IRA was well documented and not merely an issue in Tipperary. The organisation had a nationwide habit of intimidating and threatening both jurors and witnesses.

On 16 March, another disturbing incident had occurred involving Superintendent Curtin and three of his colleagues. They partially extinguished a fire that engulfed a hay shed belonging to Anthony Ryan, a farmer from the village of Donohill, just outside Tipperary Town. Ryan was another man who had recently given evidence in a court case, this time involving a charge of bribery, and it was thought that the fire had been started by members of the local IRA as an act of revenge. Curtin and his fellow Gardaí managed to save one wing of the shed. It was clear that South Tipperary was in the grip of subversives who were prepared to go to extreme lengths to ensure that people would not testify against them.[8]

Although none of the defendants received a conviction on foot of the charge brought by Superintendent Curtin, they were clearly angered that the case had gone to court at all and decided to get their revenge.

At 5 p.m. on Friday, 20 March 1931, John Curtin left Friarsfield House in his two-seater Morris Cowley motor car to go on inspection duty. He worked for some five hours before setting off home. He passed his young neighbour, Michael Doherty, who was walking home, on the way. The superintendent rounded the final bend approaching his home at around 10.20 p.m.[9] The gates to the house had been damaged by a lorry some time before and had been left open ever since so Curtin would have been surprised to discover the undamaged left-hand side of the gate was closed, obstructing his path. He stopped suddenly enough that he left an impression on the road 3ft from the gates. He then exited the vehicle to open the gate. He could not have known that it had been closed so as to compel the superintendent to get out of his car.

Curtin walked to the gate and pulled it open. As he did so, figures concealed behind the 4ft wall to the right-hand side of the driveway revealed themselves. Using the lights from the car as a guide, they identified that the figure was the Garda; his clerk also regularly delivered messages to the house. When they were satisfied that they had the right man, the gunmen fired a number of shots in the direction of Curtin. Although several bullets missed their intended target, five bullets struck the superintendent, one of them entering the area around his heart. The raiders then absconded, leaving their fatally wounded victim lying helplessly on the ground.

A few minutes later, Michael Doherty walked through the entrance gates to Friarsfield House but the superintendent was lying unconscious in the narrow space between the car and the wall and the young boy failed to see him.

Mrs Maureen Curtin and her sister Irene O'Connor had retired to bed at around 10.30 p.m. that night. As she was going to bed, Miss O'Connor noticed the reflection of headlights from the gate but took no notice, assuming that the superintendent was returning. Half an hour later, she noticed that the lights were still shining towards the house from the bottom of the avenue. She could also still hear the engine of the car. Puzzled as to why her brother-in-law was still waiting at the gate, Irene got up and knocked on Mrs Curtin's bedroom door, telling her of the unusual occurrence. After some deliberation, the two women decided to walk down the avenue to investigate.

The women walked down the avenue with the headlights of the vehicle guiding their way. They went to the car first and peered in the window but could see no one. Then they discovered the superintendent lying unconscious on the ground between the wall and the right side of the motor car. He was lying on his back and his head was facing the gate. He was still warm and the women did not at this point realise he had been shot. They quickly informed the Doherty family, begging them to send for a doctor and a priest. Doherty sent a family member to cycle for assistance. He then helped the two women to carry Curtin into the drawing room. It was here that they discovered that he was haemorrhaging blood and was riddled with bullets, even discovering a spent bullet in his sock. Dr O'Halloran arrived at 1 a.m. but later deposed that the superintendent was 'beyond human help' by that stage, having lain on the ground undiscovered for over an hour. He died shortly afterwards without ever regaining consciousness.

Detective Joseph Kelly arrived at the scene at 1.15 a.m. He found Curtin's car still running and the headlights still on three hours after the ambush. There were bloodstains on a stone near where the body had lain and bullet marks could clearly be seen on the wall opposite. It was believed that 'not more than three and probably two men' who were familiar with the superintendent's routine had taken part in the carefully planned ambush.[10]

The inquest was held by the coroner for the Fethard district, Mr Patrick Maher, the following day. He found that the death was due to shock and haemorrhage and that the victim has been 'murdered foully by some person or persons unknown'. The indication was that the shot to the heart had been fired when Curtin lay injured on the ground. It had been fired from such close range that the uniform was blackened and singed.[11] The jury then tendered its sincere regret to the widow of the deceased superintendent. Only one man was thought to have heard the shots, neighbour Cornelius Godfrey, who came out of his house at 10.15 p.m. and saw the lights of a motor car and heard six or seven sharp reports.[12]

Sympathy poured in for the deceased Guard and the Curtin household in Meelin received a steady stream of visitors after the tragedy. Amongst them was Eoin O'Duffy, who arrived at the house the day after the tragedy and expressed his sorrow. He told the media that the brazen murder of the superintendent was even more serious than the assassination of the Minister for Justice Kevin O'Higgins four years previously. The district judge in Clonmel also paid tribute to the Garda, whom he described as 'capable, efficient and fearless'. John Curtin's funeral took place in the graveyard of Clonfert near his native Meelin. A wreath from his wife took pride of place on his coffin. It read, 'To my own darling Jack, from his loving and heart-broken wife – Maureen.'[13]

This was the tenth murder of a Garda since the force's foundation nine years before and incredibly five of them had occurred within the borders of County Tipperary. In none of the cases in that county was the perpetrator brought to justice. The superintendent was the most senior officer to be killed and the media at the time covered the story extensively. The Minister for Defence, Desmond FitzGerald (father of subsequent Taoiseach Garret), also denounced the crime and described the perpetrators as a 'disgrace not only to Ireland, but to civilisation'.[14] He added that the gunmen would be hanged when they were detected. A local priest, Revd Cotter, described the killing as bringing the country back to 'the evil days of eight, ten and twelve years ago when no one's life was safe'. It was commented in the media that 'the shaming eyes of the whole country have been turned upon their locality'.[15]

Days after his death, the organisation Cumann na mBan, a women's group closely aligned with the IRA, circulated a poster in the local area which boldly stated, 'The men of Tipperary will not allow a Free State police superintendent to stand between them and freedom'.[16] The deceased superintendent was also denounced by the socialistic republican party, Saor Éire, and An Phoblacht, which stated that he had overstepped the mark and made capturing republicans his hobby. The newspaper published an article in which they described how the Special Branch should be handled: 'Members of the CID must be treated as social pariahs. That treatment must be extended to district judges and uniformed police, to every individual who is a willing part of the machine by which our Irish patriots are being tortured.'[17] Frank Ryan, editor of the same newspaper, gave an interview to an English journalist in which he defended the shooting of Superintendent Curtin and objected to it being called a murder or assassination. Ryan stated:

> The shootings were acts of war. Curtin had exceeded his duty. He went out of his way to persecute the IRA. The Civic Guard have no right to interfere in matters which don't concern them. If they ask for trouble they must not be surprised if they get it.[18]

Clanwilliam Rugby Club would be one of many organisations to express sympathy for the superintendent and cancel a match that had been due to take place shortly after his death. On 2 May an attempt was made to burn their clubhouse to the ground, a can of petrol being found inside the building.[19] Limerick Borough Council experienced similar opposition when unidentified men entered the office of the city surveyor and seized the minutes from a council meeting that had passed a resolution expressing sympathy after Curtin's death. The men made their displeasure clear and promised to delete the resolution from the minute book, resolving that further action would be taken if the council repeated their expression of sympathy.[20] Shortly afterwards the county board of Tipperary GAA, perhaps fearful of IRA reprisal, voted against issuing a resolution condemning the killing.

The IRA held a vice-like grip on parts of South Tipperary at that point and they showed their ruthlessness again just months after Curtin's death. John Ryan, a 26-year-old farm labourer who lived 4 miles away, had given evidence against the IRA in the earlier trial in Clonmel. Ryan was lured from the house where he worked in Cappawhite and shot dead on the roadside as a punishment for appearing as a witness in court against the IRA. A placard hung around his neck stating 'Spies and informers beware. IRA.' When Frank Ryan of *An Phoblacht* was asked about John Ryan, the republican replied, 'He was nothing else than a traitor'.

The government's reaction to the deaths of Ryan and Curtin was similar to earlier killings of Gardaí: legislation. On this occasion, with a large amount of encouragement from Eoin O'Duffy, they brought in a Constitution Amendment Act, which gave special powers, including the death penalty, to military tribunals in dealing with subversives. This would also compel suspected members of unlawful organisations to account for their movements when questioned by a Garda. The annual commemoration of Wolfe Tone at Bodenstown was also outlawed. Unsurprisingly, these moves were vehemently opposed by Fianna Fáil. The latest in a long line of emergency measures designed to keep the IRA at bay proved more successful than in the past; 91 per cent of suspected members were convicted of membership of the illegal organisation between 1931 and 1937.[21]

Tragically, Mrs Curtin had been pregnant with twins at the time of her husband's death and both would die within hours of their birth. The heartbroken widow eventually received £6,000 compensation from Tipperary County Council South Riding for the murder of her husband, although the government would controversially stop the £160 pension she received on her husband's death as a result.[22] It would eventually be reinstated. Maureen Curtin moved home to County Kerry shortly after her husband's death.

In the aftermath of the shooting of the superintendent, Eoin O'Duffy begged the local people to co-operate with the Gardaí and bring his killers to justice. Unfortunately for the Gardaí, hours had passed between the time of the shooting and the arrival of the first officer on the scene. The gunmen had slipped into the black night in the rural area immediately after the ambush and were presumably safely concealed by the time anyone went to look for them. The chief superintendent also lamented the circumstances, stating that the hands of the Gardaí were tied and people were unwilling or afraid to co-operate with them. He also berated the local clergy, saying, 'The Garda feel very aggrieved indeed that the Archbishop of the Diocese did not publicly denounce the atrocious murder, or the four previous members of the force in this county.' He finished his report bleakly: 'Owing to the restraint with which investigations must now be pursued, I fear it will be extremely difficult to bring the guilt home to those responsible for the murder.'[23] He was proven correct.

Confidential Garda reports indicated that Gardaí believed the killing of Superintendent Curtin had been sanctioned at a Tipperary IRA convention on 18 March, two days before his death.[24] Names were mentioned in confidential documents in relation to the identity of the killer, including one man who we shall refer to as TB. TB was a leader of the Tipperary Brigade of the IRA, although not originally from the area. He had gone missing for several weeks after the shooting, a fact that marked him out as a suspect. Rifles were allegedly distributed by IRA commanders in the aftermath of the shooting and a large number of local men were named as murderers by Garda reports. TB was amongst a number questioned. Despite the Minister for Justice's strong words, however, neither TB nor anyone else was ever charged with, let alone punished for, the crime.[25]

The lack of a conviction did nothing to improve the abysmal detection rate of Garda killers. As a direct result of Curtin's death the rules of An Garda Síochána were changed to give more protection to members of the force: 200 extra Gardaí were transferred to the Special Branch to deal with the 'increased activities of illegal association', while it was decided that revolvers would henceforth be issued to all district and divisional officers.[26] It also indirectly led to the removal of Eoin O'Duffy from his role as commissioner. O'Duffy had become increasingly militant towards the end of the 1920s and persistently called for the arming of the Gardaí. He had also allegedly been in favour of keeping Fianna Fáil away from the levers of power by virtue of a coup if they were voted into government.[27] Shortly after gaining power, de Valera's government relieved him of his post in 1933.

The weekly newspaper of Fianna Fáil, *The Nation* (precursor to the *Irish Press*), condemned unequivocally the deaths of both Superintendent Curtin and John Ryan in 1931.[28] This was something that they had failed to do in relation to previous Garda killings and a clear divergence from the position of the IRA. It would sit well with the general public, however; the vast majority of the population were shocked at the senseless killing and abhorred the idea of violence against Gardaí. The party would find themselves in government the following year with a hardened attitude to the IRA, their former comrades. The clash between the two sides of republicanism would come to a head in 1940, and again Gardaí like Superintendent Curtin would find themselves on the front line.

DETECTIVE PATRICK MCGEEHAN

*'You need not think you will frighten me
with your gun. I was never frightened.'*

The election for the Dáil of 1932 was amongst the most divisive ever seen in Ireland. Passions were running high in the country at the time, as it seemed a distinct possibility that the outgoing Cumann na nGaedheal party was going to be ousted. Even worse than that for the government was that they appeared likely to be replaced by Fianna Fáil, the reincarnation of the anti-Treaty side of the Civil War, who had fought tooth and nail to attempt to ensure that a twenty-six-county Free State would never come into being. An already tense election campaign was thrown into further disarray when outgoing government TD Patrick Reynolds was shot dead. Detective Patrick McGeehan was by his side on the day, and although not the target of the attack he would also be shot, later succumbing to his injuries. It had seemed like only a matter of time before the tense election campaign would claim its first victims; the trivial, mainly non-political reason behind the shooting was the main surprise.

Patrick Reynolds was a merchant and farmer from Ballinamore, County Leitrim, who owned a public house and a hardware shop in the town, as well a couple of large farms. The 45-year-old was married and the father of seven children. Renowned for being a talented footballer and boxer in his youth, Reynolds had spent several years in New York, where he had run a saloon on the city's docks. He had returned to the land of his birth with independence on the horizon. Reynolds then branched out into politics, running as a TD for the vast Sligo-Leitrim constituency in the election of 1927. He was elected as a government candidate, despite the fact that the area was known for its republican sympathies. Reynolds had also been appointed chairman of the Board of Health in Leitrim, and was a member of the county council. He was described as popular locally, even amongst his opponents, and his re-election in the election of 1932 seemed a certainty. Not a man to rest on his laurels, however, he had been campaigning vigorously to ensure that he retained his seat in the Dáil.

Patrick McGeehan was also a resident of Ballinamore, although the detective officer was originally from Meenamore East, outside the village of Fintown in County Donegal. Born in 1904, McGeehan was from a large family of hill farmers. The family eked out a living on a farm of 64 acres, with a horse, a few cows and a handful of sheep. Patrick was reportedly a man of powerful build who towered at well over 6ft. Like many in his district, he had joined the fight for independence at an early age and served as a teenage captain in the IRA in the 'Tan War'. After the truce, he travelled to Glenties to enlist in the National Army, although still aged just 18. He rose to the rank of corporal, his brother also serving as a lieutenant.[1] Patrick McGeehan was demobilised in 1928 after six years, at which point he enlisted in the Guards. After a brief stint training, the young Garda was posted to Cappamore, County Waterford, and then Kilakee, County Dublin. In 1931 he managed to secure a job closer to home, in County Leitrim.[2] He was described as an efficient and energetic detective officer and was supposedly engaged to be married, although he had not told his father this news. All seemed

Newly commissioned officers of An Garda Síochána, 1923. (National Library of Ireland collection)

Some of the first Gardaí on parade at their depot in the Phoenix Park, Dublin. (National Library of Ireland collection)

New recruits to the Civic Guard in Waterford. (National Library of Ireland collection)

General Eoin O'Duffy was instrumental in the setting up of the new Irish Police Force. (National Library of Ireland collection)

The gateway where Superintendent Curtin's killers lay in wait before shooting him dead. (Part of the Independent Newspapers Ireland/National Library of Ireland collection)

Detectives outside the home of Superintendent Curtin after his assassination. (Part of the Independent Newspapers Ireland/National Library of Ireland collection)

The coffin of Superintendent Curtin being carried by colleagues. (Part of the Independent Newspapers Ireland/National Library of Ireland collection)

The Square in Baltinglass, close to where Garda Patrick O'Halloran was shot dead by bank robbers. (National Library of Ireland collection)

Green Street Courthouse. Felix McMullen had the death sentence pronounced on him here. (National Library of Ireland collection)

Éamon de Valera showed little mercy to his former republican colleagues during the Emergency. (National Library of Ireland collection)

Éamonn Duggan, whose father was a policeman, was chosen as one of the architects of the Civic Guard. (National Library of Ireland collection)

The funeral of government minister Kevin O'Higgins. In 1927 O'Higgins was shot by the IRA, a group he had months earlier referred to as 'foolish young boys'. (National Library of Ireland collection)

Ballinamore, County Leitrim. Republicans accused Gardaí in the town of overseeing a reign of terror. (National Library of Ireland collection)

The RIC preceded the Gardaí but found themselves one of the main targets of the IRA in the War of Independence. (National Library of Ireland collection)

The Cumann na nGaedheal cabinet refused to commute the death sentence of Felix McMullen, who was hanged on the 1 August 1924. (National Library of Ireland collection)

to be going well for the young Garda, although Officer McGeehan and some of his comrades had found themselves in a spot of bother in early 1932.

Ballinamore had quickly become a republican stronghold and a crime blackspot after independence and the newly formed Gardaí suffered raids, robberies and kidnappings throughout the 1920s. The Gardaí, with a number of detectives from the Special Branch, had attempted to crush the IRA forcefully by fair means or foul ever since and had on occasion shot and killed members of the local IRA. On 7 February 1932, McGeehan and several other Gardaí appeared in court, where they denied a charge of beating a republican named John Vaugh in custody in Ballinamore Garda Station. The young man had died shortly after being released from custody after coming home looking 'battered and starved'.[3] His family claimed that he had been beaten within an inch of his life in the barracks and that this had contributed to his early death. The defendants were acquitted of the charge, although up to twenty men had complained of widespread beatings in Ballinamore Garda Station. The Gardaí in the area were accused of overseeing a reign of terror. Patrick Reynolds TD was amongst the witnesses giving evidence in support of the Gardaí during this inquest and was described by the deputy coroner as having 'a truculent attitude'.[4]

A week later, on Valentine's Day, Sunday 14 February 1932, Patrick Reynolds addressed a Cumann na nGaedheal election meeting held in Carrick-on-Shannon, County Leitrim. It was only two days from the vote and the meeting was a last-minute attempt to garner support. The engagement ended at 2.30 p.m. and afterwards Reynolds met Detective Officer McGeehan who had been on business in the town. McGeehan asked the TD for a lift to nearby Ballinamore. Reynolds agreed readily, although he informed the Garda that he would be stopping to canvass first. A barrister named Mr Barry O'Mahony from Dublin and an organiser from the Cumann na nGaedheal party called Mr Wrynne also accompanied the men. John McKeogh, a 43-year-old Dublin native, was the driver of the crowded vehicle.

The car made a detour to Foxfield, a townland just outside the village of Fenagh and 4 miles from Ballinamore. The TD canvassed several local houses. It was at this point that Reynolds called to the home of Joseph Leddy in an attempt to secure his vote. Leddy was about 45 years old and described as tall and well built.[5] A married man with two sons aged 10 and 12, Leddy was himself a Leitrim native and a former police officer, having joined the RIC in peaceful times in 1910. He also had three brothers in the force. He was first stationed in County Clare, as well as spending four years in Glenravel Street, Belfast. While in Belfast he had been struck on the head with a brick after being called to a house, after which his baton was wrenched from his hand and used against him. He spent six weeks in hospital and he would later depose that the attack had made him 'short-tempered and hasty'. One of his brothers had also been killed in the line of duty.

Like a large cohort of his colleagues, Leddy resigned from the force in 1920. The War of Independence was starting to heat up at that stage and RIC officers found themselves on the front line in a war with their fellow countrymen that they had never foreseen. Leddy had spent a total of ten years serving with the RIC. After demobilisation he married and moved to a small farm in Foxfield. Along with the income he derived from agriculture, Leddy received a small pension for services rendered to the IRA after he had resigned from the RIC, the former policeman having assisted republicans by giving over his revolver and ammunition. He had also taught younger republicans how to drill. It was a difficult task to obtain a pension for ex-RIC officers in those strained financial times, especially for a man who had been in the pay of the British up until 1920. Several TDs had helped him to receive the payment. Patrick Reynolds stated that he had interceded on Leddy's behalf and helped him to obtain what he felt was rightfully his. Leddy disagreed, saying that Reynolds had never proven that he had helped with the application, unlike other TDs.

At about 4.15 p.m., Reynolds left his four compatriots in the car and approached Leddy's door alone. As the TD felt that he had

helped his constituent with his pension application, he was ada-
mant that he deserved Leddy's support in the upcoming election.
The Leddys, who were sitting down waiting for the kettle to boil,
greeted the TD warmly, saying, 'Welcome, Mr Reynolds.'

Reynolds did not return the greeting, apparently immediately
accusing Leddy of double-crossing him, saying, 'You are out canvassing against me.' Leddy refuted this, claiming, 'I never went out
canvassing against you. I was always planning on giving you my
number one.' Reynolds was not placated. He repeated the accusation before attempting to strike Leddy. A furious Leddy then stood
up and said, 'Don't come into my house to beat me or I will shoot
you.' Reynolds retorted, 'I dare you to shoot me', and grabbed
Leddy by the scruff of the neck, shouting, 'I'll kill you, you bastard.'
Mrs Leddy, who was crying, helped her nephew, Francis McNamee,
try to pull the two men apart. It was at this point that the occupants
of the car heard the commotion from the house. Leddy's two sons
then came to the door shouting, 'Save my father.'

Wrynne and McGeehan got out quickly and entered the house,
where they found Reynolds and Leddy fighting, and McNamee
attempting to separate them. Eventually McGeehan and Wrynne
managed to pull Patrick Reynolds away. As Reynolds was being pulled
out the door, he threatened Leddy, 'You bastard. I took a wrong oath
to get you the pension and by God, I will see you broke off it.' Leddy
then rushed to the corner, where he picked up a double-barrelled
shotgun and threatened to shoot everyone in the house. Reynolds
sneered, 'There are more guns than yours.' Detective McGeehan also
warned Leddy that he was in the presence of an officer of the law
and put his hand into his inside pocket. At this, Leddy quietened and
Reynolds left the house with the driver McKeogh. The men stood
alongside the vehicle, although McGeehan and Wrynne stayed in the
house for up to three minutes talking to Joseph Leddy.

The car had been turned and was nearly at the door when
McGeehan and Wrynne got outside. McGeehan stood at the front
while Reynolds was standing at the back, reluctant to enter the
car and leave the scene. Suddenly, Leddy came to the door with a

shotgun and repeated, 'The first man that comes inside the door I will give him what is in the gun.' McGeehan shouted, 'I'll fire, Leddy, if you fire.' Reynolds then said to Officer McGeehan, 'Give me that gun, by God I will plug him in his own door.' He had hardly the words out of his mouth when Leddy aimed the gun at the Garda and fired at him. It struck him square in his chest.[6] The Garda somehow managed to stumble over 50ft down the road to the mouth of the laneway, where he crashed face first into a pile of rocks, leaving a trail of blood along the ground behind him.

Reynolds watched in horror. He then turned towards the house owner, shouting, 'You need not think you will frighten me with your gun. I was never frightened. I faced better than ever you were.' Despite his nephew's best attempts to pull his arm back, Leddy managed to raise and fire his shotgun, shouting, 'Reynolds, take that.' The bullet struck Reynolds in the back and the TD fell where he stood. Leddy then calmly walked four or five steps to where McGeehan lay and picked up the Garda's revolver. He emptied the five bullets onto the ground and handed the empty gun to McNamee, who asked him what he should do with it. Leddy replied, 'We will soon be called for.'[7]

Wrynne and McNamee immediately went to the injured men's aid but in both cases the situation was hopeless. O'Mahony, who had been asleep in the back of the car, tired out after addressing meetings all week, had woken by this point and witnessed the second shot. Bravely, he got out of the car and went to Reynolds who was lying on the ground. 'Paddy, have they got you?'

'A priest, a priest,' answered the injured man. O'Mahony told him he would try to get one, before going to McGeehan. He believed the Garda was dead. McKeogh started the car and drove off with Wrynne at this point. O'Mahony chose to stay with the Leddys and the two fatally injured men.

O'Mahony then turned around to see Joseph Leddy standing there with the shotgun, smoke still billowing from the barrel. O'Mahony pleaded to the gunman, 'Don't shoot, don't shoot. Why should brother Irishmen shoot one another?'

Leddy replied, 'Are you a CID too? Produce your gun, produce your gun.'[8] O'Mahony spent the next eight to ten minutes pleading with Leddy not to put another cartridge in the gun. He asked Leddy to hand the firearm over to him so the Gardaí would not come and shoot him. Leddy replied with the words, 'I will shoot you too. Who are you and what brought you here?' O'Mahony later described a wild look in Leddy's eyes which made him look like a madman. The barrister was afraid and desperately waiting for the return of his comrades. He quoted a line to Leddy about peace that had been said by Abraham Lincoln, 'I came with malice in my heart towards no man, and charity towards all.' Unsurprisingly, this failed to calm the gunman down. Two women then came up behind Leddy to the door, begging him not to shoot anymore. His wife then asked O'Mahony why they had come, saying, 'You were looking for trouble and got all the trouble you wanted.'[9]

O'Mahony said that he had sought no trouble and neither had Paddy Reynolds. The woman said, 'Why did you come here trailing a flag?' in a reference to the tricolour McGeehan had been carrying. When O'Mahony tried to tell her that that was a flag for every Irishman, she replied, 'Go boy, now, while you still have your life,' before saying to Leddy, 'Let this chap go. You have shot enough men for today.' O'Mahony refused to go. He demanded that Leddy give him the gun so as to prevent others being shot, either the policemen who were surely on their way or Leddy himself.

Leddy, who seemed to have calmed down, again grew agitated after hearing this statement. O'Mahony put his hand on the barrel of the gun and Leddy used it to hit him below the breast. He then punched him in the face several times, causing O'Mahony to fall to the ground. Leddy next attempted to reload the gun but his wife knocked the cartridges out of his hand and an injured O'Mahony got up and ran to the neighbour's house. Leddy then sent one of his children for a priest and walked back into the house, pacing up and down the kitchen. McGeehan was in all likelihood dead at this point, but Reynolds was still alive and he called out to the man who had shot him, 'Joe, lift me', several times. Leddy ignored the calls and did not leave the house.

Fr O'Connor from the nearby village of Fenagh was the first on the scene at some point after 4.30 p.m., finding Reynolds lying in the middle of the road, twitching. He appeared to be close to death. Leddy's wife and children were on the road crying when the priest arrived and Leddy himself came out of the house on seeing the priest. He said, 'This is terrible. It had to be done, they came into my house to beat me.'[10] O'Connor reassured him that it had all been an accident. Leddy agreed. He then asked Leddy calmly to put away the gun before the Gardaí arrived, saying later that he believed that Leddy 'was in a dangerous frame of mind and would shoot indiscriminately'. Leddy acquiesced, taking two cartridges out of the gun, saying, 'I won't want them.'[11] At the request of Fr O'Connor, Leddy also took the boots off the feet of Reynolds so that the priest could administer the Last Rites to him. He then did the same for McGeehan, although the Garda appeared to be dead.

The doctor was also quick to the scene. He arrived at 5.15 p.m., confirming that both McGeehan and Reynolds were now deceased. He was swiftly followed by several Gardaí from Ballinamore who had heard two men were dead. They did not know the circumstances of the shooting or that one of their colleagues was amongst the dead men. The Gardaí found Leddy calmly smoking a pipe, although they did not know he was the wanted man. Detective Kenny asked, 'In the name of God, what happened here?'

Leddy responded calmly, 'I suppose you know what happened. I will make no statement. The men are dead and we cannot bring them to life.'[12] Leddy was quickly placed under arrest.

Reynolds' body was examined and a ragged gunshot wound was found on his inside right thigh. Death had been due to shock and haemorrhage, the principal artery of the thigh having been severed. McGeehan's cause of death was a circular wound underneath his chest. Reynolds' funeral took place in Ballinamore on 17 February while Detective Officer McGeehan was buried in his native Fintown two days later. Both occasions were well attended.

The shootings caused uproar in an already fraught election campaign. De Valera and the Fianna Fáil opposition were quick to offer their condolences and condemnation and the election in the Sligo-Leitrim constituency was deferred for two weeks out of sympathy for the deceased TD and to allow Cumann na nGaedheal to find a suitable replacement candidate. The Taoiseach, W.T. Cosgrave, sent his sympathy to the dead men's families.[13] There was widespread interest in the affair and large crowds were present outside the Garda station where Leddy was held and at all subsequent hearings. Patrick Reynolds was not the first member of the Oireachtas to be shot dead but the circumstances of his death were bizarre enough to capture the imagination of the public.

Leddy himself was initially interned in Ballinamore before spending a month awaiting his trial in Sligo and Mountjoy prisons. The trial would concern itself only with the murder of Patrick Reynolds and began on 7 March 1932 in the Central Criminal Court on Green Street in Dublin in front of Mr Justice Meredith. Leddy pleaded not guilty to the charge of wilful murder.

The prosecution called as witnesses all the men who had been in the car with McGeehan and Reynolds. None of them alluded to the threats that Reynolds had supposedly made to Leddy. Mr Wrynne took the stand and downplayed any remarks made by the deceased politician, saying he 'did not hear a single threat from Reynolds'.[14] He was given a particularly stern cross-examination in which he admitted that his story had changed slightly since the first day he had given it. He hesitated when asked if someone was schooling him on the answers he was giving the court. He was also accused of discussing the case with members of the Civic Guard, which he denied. Wrynne did admit that he and Reynolds had stopped at several hotels and drank pints during that day in between political engagements and that they were somewhat intoxicated by the afternoon.

Mr O'Connor, defending, put it to the jury that Reynolds was a domineering bully who would do anything to get elected.[15] He accused the deceased TD of having paid men a barrel of porter in return for breaking up the meeting of a rival candidate the day before he was shot. O'Connor added that the shooting had:

taken place under circumstances of the greatest provocation and in necessary self-defence ... if a blackguard (like Reynolds) came into one of your houses, and polluted the ears of your wife and children, would you not feel that you would revenge yourself?'

He went on to say:

I don't think that outside Mexico there has ever been an election campaign conducted in such a state of bravado as this man Reynolds who could be described as the Big Bill Thompson of Ballinamore.[16]

Similar to in County Clare, O'Connor insisted that the Gardaí, in league with Reynolds, were inflicting a reign of terror in that part of County Leitrim. He reminded the jury about the death of John Vaugh and the more than twenty men who had complained about being beaten in Ballinamore Garda Station in the previous year. He also cast aspersions on whether McGeehan was actually getting a lift on the day in question or if he was in fact acting as the gunman and enforcer for Reynold's violent campaign.

James Leddy, a neighbour of (but no relation to) the accused, also took the stand, repeating the story of Reynolds' threats. When giving his account of the day, he told the court that he heard Joseph Leddy's wife saying, 'We will vote for you.' Reynolds had apparently responded, 'You will not vote for me, you bitch. I will kill you.'

Joseph Leddy also chose to take the stand. He deposed that on the morning of the incident he had been out fishing and hunting with his nephew, Francis McNamee, and on his return he had left the gun in the corner of the kitchen and eaten his dinner. A knock on the door came some minutes later and Reynolds came in. The couple welcomed him – Reynolds shook Mrs Leddy's hand but clenched his fist when Joseph Leddy extended his hand to him. The TD then called the houseowner a cur and again accused him of canvassing for his rival, Carter. Leddy denied canvassing and assured Reynolds he would get his number one. Reynolds then said, 'I will kill you in your own house', before grabbing him by the throat and punching him. After McGeehan and Wrynne managed to remove Reynolds from the house, McGeehan had taken his gun out of his pocket and said, 'Keep quiet you, Leddy.' Leddy followed them to the door and said, 'Go home Paddy, that is the bad way for getting votes.'

Leddy described how he then noticed McGeehan's revolver and grabbed his own shotgun, threatening to shoot whoever came near his door. Leddy claimed that at this point Reynolds had asked the detective for his gun to shoot Leddy. Leddy stated that he was in fear of his life. He asserted that it was Reynolds he had shot first, aiming for his leg. He had then shot McGeehan. 'I had no intention of killing either of them, I thought I was going to be shot myself.' Leddy went on to say that he felt sorry after he saw Reynolds fall but that he had been trying to protect his wife and children. 'I had no resentment against Reynolds but I saw myself in danger.'[17] He next described how he stayed on the road, waiting for the Gardaí. He did not wait in his own home as he wanted a witness, being afraid that the Gardaí would shoot him when they found out what he had done.

Leddy accused the Gardaí of roughing him up after his arrest, claiming he was hit with a revolver in a car multiple times, including by the driver. He was also beaten frequently at the barracks by large groups of Gardaí who threatened to kill him like John Vaugh. They also took out his bed on the first night, forcing him to sleep on the flagstones. He had asked to be escorted by uniformed officers to Sligo Gaol as he was afraid of Officer McGeehan's colleagues, the detective officers. The Gardaí flatly denied all of these allegations. Leddy went on to divulge to the court that he had supported Reynolds in the 1927 election but in 1932 was supporting Michael Carter, an independent candidate. He also admitted to canvassing some of his Protestant neighbours in nearby Ballyduff to support Carter, an act which Reynolds had tackled him about previously when he had been in his pub.[18]

The prosecution disagreed wholeheartedly with the defence's version of events, insisting that the malice involved made this a straightforward murder case and reminding the court that Reynolds was an unarmed man who was shot down. The judge gave the jury options of murder or manslaughter, if the provocation had been enough to render Leddy in fear of his life. The jury retired at 2 p.m. on 10 March and were absent for an hour and forty minutes. A crowded courtroom waited for the result, a hush falling on the onlookers when the prisoner was brought forward. Leddy was found not guilty of murder but guilty of manslaughter. The jury also gave a strong recommendation to mercy on account of the provocation before the incident. Judge Meredith announced his agreement, telling the jury that he could impose anything from three years to a lifetime of penal servitude. The foreman urged him to go beyond that and give 'the lightest sentence possible'.[19] Joseph Leddy, who agreed at that point to plead guilty to the wilful manslaughter of Detective Officer McGeehan, was thus sentenced to two sentences of twelve months in Mountjoy Prison, to run concurrently. He left the dock, nodding to his wife and children as he passed. The court had shown great leniency and obviously had sympathy with Leddy's version of events – the judge even agreed to write a letter to the government asking them not to cancel the prisoner's pension.

Mrs Mary Reynolds was selected to run for TD in place of her late husband and she was elected with over 5,000 first-preference votes. It would not be enough for Cumann na nGaedheal, who lost out to their bitter rivals Fianna Fáil for the first time. They would not revisit the corridors of power for sixteen years. In March 1933, newly elected Mrs Reynolds sued Joseph Leddy. Leddy's defence was again insistent that he had committed the act in self-defence after being violently assaulted and after threats were made to his life. They also argued that Reynold's business was not profitable and that the family had not suffered much financially on account of his death. The judge disagreed, finding in favour of the widow and awarding her £1,050. McGeehan's father would also seek £1,000 compensation for the loss of his son, stating that Patrick had contributed £50 a year to his father, telling him to ask any time he needed support. Despite this, on 27 July 1932, the claim was refused. The reason given was that it had not been proven that there was any malice towards Detective Officer McGeehan and therefore the issue of compensation was not relevant. It was also stated that 'the parents of the deceased were not mainly dependent upon him'.[20] Yet again a slain Garda's dependents were left disappointed by the response of the state.

Unusually for killings of Gardaí in the early days of the state, there was no paramilitary involvement whatsoever in the death of Detective Officer McGeehan. It appears that he simply found himself in the wrong place at the wrong time and in the middle of an argument between two headstrong men. He was the first Garda killed in Connaught, the western province.

11

DETECTIVE
JOHN ROCHE

'I will go quietly now.'

After the death of Patrick McGeehan in 1932, the Gardaí would
have a relatively peaceful eight years, although there were unavoid-
able tragedies within their ranks. On 8 January 1933, Garda Eugene
McCarthy was drowned when attempting to rescue a man from
the River Lee in Cork City. A year later Sergeant Patrick Forde and
Garda Michael Kennelly were travelling towards their station in
Maam in County Galway when their hackney car slipped into the
River Corrib. Both men were drowned, along with two civilians.
Thankfully no member of the force would be deliberately killed
in this period, although the IRA was still active and would injure
Gardaí on more than one occasion.

The majority of the IRA had followed de Valera in 1926 and left
Sinn Féin to form Fianna Fáil, vowing to turn their backs on violence and use purely political means to achieve their ambitions.
However, many members of the IRA remained steadfastly committed to a republic and the relationship between the Gardaí and the

organisation deteriorated rapidly throughout the 1930s. A sergeant named Bevan got a bullet in the back from the organisation outside his own home in Tralee in 1933. Two years later, Garda Egan was shot in Leeson Street in May 1935 after arresting men writing republican slogans. Neither man's injuries were life threatening. Two RUC officers in Northern Ireland were less fortunate, both being shot dead by IRA volunteers in Northern Ireland during separate incidents in 1933.[1]

In 1936 two incidents occurred that forced the government to deal with IRA violence. The first was in Castletownshend, County Cork, when republicans shot dead Vice-Admiral Somerville due to his habit of giving references to local men who wanted to join the British Army. A month later, in County Waterford, the organisation killed John Egan, a suspected informer. Within weeks, dozens of members of the organisation were arrested by Gardaí and the IRA was banned once again, this time by their former Fianna Fáil allies. The schism in republicanism was complete.

By 1939 Éamon de Valera's government found itself in a dire predicament. The Second World War, or the Emergency as it was known throughout Ireland, had been declared in Europe. Although the Free State was officially a neutral country, they gave tacit support to the British, co-operating with them on such matters as weather reports and intelligence. Unfortunately for de Valera, a significant number of IRA men considered their former leader little more than a treacherous puppet of the British Empire. Worse again, many of them viewed a German victory in the war as a sure-fire way to achieve their dream of a united Ireland. Consequently, the dawning of the 1940s would see a new era of conflict between the Special Branch of An Garda Síochána and the IRA.

The republicans had made contact with the German military secret service, the Abwehr, early in the conflict.[2] On top of this, they declared war on England and started a bombing campaign across the Irish Sea to aid the German cause. Although the whole of Britain had entered the war, the IRA decided that 'on the basis of Celtic solidarity the war was confined to England only, Wales and Scotland being excluded'. There would be over 200 bombings, although only a handful of people were killed.[3] The IRA was also active in Ireland and in Christmas 1939 they stole over 1 million rounds of ammunition from the Phoenix Park Magazine Fort. Although most of it was recovered swiftly, it would still prove a highly embarrassing incident for the establishment.[4] The IRA sent emissaries such as Chief of Staff Seán Russell to Germany, while republican publications expressed the desire that Germany would win the war, even referring to the Nazi regime as their 'gallant allies'.[5] The Fianna Fáil government, fearful of a backlash from the British, clamped down hard on the IRA by introducing the harsh Emergency Powers Act. The stage was set for a period of violence between the Gardaí and the IRA as bad as anything seen since the days of the Civil War. Detective John Roche would be one Garda tasked with keeping tabs on known republicans.

John Roche was born in Ballybehy South near Abbeyfeale in Limerick, just yards from the border with County Kerry. As a young man he had worked on his family farm and was a keen Gaelic footballer. He decided to leave the agricultural life behind in 1923 to enlist in An Garda Síochána. Roche completed his training and served in numerous postings, initially in Kinnegad, County Westmeath, and then around the Cork City area in 1932. Five years later, aged about 32, Roche was promoted to detective and moved to the Detective Branch in Union Quay in the city. It was here that he was to come into contact with Tomás Óg Mac Curtain.

Tomás Óg Mac Curtain was born into republican royalty. His father, also Tomás, was commander of the Cork Volunteers during the 1916 Easter Rising, although little revolutionary activity occurred in the city due to confusion and a lack of orders from Dublin. Mac Curtain Snr remained popular amongst the nationalists in Cork, however, and was elected councillor and subsequently Lord Mayor of the city. He was assassinated just two months into his tenure on 20 March 1920 by a group of men with blackened faces. His death appeared to be in reprisal for the fatal shooting of an RIC man in the city and his house was then ransacked.

The official report stated, 'He was wilfully murdered under circumstances of most callous brutality, that the murder was organised and carried out by the Royal Irish Constabulary, officially directed by the British Government.'[6] Mac Curtain's death caused uproar throughout the country and led to a heightening of republican feeling in Cork and further afield. Tomás Óg was just 5 years old at the time of his father's death. He was far too young to take sides in the Civil War but as he entered his teenage years he found himself a leading member of the IRA.

By 1935 Mac Curtain Jnr was enrolled as a medical student in Cork University and well known in republican circles. At one stage, a Garda commanded the medical student to stop attacking a member of the Blueshirts when Mac Curtain turned and pointed a gun at him. He was arrested and charged with the offence, as well as membership of an illegal organisation. The teenager was defiant in court, but the judge extended leniency to him on account of his family history, suspending the sentence for twelve months to allow him to finish his studies.[7] After his release Mac Curtain was kept under Garda surveillance. Although he was known to be involved with the IRA, even leading their drilling on occasion, a Garda report in 1937 stated that 'the term of imprisonment he underwent put a good deal of sense into him'. It was also noted that Mac Curtain seemed like a normal teenager, spending 'a good deal of time walking around this city, particularly so at night and on Saturday evenings, usually in the company of young fellows and girls about his own age'.[8] Nevertheless Tomás Óg continued to be involved in the IRA. By 1940, Mac Curtain was living on Wellington Road in the city. He was 22 years of age and was occupying the same position, commandant of the No. 1 Cork Brigade of the IRA, as his father had two decades before.

The city had a strong republican presence and the relationship between the IRA and the Special Branch was poisonous by the time the Emergency began. Detective Roche was particularly well acquainted with Mac Curtain, having arrested him on multiple occasions, the first in 1932 when the republican was just 14. He had also given evidence against the IRA man on more than one occasion. On 15 September 1939, over fifty leading figures in the IRA were arrested under the Offences Against the State Act, including a number in Cork. Shortly afterwards a document was issued by the organisation in which ill treatment of volunteers and attempted bribery of prisoners by the Gardaí was alleged; Detective Roche was amongst the names of the men accused of such acts.[9] Mac Curtain would not be seen for the next few weeks but would give a chilling public speech in December 1939 in which he threatened, 'We have something the Free State are afraid of. We have guns and we have money and we have got men to use them.'[10] The Gardaí at that point were looking for Mac Curtain for questioning but would not catch up to him until January 1940.

On the evening of 3 January 1940, Éamon de Valera's Fianna Fáil government were discussing the details of an Emergency Powers Bill, which would give the state the 'authority to detain suspected persons without trial, including Irish-born citizens'.[11] Although the law seemed contrary to a democratic state, de Valera argued that the steps were necessary to keep control of the country in a time of unprecedented war in Europe. It would pave the way for mass internment of suspected members of the IRA. Meanwhile the Gardaí in Cork had heard news of the whereabouts of Tomás Mac Curtain.

Detective John Roche, Detective Sergeant Teahen and Detective Sergeant Collins drove from the station to the city centre, where they parked at Merchant's Quay. They were instructed to apprehend Mac Curtain, an arrest that would be 'both desirable and necessary in the interests of the peace of the city'.[12] The Gardaí were then to detain him under Section 30 of the Offences Against the State Act and bring him back to the station to answer questions about his alleged membership of the IRA. He was also wanted in connection with the movement of arms and ammunition in the county. Detective Roche knew the suspect well and had a long history with Mac Curtain, having arrested him and his comrades several times over the previous years. He had also searched his house on more than one occasion. The Gardaí took the Special Branch car and searched for Mac Curtain without success until 8 p.m. At that point Sergeant Teahen left the vehicle on foot to search for the suspect on Patrick Street, one of the main thoroughfares of Cork City.

At about 9.10 p.m., Teahen made a hurried phone call from the Savoy Cinema to Union Quay Barracks to say that he had found Mac Curtain and was watching him talking to two other men at the statue outside Mangan's Jewellers on Patrick Street. He added that Mac Curtain, dressed in a grey tweed overcoat and cap, did not realise he was being monitored and implored them to come quickly. Sergeant Collins and Detective Quinlan immediately rose to leave. As they were departing the station, they happened to see Detective Roche beside the day room window. They informed him of the developments and he readily agreed to go with them.

The three officers set off from the Garda station, arriving at the corner of Patrick Street within minutes. Detectives Roche and Quinlan alighted from the car and walked the 30 yards to Mangan's. As they came nearer the building they saw Tomás Mac Curtain, with his hands in his pockets, in deep conversation with two men they did not recognise. He had his back to the street.[13] Both detectives managed to reach Mac Curtain before he saw them. They placed their hands on his shoulder, one uttering the words, 'I want you to come to Union Quay.'

Mac Curtain immediately made a grab for his right pocket. Quinlan grabbed him with his two hands and shouted, 'Don't pull a gun.' Roche also reached out his hand and grasped Mac Curtain's arm. Suddenly Mac Curtain jumped backwards, managing to free himself from the grip of the detectives. He produced a gun from his coat and shot once. The bullet struck Roche in the upper abdomen. He slumped to the ground and groaned, 'Oh, God, I am shot.'

Detective Quinlan, who had at this point been joined by Teahen, immediately grappled with the gunman and managed to hold his right arm, in which the gun was held. The men struggled down the street as far as Fisher's Lane. The detective later stated:

He seemed, all the time, to be trying to turn the gun towards my body. I saw the muzzle of the gun was almost touching my head and I put my left hand over the muzzle to push it away. I was becoming exhausted at the time and I drew a kick at the defendant's stomach. He seemed to struggle less violently after this and he was knocked on the street.[14]

The detectives then drew their own firearms and kneeled on Mac Curtain, who said, 'I will go quietly now.' Meanwhile, a large crowd had assembled around the struggle in the roadway. Some who were present attempted to administer medical assistance to Roche, who was haemorrhaging blood. Meanwhile Mac Curtain was taken to the waiting patrol car with a gun pressed into his back. He was then searched, all the while assuring the officers, 'I have no other firearms on me. You have got the only one I had.' The detectives then berated him, saying, 'It is a cowardly thing to shoot an Irishman as you have shot Sergeant Roche.' Mac Curtain retorted, 'I don't know why you think it cowardly. Wasn't it three armed men against one armed man?' When reminded that the Gardaí had not drawn their weapons, Mac Curtain protested, 'I am surprised that you did not know before now that we are armed and that we are bound to use them.' Mac Curtain was searched at this point and was found to have no other arms, although he did have lists that appeared to refer to IRA activity.[15]

The prisoner was taken to Union Quay Barracks, the station of the man he had shot, and asked again why he had shot the Garda. Mac Curtain answered, 'There were four armed men there. I thought I would take a chance and get away. As man to man wasn't that a fair break?' Mac Curtain asked to see his solicitor, who arrived and examined his client before asking that a medical professional be summoned. At 1.30 a.m. that night, a doctor was brought to the barracks to examine Mac Curtain who said he had been threatened by Gardaí and was 'afraid to be beaten'.[16] The doctor found no marks on the prisoner. Mac Curtain was told the following morning that Detective Roche had died. He did not express remorse, merely replying, 'I make no statement.' His words were written down and the prisoner was asked to sign them, to which he replied, 'I will sign nothing.'[17]

An ambulance had arrived within minutes and John Roche was rushed to the South Infirmary where he was quickly treated by three doctors.[18] Although he was conscious initially, he was thought to be in a critical condition. The detective was in severe pain and bleeding from the side. The bullet was found to have lodged just inches below his heart, causing him to also bleed internally. The bullet was extracted and a successful appeal was made to other Gardaí to donate blood for a blood transfusion. The detective received three pints of blood but to no avail. John Roche died at 2.25 a.m., before the operation could be completed.[19]

An inquest, which was held on 8 January, established that Roche's death was caused by haemorrhage from the portal vein, liver and lung as a result of a bullet to the chest, the wound being 13ins long, with the bullet ending up in the unfortunate detective's back. It was ascertained that the bullet had come from the gun taken from Mac Curtain, which also had his initials etched into it. The funeral on 7 January saw the procession travelling 60 miles north from Cork City to the slain Garda's hometown of Abbeyfeale. The coffin, draped in a tricolour, 'bore a wealth of wreaths and floral tributes'.[20] The newspapers described how the sight of his 'young widow prostrate with grief and his grey-haired father aroused deep sympathy'. Ironically, the procession wound its way through Mac Curtain Street in Cork City, the street named in honour of the father of the man who had caused the detective's death.

The Gardaí were busy in the aftermath of the arrest. A lorry-load of army personnel were called into the city, arresting up to two dozen suspected republicans in the area. Mac Curtain's home was also searched by a party of Gardaí. His sisters were present and verbally abused the raiding party. One of them was found to be in possession of a revolver, which was forcibly taken from her. She shouted, 'Give me that, that's mine.'[21] Items of the uniform of the National Army were also discovered in the house. Despite an extensive search of the wider Cork area, the two men that had been talking to Mac Curtain on the evening in question were not found or identified.

Mac Curtain was charged with murder on 4 January. He had been brought to Cork District Court in a covered lorry. The prisoner, handcuffed and surrounded by several uniformed Gardaí, was brought again on 13 January and placed on remand. A feature of each of his journeys to the courthouse was the large armed presence around the court, the Gardaí presumably mindful of a possible IRA attempt to free their colleague.[22] On each occasion, a relaxed-looking Mac Curtain chatted happily with his sisters, who were present. His defence team also insisted that they wanted the case to be dealt with as quickly as possible.

The preliminary hearing began on 1 February, almost a month after the shooting. The public were not admitted. The defence began by asking that all Gardaí, except those on the stand under examination, be excluded from the court. They claimed that the reason for this was that at least two of the defence witnesses had been intimidated before the trial. The prosecution argued that there were no grounds whatsoever for the charge of intimidation. Nevertheless, it was decided that just one prosecution witness would be permitted in the courthouse at any given time. The case was then returned for trial to the Special Criminal Court.

On 25 February, Mac Curtain and six other IRA prisoners went on hunger strike in an attempt to achieve political status. This was just two weeks after Peter Barnes and James MacCormack, IRA volunteers convicted of aiding in the planting of a bomb in Coventry, were hanged. The hunger strike had long been a popular method of protest by the IRA and had been used to great effect by the former Lord Mayor of Cork Terence MacSwiney (who replaced Tomás Mac Curtain Snr after he was assassinated). It was Mac Curtain Jnr's second hunger strike, having undergone the gruelling ordeal previously in 1935.[23] On this occasion, however, the protest was strictly censored, the government refusing to allow the media to report on the condition of the prisoners. Mac Curtain's hearing was delayed due to his weak condition and on the forty-fourth day of the strike he was removed to hospital. The strike was only abandoned after the death of two of his fellow hunger strikers. They were Tony D'Arcy and Seán MacNeela. Embarrassingly for the government, the latter was a nephew of government TD Michael Kilroy and he died hours after the strike had been called off.[24] Meanwhile, on 17 March 1940, a plaque was dedicated to Tomás Mac Curtain Snr at his former residence in Cork City.

The trial finally began in Collins' Barracks on 11 June. Mac Curtain was deemed fit to face the court although his defence argued that he was still too weak after his prolonged fast. The accused refused to plead, saying, 'I do not recognise the jurisdiction of this court at all.'[25] A plea of not guilty was thus entered on his behalf. Mac Curtain's family had been anxious that he would appoint a defence team, to include the outspoken campaigner against the death penalty, Seán MacBride. Mac Curtain initially refused but would eventually relent. MacBride's first grievance was that his client was not tried in an ordinary criminal court but 'returned to a non-legal tribunal'. He implored the judge to downgrade the charge to one of manslaughter, as security against 'a gross miscarriage of justice'. MacBride, who had himself been imprisoned for membership of the IRA, added that there was 'an inherent improbability with regard to the truth of the case of the Gardaí'.[26]

The Gardaí present on the day all gave their version of events, but were given a stern cross-examination by Mac Curtain himself, who contended that he had been hounded by the Gardaí for several years before the shooting of Detective Roche. Mac Curtain wrangled an admission from Sergeant Collins that at one point the accused had been arrested for three days without charge, while on another occasion he had been brought to trial and the judge had dismissed the case without even asking the jury to retire.[27] Another detective admitted that he knew that Mac Curtain had been shot at and beaten on several occasions on his way home.

The following day the court informed Mac Curtain that a *prima facie* case against him had been proven and that he was about to be found guilty if he did not prove his innocence. He was given time to prepare a case. Despite the fact that the death penalty was certain to be the outcome, Mac Curtain answered, 'I don't think there is any necessity.'[28] Three hours later the court again met, Mac Curtain still refusing to recognise its jurisdiction. He did agree to give a short statement from the dock to let his side of the story be known.

The prisoner asserted that he had been arrested on several occasions before that January night and never offered resistance. On this particular evening he had been quietly talking to two friends on a crowded street when without warning he had been grabbed from behind by men with no uniform. He went on:

> I had been fired on on two occasions. I had been beaten on numerous occasions. On one occasion I had four teeth broken. What was my natural reaction? There were three men piled on top of me in that moment. It all happened in a fraction of a second. I leave it to the court to decide if it was murder or not.[29]

Mac Curtain would claim that the Gardaí had harassed and stalked him in the years leading up to Detective Roche's death. He insisted that he was permanently followed by detectives after his release from prison in 1937. They would even sit behind him in the cinema. They raided his house continually. He said he was arrested on multiple occasions, including for smashing up the presses of *The Irish Times* and for shooting at the Union Quay Barracks, despite the fact that he had been in different places in plain view of Special Branch officers at the time those offences were being committed. He also claimed to have been warned by a Mrs Hurley in 1939 that the Special Branch wanted to get him 'dead or alive'. He added that as the Brigade Commander of the Cork No. 1 Brigade he made no apologies for carrying weapons, adding that it had never been shown that he had any animosity towards Gardaí. It was a heartfelt oration but it was in vain.[30]

The following morning the court reconvened and announced the case had been proven. Tomás Mac Curtain had deliberately fired his gun at Detective Roche and was thus found guilty of murder. When asked if he had anything to say, Mac Curtain answered, 'It is a proud moment that I can face my death knowing that I have done my duty to the army to which I belong and to Ireland. I am happy to die and I assure you that I die a soldier.' He was sentenced to death by hanging for 5 July, his sister Eibhlín shouting at the court, 'May the Lord have mercy on your souls'. Mac Curtain himself, defiant as ever, turned to a witness in the trial and said, 'You may see me down in Cork yet, or if you don't I have plenty of friends there.'

An enormous campaign was mounted to secure a reprieve for the young IRA man. The Mac Curtain family were still highly regarded within republican circles and counted Fianna Fáil cabinet members like Seán T. Ó Ceallaigh amongst their family friends. The initial meetings to overturn the sentence failed to receive a cabinet majority, Ó Ceallaigh appealing to Seán MacBride to secure a delay in order to give him time to convince his colleagues.[31] MacBride chose the last available moment on the day before the hanging to submit his appeal, a ploy that would prove fruitful. Although the hangman, Thomas Pierrepoint, had made the journey on the eve of the hanging, Mac Curtain was given a two-day stay of execution as the Supreme Court met to consider an appeal. At this point the *Washington Evening Star* wrongly reported in America that Mac Curtain had been hanged, an announcement which 'caused dismay, the general feeling being that it would strengthen the IRA'.[32]

MacBride went to inform his client that he had received a stay of execution. Rather than relief, Mac Curtain was angry at his counsel. He fumed:

> It's all very well for you lawyers to amuse yourself with your tricks. Now I've got to go through it all over again. I've had to say goodbye to my mother, my sisters, my girlfriend. I've had to make my peace with God, which was no easy matter. And now I've got to go through this all over again in a fortnight while you fellows are having fun arguing over my dead body.[33]

Whether or not the court was mindful of the outcry that would come from executing Mac Curtain, the appeal was rejected, the announcement being that the law must take its course. The date with the hangman was fixed for 13 July. Further petitions for a reprieve were received and considered by the government but also dismissed. To execute the son of an Irishman who had himself been assassinated by the British during the War of Independence may have been a step too far for Fianna Fáil under de Valera. Mac Curtain's reprieve did finally come on 10 July, the sentence being commuted to one of penal servitude for life. He had been just three days away from the gallows.

By 1946 it was stated that Tomás Mac Curtain had been in solitary confinement for six years in Portlaoise Prison as punishment for his refusal to wear prison clothes. His health was also failing. Various groups had lobbied that he be released forthwith, including the Kerryman's Association in New York. Several TDs also mentioned his plight, Seán MacBride contending that the treatment he received in prison 'would not be meted out to a dog'.[34]

By 1948 Fianna Fáil had lost their mandate and a new coalition government was elected that included Clann na Poblachta, a republican party with Seán MacBride at its helm. Unsurprisingly, the release of IRA prisoners was one of their main objectives and Mac Curtain was released just weeks after they gained power on 9 March of that year. He travelled home to his native Cork shortly afterwards, where an open-top bus would be used to return him to the city as an estimated crowd of close to 4,000 men and women cheered him on.[35]

Tomás Mac Curtain was quick to re-join his old comrades and went on to become one of the most important IRA figures of the 1950s and 1960s, even proving instrumental in planning the IRA's border offensive in Northern Ireland. He died in 1994. Detective Roche's wife, meanwhile, applied for compensation the year after her husband's death, claiming that he had been specifically targeted and that IRA documents discovered had mentioned beatings meted out to republican prisoners and seemed to single Roche out for blame. She initially received £1,300 in compensation for her loss, increased to £2,475 in 1945.[36]

12

DETECTIVE RICHARD HYLAND & DETECTIVE SERGEANT PATRICK MCKEOWN

'We are taking no chances now.'

Tomás Mac Curtain may have escaped the hangman by the skin of his teeth but the IRA's objective of undermining Irish neutrality remained in place. The Fianna Fáil party and their former colleagues in the republican movement were on a collision course, and the Gardaí found themselves on the front line in the war against the subversive organisation. The Special Branch took the lead in the search for republican suspects, detaining over 170 alleged IRA members in 1940. In April a bomb rocked Dublin Castle, headquarters of the branch, although miraculously no one was seriously injured. Four months later, two detectives, Patrick McKeown and Richard Hyland, were gunned down.

Patrick McKeown was born in the townland of Clea, just outside Keady in South Armagh. The passing of the Anglo-Irish Treaty by the Dáil dictated that McKeown's home place would be situated within the British-controlled six counties. Rather than rebel against the arbitrary line drawn through Ulster, Patrick and his brother Felix decided to join the Free State Army, enlisting in Monaghan Town in early 1922.[1] After the ceasefire in the Civil War, both men moved south to enlist in the Gardaí in 1923. Although he was initially an officer in the Dublin Metropolitan Police, Patrick was moved to An Garda Síochána after the DMP was subsumed into the force. He attained the rank of detective in 1933 and six years later, as the Second World War began, the northerner was made a detective sergeant. A single man, McKeown had served in Blackrock and Dún Laoghaire in County Dublin before being moved, along with his brother, to the Special Branch in Dublin Castle.

Richard Hyland had a slightly different background to many of the Gardaí mentioned heretofore. Born in the village of Manulla in County Mayo in 1903, Hyland lived in Maynooth, County Kildare for much of his youth. He had served as quartermaster of the IRA's 'E' Company in the Dublin Brigade during the War of Independence. What marked Hyland out from many of the Gardaí was that he had fought on the republican side in the Civil War against the government. He had even acted as a bodyguard for Éamon de Valera himself when the politician had escaped custody from the Hammam Hotel in July 1923. Hyland had assisted de Valera's safe passage under heavy gunfire from Free State Forces in a raid that cost Cathal Brugha his life. The Gardaí had remained a cold house for republicans for the next decade or so.

After Fianna Fáil were elected to government in 1932, however, an appeal was made to the ranks of the anti-Treaty IRA to join An Garda Síochána to transform it into a force for people from all sides of the political spectrum, a controversial venture at the time. Hyland answered the call in 1933, leaving his job as manager of a pawnbrokers in the capital. He was stationed for a time in Dundalk after his training. By 1940, Hyland, who was well known in coursing and racing circles, was 36 years of age and a married man living in Drimnagh. He juggled being a father of two children under the age of 3 with being a detective stationed at Dublin Castle.[2] The ex-republican had dealt with his former comrades in the IRA many times in his policing career and on 16 August 1940 had been due to give evidence against three men he had arrested after they were found with a lorry-load of ammunition.

At about 7.45 a.m. on the morning of Friday 16 August, five detectives drove in a 1938 Ford V8 patrol car to house No. 98A on the Rathgar Road, 4 miles south of the city centre. The contingent were under the direction of Detective Sergeant McKeown and included Detective Hyland. The premises in question had been under observation by the Gardaí for some time as a suspected IRA safe house and the plan was to search it under the Offences Against the State Act. The IRA had been particularly active over the previous months, bombing Belfast on seven occasions and conducting a number of bank raids and the Gardaí believed that No. 98A was also being used by the subversives for training purposes.[3]

The house was unassuming and unlikely to arouse suspicion. To a passer-by, the building resembled nothing more than a small and rarely visited tobacconist shop on the ground floor. The premises was bigger than it appeared, however. A plywood partition separated the shop from the living quarters behind it on the same floor; these included a small room and kitchen as well as stairs leading to the flat above, which had three bedrooms and a bathroom. It was in this flat that the Special Branch suspected illegal activity was going on.

The Gardaí parked the car 30 yards up the road to avoid notifying the occupants of their presence and walked quietly to 98A. While two of the Gardaí went to the rear of the house via a laneway, Detectives Brady, McKeown and Hyland stood waiting at the front door. All three men were armed: Hyland had a .38 revolver on his person while his two colleagues carried .45s. The door had an electric bell, which the men rang. There was no answer for about five minutes until a teenage girl came down and looked out by pulling the blind quickly to one side. The Gardaí heard her talking in a muffled fashion to others in the building. She did not open the door and there was the sound of footsteps going back upstairs. McKeown then walked around the back and had a conversation lasting about thirty seconds with the other two detectives before returning to Hyland and Brady. Meanwhile, there was the unmistakable sound of rustling and rummaging coming from upstairs.[4]

The Gardaí were now able to hear loud noises inside, including running water, which continued for three to four minutes. Footsteps were then audible coming down the stairs and a boy, who appeared to be aged about 15 or 16, approached the door and attempted to open it. He fumbled with the lock for about two minutes and appeared to be deliberately delaying, causing Detective Brady to tell him to, 'Hurry up.'[5]

When the boy finally opened the door, he asked, 'Who are you? What do you want?' He then bent down to pick up six milk bottles that were left on the doorstep. Hyland told him to leave the milk where it was and pushed him backwards into the shop. The boy, who appeared nervous, stood with his hand on the door of the shop and asked the men for their authority. Hyland produced his identification card. Detective McKeown next held the boy while Brady and Hyland walked towards the partition between the shop and the back. At that point, from a range of about 7ft, a burst of gunfire was heard.

Detective Hyland managed to shoot one bullet in response, which embedded itself in the wall. Neither of the other Gardaí had time to fire their guns. Hyland, who had been walking behind his colleague Brady, was shot seven times by the machine gun. He collapsed between the door and the counter, his blood haemorrhaged over the shop's floor. Sergeant McKeown was also struck by a bullet into the stomach, but somehow managed to turn and run out the door. Garda Brady was shot near the spine and crawled out the door, where he collapsed in front of the house. It was later contended that the delay opening the door was to give those inside an opportunity to get their guns and ammunition ready.[6]

The detectives at the rear of the shop heard the barrage of shots and ran around the front to be met by a disorientated Detective McKeown running in the direction of Terenure and waving his hand in the air. The Gardaí were talking to the milkman who happened to be passing when suddenly three men came running out of house 98A and almost stepped over Hyland and Brady. They then fled in the direction of Rathmines. They were just 8 to 10 yards from the Gardaí and one of them was carrying a machine gun. Another of the gunman fired over his shoulder as he ran.[7]

The two detectives who had not been shot immediately gave chase, shouting at the fugitives to halt. As the first Garda reached the corner of Wesley Avenue, he opened fire. He fired six shots from his revolver, a single bullet managing to strike one of the fugitives. One of the men took cover behind a car but the Garda shot several times and a bullet shattered the windscreen. The other detective, after talking to a civilian, received information indicating that a suspicious-looking man had gone through house No. 56. Sure enough, he found trampled wire netting, convincing him that someone had just passed this way. As he got into the laneway behind the house, Winton Avenue, he saw two men whom he recognised as the fugitives. One of them was limping, having been shot in the leg in the fire fight. The Garda shouted, 'Hands up', an order both men had ignored earlier. This time, they complied. He shouted for his fellow detective, who heard his cry and rushed toward the avenue. The third man had meanwhile managed to escape in the direction of Harold's Cross.

One of the men was fair-haired and he told the Gardaí that his name was Thomas Green. He was unarmed when arrested and the shotgun he had been carrying when fleeing the house was nowhere to be seen. The older man was Patrick McGrath and was well known to the authorities. He had a loaded .45 Webley revolver in his pocket, which, along with his hands, was covered in blood. It had been recently fired. At this point the detectives were unaware that three of their colleagues had been shot, two fatally. The men were taken into custody regardless.

A search of the area was quickly conducted and a 1921 Thompson submachine gun was found at No. 57 Rathgar Road, where McGrath had been running. There were seven rounds in the magazine and the safety catch was off. The gun was also cocked for use. It appeared to have been thrown into the hedge of the garden from the street. The machine gun showed signs of recent use, so much so that any further use of it was likely to cause it to burst. The house at No. 98A Rathgar Road was then searched. It contained an array of subversive material, a wireless transmitting set, two typewriters and a duplicating machine. There was also a large quantity of guns and ammunition present, which would be described in court as 'a minor arsenal, controlled by the two accused'.[8] It was ascertained that three men and a woman had been sleeping in the house the night before the shooting, two of whom were now in Garda custody.

The man who called himself Thomas Green was brought to nearby Wesley Road, where a house with its door open was chosen to host the prisoners. Green had been shot in the leg and was attended to by a doctor, although the wound was not serious. McGrath was also brought into the house after his surrender and he was said to have approached Green and shook him by the hand. He said 'Congratulations' and 'Good-bye' to his compatriot. Green was then taken to hospital while McGrath was removed from the house to Bridewell Garda Station.

Patrick B. McGrath was a native of Rathmines but by 1940 lived in No. 17 Aungier Street in Dublin City, where his family owned McGrath Brothers Blinds Ltd. He was a veteran of the Easter Rising of 1916 and had one hand incapacitated as a result of injuries suffered in the campaign. He had also fought in the War of Independence. McGrath stayed true to the republican cause after the Treaty, training many of the younger volunteers throughout the 1920s and 1930s. He was also a member of the IRA headquarters staff, described as the Chief Operations Officer. He was therefore well known to the Special Branch, Detectives Brady and Hyland having previously arrested him. On 9 September 1939, he had again been arrested in Rathmines after being found at a suspected IRA safe house in possession of firearms and illegal documents. He was conveyed to Mountjoy Prison, where he was detained under the Offences Against the State Act.

The elderly republican had decided to go on hunger strike on 22 October of that year along with three IRA men from County Cork. The protest was against the Emergency Powers legislation that allowed the government to detain citizens without charge. By 10 November 1939, McGrath's condition was described as 'exceptionally grave'. The National Association of the Old IRA visited de Valera himself, begging him to show mercy to their former colleague. The opposition Labour Party also petitioned for mercy for McGrath and his fellow strikers. The Taoiseach, despite knowing McGrath personally, declined. He said that in the interests of public order and security they could not allow themselves to release the prisoners as it would encourage similar tactics in future. 'The government had to choose the lesser of two evils and that was to see the men die rather than the safety of the whole community be endangered.'[9] Mercy was ultimately shown, however, and McGrath was released into Jervis Street Hospital on the twenty-third day of the strike. He eventually recovered but the government decided not to proceed with a prosecution. Patrick McGrath was free to go.

Now, less than a year later, he was back in police custody. On the journey to Bridewell Garda Station McGrath spoke freely, saying to the Gardaí:

> I suppose you men don't know who I am. I am Patrick McGrath. You got the spoils this morning. I am surprised at you men coming to a house where there are Republican soldiers, knowing that they were armed. You have started the shooting by shooting the last two of our leaders that were arrested. We are taking no chances now.

Meanwhile, the Gardaí had realised that 'Thomas Green' was not the name of the other prisoner. He was visited in Mountjoy Hospital by a policeman shortly after the shooting. The Garda, recognising the injured man, showed him a picture of himself and asked him if that was him and if his real name was Thomas Gordon Harte. Harte replied, 'It is', but would not answer any further questions relating to his background. It would later transpire that the prisoner was from the Edward Street area of Lurgan, County Armagh, and was aged just 25. Despite his youth, Harte was a seasoned IRA activist with several aliases who had played a part in the IRA bombing campaign in England in 1939. In early 1940 Harte was appointed to the staff of the GHQ under the stewardship of Paddy McGrath.

The three detectives, meanwhile, had been rushed to hospital. Richard Hyland was pronounced dead on arrival. Dr John McGrath, the state pathologist, performed a post-mortem examination on the deceased Garda. He had been riddled with bullets. Seven in total had entered his body, just five of them exiting. One of the bullets had struck him on the forehead, causing an extensive fracture to the skull. His brain was also lacerated, giving Hyland no chance of survival. His death was caused by shock and haemorrhage. The pathologist later produced two of the bullets extracted from Hyland's body and showed them to the courtroom, explaining that four of the shots would have proven instantly fatal.

Patrick McKeown was brought to the Meath Hospital in a milk van. Unlike his colleague, he was conscious on arrival. The detective was treated for shock and operated on that afternoon but died of his injuries the following morning. McKeown had been struck by a bullet at the tip of his twelfth rib, which had then entered his abdomen. Peritonitis had set in, inflaming his abdomen, and death had followed shortly after. The third man, Detective Brady, had managed to crawl outside after being shot. His injuries, although serious, would not prove to be life-threatening.

The funerals of the two Gardaí took place on 18 August, when the remains were removed to the Carmelite Church on Whitefriars Street. Between 400 and 500 Gardaí attended the service, as well as four ministers of government. McKeown's body was buried afterwards in his family's plot in Keady. Several Garda stations en route paid tribute to their fallen comrade. Hyland was buried in the Republican Plot of Glasnevin Cemetery in County Dublin.

It was announced that the case of the two IRA prisoners would be heard immediately, despite Harte's injuries.[10] As it was considered a political crime, the trial took place in Collins' Barracks as opposed to Green Street in Dublin, where ordinary murder cases were tried. The Military Court, established under the Emergency Powers Order 1940, had only been set up the day of the Rathgar Road shootings. The case of McGrath and Harte would be its first assignment. It was no ordinary court of law. The judges were three military officers, all members of the Special Criminal Court. Similar to the trial of Tomás Mac Curtain, a guilty verdict meant only one likely outcome – the death penalty.

Harte was brought to the court in an ambulance and under armed escort, before being carried into the building on a stretcher and placed on a chair to observe the proceedings. The trial would focus only on the shooting of Detective Hyland, who was believed to have been gunned down by Harte's weapon. Mr J. McCarthy, outlining the state's case, described how the 'loyal servants were murdered in the prime of life … in the execution of their duty to the people and to the state'. He also told the court that if they were satisfied that the men had planned to escape by shooting, it was immaterial which of them had fired the fatal shots. 'Everyone who took part in this conspiracy to shoot their way to liberty was liable for the consequence of the act of the others, whether they themselves fired the shots or not.' The bullets that were taken from Hyland's body were from a Thompson machine gun, while those that killed McKeown came from a Webley revolver. McCarthy went on to speculate that, 'It might well be that each marksman in this ambushing party selected out his own victim and fired accordingly.' He also detailed McGrath's comments in the car after his arrest. 'You have started the shooting. We are taking no chances now.'

The President of the Court informed the two men that they would be given every opportunity 'to prepare their defences and to obtain legal assistance', but like many captured IRA volunteers, McGrath and Harte refused to plead to the charge or recognise the court. A plea of not guilty was thus entered on their behalf.

When the president of Arbour Hill Prison enquired about what facilities the men would want to fight the charges against them, both replied that they did not want any assistance.

The state continued with its case regardless. They produced numerous witnesses, including the two detectives and medical officers, to vouch for the identification of the two prisoners as the armed men who had fled from 98A Rathgar Road. There was also an adjournment to the Meath Hospital to interview the injured Garda Brady, who was unable to be moved to Collins' Barracks at the time due to the seriousness of his injuries. The court, including the two prisoners under heavy armed escort, assembled in one of the hospital wards, where the Garda was wheeled in on a bed. He described the traumatic events of the day 'in a low voice and seemed to have some difficulty in speaking'. After the state concluded its evidence, both prisoners were offered the opportunity to speak in response to the evidence or call witnesses for the defence. Both men stayed silent.[11]

After just fifteen minutes' deliberation, the Military Court returned. They announced a guilty verdict for the two accused men. 'This court finds you guilty of murder and the order and sentence of this court is that you suffer death by shooting.' It was just four days since they had committed the killings for which they were now under sentence of death. The President of the Court announced that a record of the trial would be sent to the government and if the cabinet 'declined to remit or commute the sentence then directions must be complied with not later than forty-eight hours after such directions are given'. There would be no appeal under the terms of the Act and the prisoners were removed to Arbour Hill Prison under armed escort to await the government's decision on a reprieve.

The day after the trial the Fianna Fáil government released a statement announcing that they would not be commuting the death sentence of either man. It was unsurprising that they would refuse to intervene in the Military Court's ruling, a body that they had masterminded. De Valera had shown leniency to Mac Curtain earlier in the year and was undoubtedly rueing the previous act of mercy towards Patrick McGrath. On this occasion he would not countenance repeating the gesture. The execution would thus have to be carried out within forty-eight hours. The death sentence having been procured on a charge of killing Detective Hyland, the Military Court decided against proceeding on the case of McKeown, adjourning it *sine die.*

A last-ditch attempt to save the two men's lives was inaugurated. Seán MacBride demanded that the warrant of commitment and detainer be produced in relation to the two men. MacBride, outspoken opponent of the death penalty and future winner of the Nobel Prize, again took charge of the campaign to save the lives of IRA men under sentence of death. He managed to get their death sentence postponed; a judge granted the men a conditional order of *habeas corpus* amid doubts over the legitimacy of the Military Court and the validity of the emergency legislation, which MacBride asserted had not even been in place at the time of the men's arrest.[12] MacBride insisted that there was no state of war in the country at the time of the shootings and therefore the Military Court was unlawful. He further claimed that McGrath and Harte, as ordinary citizens, could not be amenable to military law and were thus unjustly detained in military barracks.[13] He added that there had been no mention of the Emergency Powers Order in the prisoners' committal order, thus rendering it invalid.

The stay of execution was to be short-lived. On 26 August 1940, Mr Justice Gavan Duffy decreed that the detention and sentencing of the two men was indeed lawful and that the law, having been passed by both Houses of the Oireachtas in a time of national emergency caused by war, must take its course. He added that the appeals had been mainly on technical points and pronounced himself disappointed that the defence could not see 'the public importance of this emergency legislation'.[14] The men appealed the decision but this was unanimously dismissed by the Supreme Court on 4 September. Their date with the firing squad was set for 6 September, just two days after the appeal was rejected.

Widespread protests were held in the days leading up to the executions but Fianna Fáil stood their ground and no commutation was granted. Paddy McGrath, believed to have fired the fatal volley into Detective McKeown, was considered to have served his country especially well. He had fought in the Easter Rising and the War of Independence, been shot in a fire fight with the British and been interned in Frongoch. The thought of his execution by an Irish government was therefore greeted with horror by many. No IRA volunteer had suffered the death penalty in Ireland since the Civil War and the death of Easter Rising veteran McGrath by firing squad, followed by burial within the prison grounds, drew uncomfortable comparisons with the fate of the leaders of 1916 by the British regime.

Thomas Harte (alias Green) and Patrick McGrath were executed by firing squad at 6.45 a.m. on the morning of 6 September in Mountjoy Prison. It was just three weeks after Hyland and McKeown had been killed. The news in the country was strictly censored at the time but the shootings aroused equal amounts of interest and outrage.

Searches had continued for the third man who had been seen running from 98A Rathgar Road after the detectives' death. Buses and cars were stopped on the day of the shooting and men and women searched but the fugitive remained at large. The day after the executions, English-born Thomas Hunt was identified by Brady as having been in the house at the time of the shooting and charged with Garda Hyland's murder. A British detention order with his name on it had also been found in the 98A Rathgar Road address and had led the Gardaí to him. He pleaded not guilty to the charge but evidence was heard that he had arrived at Gloucester Street at 8.45 a.m., allegedly having run all the way from the crime scene. He was arrested on 22 August, six days after the shootings, and found to have keys for 98A Rathgar Road in his possession. He was tried by the Military Court and was also represented by Seán MacBride.

MacBride complained bitterly that Hunt's trial had not been convened until the day after the executions of Hunt and McGrath, 'the only two people who could have given evidence of his innocence'.[15] He also questioned Brady's identification of the prisoner. The Garda now said that Hunt had opened the door, but at the time of the shooting he claimed a small fair-haired boy had done this; Hunt was 21 and dark-haired. It made little difference and after half an hour's deliberation the prisoner was found guilty of murder. Hunt, too, was sentenced to death on 23 September. He replied, 'I am innocent of this charge.'[16] Perhaps cognisant that enough lives had been lost, the government commuted his sentence to one of penal servitude for life at the last minute.

Detective Michael Brady's condition was described as favourable after the trial and he went on to fully recover from his injuries. Claims for compensation totalling £6,000 and £5,000 were submitted against Dublin Corporation by Detective Hyland's wife and Detective McKeown's mother, respectively. The claims were dismissed, the judge ruling that there was no evidence to prove that the gunmen had harboured any 'special malice' against the detectives.[17] Five years after the shootings, Mrs Hyland received £2,677 while Mrs McKeown was awarded £620 for the death of her son.

With the Second World War and the Emergency coming to an end, the National Graves Association made tentative overtures to the government, asking them to release the bodies of all IRA men executed during the conflict. The government agreed and Patrick McGrath's body was brought from Mountjoy on 17 September 1948 to the Franciscan church on Merchant's Quay. He was reinterred in Glasnevin Cemetery the following day, with Seán MacBride in attendance. Thomas Harte's body was released in the same month and a cortège wound its way to Lurgan. When it reached the border, a northern party of police stopped the procession and insisted that the tricolour be removed from the coffin. The mourners refused and the RUC opened the hearse themselves and took off the flag. Harte was then buried in St Colman's Cemetery in his home town of Lurgan.[18] The events of a summer morning in 1940 had ultimately led to the deaths of four men.

DETECTIVE SERGEANT DENIS O'BRIEN

'If this is an example of justice, freedom and democracy, then I would like to know what dictatorship and militarism are.'

Detective Denis 'Dinny' O'Brien and the IRA had a long history. O'Brien had been an anti-Treaty fighter and had only joined the Gardaí in 1933. He was not a man of divided loyalties, however, proving himself to be a detective capable and willing to target his former colleagues in the IRA. He had a hand in snaring some of the organisation's most important officers in the war years but this devotion to duty convinced some members of the illegal army that he deserved the ultimate punishment.

Denis O'Brien was born on 17 June 1899 on Pim Street in Dublin's south-inner city, attending a school in nearby Marrowbone Lane, which was run by the Christian Brothers. The order was known for their republican sympathies and it is perhaps not surprising that O'Brien, along with his two brothers, fought in the Easter Rising while his sister was a member of Cumann na mBan. Dinny was just a teenager at the time of the conflict and was released after a short term of imprisonment on account of his youth. He continued to espouse the republican cause, acting as Officer Commanding of the 'C' Company of the 4th Battalion in the Dublin Brigade. O'Brien refused to accept the partition outlined in the Treaty, and acted as Director of Communications in the Four Courts against the Free State government. The eventual surrender would lead to him being imprisoned in Mountjoy and Newbridge internment camps until 1924.[1]

The Civil War was particular devastating for Dinny as his brother Paddy was killed while fighting government troops in Enniscorthy in July 1922. Dinny was imprisoned in Mountjoy at the time and had to apply for parole in order to attend the funeral. A few short months later, his good friends Rory O'Connor and Liam Mellows were executed by the Free State government.[2] Nevertheless, O'Brien took no further part in the violence after his release. He had married Annie Cooney, a former Cumann na mBan member, in the meantime and secured work as an accountancy clerk with the Electricity Supply Board (ESB). Although he remained nominally associated with the IRA up until the early 1930s, O'Brien chose to devote the majority of his time to his family and his job.

By 1932, the Fianna Fáil party had seen a large growth in popularity, despite attempts by their Cumann na nGaedheal opponents to tarnish them as Communists.[3] The election of that year came in the midst of a worldwide depression, during which the outgoing government had made a series of swingeing cuts to expenditure, including old-age pensions, unemployment subsidies and public sector pay. Garda salaries had also been in the line of fire. Fianna Fáil, promising an end to austerity measures, vowed to improve infrastructure and update economic policy to restore prosperity to the masses. The electorate were sufficiently impressed and Fianna Fáil's vote increased substantially, leading to the attainment of seventy-two seats. With the help of the Labour Party, they were able to get their hands on the levers of power and oust their bitter rivals in a peaceful transfer of power.

The Republican Party had more on their mind than a shift in economic policy, however. They were unhappy with many things about the Free State, the police force foremost amongst them. De Valera himself stated that, 'There would of course be a police force in a republican Ireland. The objection to the current police force is that it is too numerous and that it acts politically on many occasions.'[4] His main problems were with the Special Branch and the upper echelons of the force, which he felt were run by pro-Treaty officers with sympathies towards Cumann na nGaedheal. De Valera and his cabinet decided to purge the hierarchy of the Gardaí of several high-profile figures, such as Commissioner Eoin O'Duffy. Calls from rank-and-file party members for the government to disband the Special Branch were rejected, although David Neligan, the famous spy in the castle during the War of Independence and head of the organisation, got his marching orders and he was moved to a job in the civil service.

Another strategy to even up the numbers was the coaxing of loyal anti-Treaty republicans into the force. Dinny O'Brien was exactly the kind of man Fianna Fáil were looking for. He had extensive experience with the IRA and the O'Briens were steeped in the party, his brother Larry eventually becoming private secretary to Seán Lemass. Dinny was thus accepted into the Gardaí and the infamous Broy Harriers. He was found to be a capable officer and was quickly promoted to detective in 1937 and stationed in Dublin Castle.

The harriers were a group of former anti-Treaty IRA men within the Gardaí who acted against the Blueshirts, a group loyal to Fine Gael who were suspected of having fascist sympathies. Along with the Fianna Fáil government, the Harriers initially targeted their political rivals, taking a hands-off approach to their old comrades in the IRA. Some of the new government's first acts in 1932 had been to release republican prisoners and abolish the military tribunals. The first few months of governance seemed to suggest that Fianna Fáil would allow the IRA leeway to conduct republican operations. De Valera did meet with republican leaders on several occasions and implored them to abandon physical force and join in Fianna Fáil's democratic campaign. He was rebuffed.

A subtle change in attitude could be felt towards the end of the 1930s. The number of Blueshirts had declined markedly by then and gradually it was more often the IRA that was coming into conflict with the Gardaí. By the advent of the Emergency, relations between the Special Branch and paramilitaries were toxic. The IRA was determined to scupper the state's attempt to stay neutral in the Emergency and the government decided that they must be stopped. Gardaí like Dinny O'Brien started to clamp down hard on the group. It was the detective's leading role in combatting republicans that would cause them to hit back at him. Harry White said that O'Brien was 'as rapacious as the most dyed in the wool Stater' and insisted that the detective had been instrumental in the shooting of high-profile republicans like Liam Rice and Charlie McGlade.[5]

It was decided that ambushing and shooting Detective O'Brien as he left home for work would be the simplest course of action. O'Brien, who lived with his wife, two daughters and his father-in-law, had built a bungalow in the suburbs of Ballyboden four years before. At the time Ballyboden was a country village and the secluded house, which was in the shadows of the Dublin Mountains, was 50 yards from the road and shielded by trees. It was here that the pre-planned attack was mounted by several experienced volunteers.

At about 10 a.m. on the morning of 9 September, Denis O'Brien left home as usual to travel the 4 miles into Dublin Castle. Four men lay in wait, having left bicycles behind the Bolton Hall Lodge, the manor beside the O'Briens' home, and concealed themselves behind a low wall halfway down the driveway. O'Brien entered his car and drove down the path, completely unaware of the ambush party.

As the vehicle crossed a small bridge over a stream, several bullets were aimed at it from the left, smashing the glass of the windscreen. O'Brien jumped out of the car and crouched behind a wall where he drew his gun and returned fire. He then tried to reach the relative safety of the gateway. Unfortunately, he was not able to make it in time. Another burst of machine-gun fire was unleashed and a bullet struck the detective in the back of the head. He slumped to the ground and the ambush party, satisfied that they had finished off their target, went quickly through the hedge and across a field, jumping over a wall before fetching their concealed bicycles.

As Dinny had left for work, his wife Annie was sweeping in the kitchen while her elderly father was outside. Annie heard the first shots but assumed that it was her neighbour shooting pigeons nearby. The sound of machine-gun fire roused her, however, and caused her to drop the sweeping brush. She hurried outside, asking her father, 'Did you hear a shot?' The pair then ran down the path towards the sound of gunfire. Mrs O'Brien and her father heard three more revolver shots and machine-gun fire as they ran. They also saw three men in the distance running away from the bridge towards Bolton Hall Lodge. When they reached the bottom of the driveway, they were met with the sight of the detective lying on the ground beside the gate, haemorrhaging blood from a wound in his head. Mrs O'Brien ran knelt beside him, stating later that his 'hand was just loosening from his hold on his revolver'.[6] She knew immediately he was dead and whispered an act of contrition in his ear.

As they stood beside the body, the same men they had seen earlier came cycling past, one with a long object covered in a sack on the front. Mrs O'Brien shouted, 'There they are, I know you.' The men did not respond but increased their speed. Mrs O'Brien shouted after them, 'They are the two men who did it.' A third man wearing glasses followed quickly after. Some distance up the road, the men separated, two going towards Rathfarnham while the third cycled in the direction of Dundrum. A fourth bicycle was later found near the scene, indicating that one member of the raiding party had left the scene on foot. One Garda did spot the suspicious-looking men and followed them on his bicycle. When he realised that he would not be able to overtake them he hailed a lorry but by the time it had turned around the men had vanished. The third cyclist, who was wearing green glasses, had been behind the Garda, but turned around when he saw him in pursuit of his comrades and escaped.[7]

Detective O'Brien was brought to hospital immediately but he was pronounced dead on arrival. His death was due to shock and haemorrhage caused by a gunshot wound to the back of the head, 2½in above the collar, which had lacerated. The Gardaí was looking at a murder investigation and a shocking daylight ambush on a detective. They immediately threw a cordon around the area, mounting checkpoints and interviewing passers-by. Up to fifteen Garda cars were on the scene within an hour and after a search an automatic revolver was discovered in a field 20 yards from where the assailants had waited.[8] Four cyclists had been seen by locals loitering in the area at about 9.15 a.m. and the four bicycles had been seen by several people behind Bolton Hall.

O'Brien's funeral took place on 11 September. The coffin, covered in the tricolour, was followed by thousands of mourners to Mount Jerome Cemetery in Harold's Cross while members of the detective force who had served in 1916 fired volleys over the grave.[9] Similar to the killing of Superintendent Curtin a decade before, the death of Detective O'Brien had been the result of a targeted attack. The government, and indeed large swathes of the country, were incensed by the audacious attack and the Dublin County Commissioner even described it as a 'Murder that has shamed the nation'.[10]

The Taoiseach Éamon de Valera sent a telegram to Larry O'Brien shortly after Dinny's death in which he wrote, 'the dastardly murder of your brother, who served the Irish people so bravely, has shocked every decent citizen and filled every just mind with anger', before going on to describe how he had a 'firm determination that those who are responsible will be brought to account'.[11] The story even made it to the other side of the Atlantic; the New York Times reported on the shooting of the Detective Sergeant the day after his death.[12] A reward of £5,000 was quickly offered for any information that would lead to the apprehension of the killers, a huge sum of money in harsh economic times.

The Gardaí mounted an intense manhunt in the weeks after the killing. The description of two of the men wanted for the actual ambush mentioned that they were between 20-25 years of age, wearing waterproof belted trench coats and grey caps, fairly tall and riding two high-framed bicycles. Despite the description and the generous reward on offer, information about the killing proved difficult to obtain. On 10 October, the Gardaí released another description. This time they named eight IRA men who were wanted for questioning: Francis Duffy, Henry White and Liam Burke, all from Belfast; Thomas Kealy from County Kildare; Hugh McAteer from Derry; and Michael Quille, Timothy Drummond, and the name that would become the most famous of all, Charles Kerins, all from Kerry.[13] Quille, a 25-year-old native of Listowel, was the first to be discovered and arrested.

He stood trial for the murder in January 1943 in the Military Court, pleading not guilty. Quille, although admitting he was a member of the IRA, claimed that he had been in Belfast on the day of the shooting and had nothing whatsoever to do with the affair, adding that the Gardaí had threatened to falsely claim that he was an IRA informer if he did not co-operate with them. If the IRA had believed this allegation, it would almost certainly have meant death for Quille.[14] The detectives denied this accusation, saying that in all their interviews with Quille he had refused to deny having a role in the shooting of O'Brien. The known IRA operative had been a wanted man at the time of the killings, having escaped from police custody in Listowel shortly before the incident. He had been picked out of a line up by Mrs O'Brien as the third cyclist who was present on the day and a detective also identified him as being at the scene of the murder.

Seán MacBride put up a spirited defence for his client, saying that he was being forced 'to defend himself of being two persons', asserting that Mrs O'Brien and the detective in question had identified two different cyclists as his client. Quille was found not guilty after several days of giving evidence due to a 'doubt in the mind of the court as to the guilt of the accused'. He did face jail for membership of the IRA but he had escaped the death sentence.

The Gardaí conducted searches of several areas of Dublin in their hunt for the perpetrators. One visit to a house at 12A Grosvenor

Square in Rathmines yielded correspondence that related to the IRA and arms and explosives it possessed in parts of County Kerry.[15] The notepaper was linked to a man named Charles Kerins. Kerins had stayed in the house frequently in the summer of 1942 under the alias Charlie Hanley, until around the date of O'Brien's murder. From that point, he had not been seen there again and the Gardaí felt that his sudden disappearance was linked with O'Brien's death.

The Gardaí scoured Dublin for the young Kerryman. As the IRA was down to just four safe houses in the capital, it did not take long to find him. Kerins was eventually apprehended at 4 a.m. on the night of 17 June 1944 in the house of Dr Farrell on the Upper Rathmines Road. A group of detectives burst into his room, where they found the suspect lying in bed asleep with a Colt automatic pistol in the chest of drawers beside him, within easy reach of his hand. It was loaded and the safety catch was off but he would not get a chance to use it. Large quantities of arms, over 1,000 rounds of ammunition, explosives and IRA documents were also discovered in the house.

Kerins had evaded detection for two years by using the aliases of a student called Mr Kearney and a Christian Brother named Brother McSweeney. When arrested, he admitted responsibility for the IRA documents, some of which mentioned various safe houses, with others alluding to attacks that had been planned against various targets and the trial of Michael Quille. It was alleged that finger-prints found on the handlebars of the bicycle left at the scene of the crime in Ballyboden were those of Kerins and he was arrested and charged with murder. When asked about his movements on the day in question he responded, 'I haven't the faintest idea where I was.'

Kerins was born in Caherina on 23 January 1918. He had two sisters, Lena and Elsie.[16] A plasterer's son, Kerins had excelled at school, winning a County Council scholarship and attending the Christian Brothers School in Tralee, where he achieved honours in his Intermediate Certificate. He also had a long history of involve-ment in the republican movement, having joined in his late teens. Kerins, described as a stocky young teenager, had also been a fan-tastic Gaelic footballer with his local club O'Rahilly's, even being part of the team that won the County Championship in 1939. He was employed as an assistant radio engineer in his home town for the three years up until May 1942. He would step up his republican activity afterwards, however, spending most of the years between 1942 and 1944 in active service or on the run. The IRA was in disarray towards the end of the Emergency, even suspecting their own chief of staff, Stephen Hayes, of being a paid informer. His successor, Hugh McAteer, was arrested and the IRA needed a replacement quickly. Charles Kerins was deemed suitable and appointed to the position by the IRA in July 1942, despite being just 24 years of age.[17]

Kerins' murder trial began on 1 October in the Special Criminal Court in Collins' Barracks, where he was charged with the murder of Dinny O'Brien. It had been over two years since the detective's death. Kerins did not go the way of his colleague Michael Quille, instead refusing point-blank to plead in court or give an account of his movements on the day of the shooting. When presented with maps and photographs of the scene of the crime, he replied that he was 'not interested'. A plea of not guilty was thus entered on his behalf. He refused to cross-examine most witnesses, remarking, 'I have no interest in the proceedings.' He did assert that he believed he should have been tried in an ordinary court of law, rather than the special Military Court, also telling the judge that his refusal to allow counsel to be assigned for him was on account of the 'insult to [my] intelligence to be expected to recognise this as a court'.[18]

Although there were numerous eyewitnesses to the ambush, no one was able to definitively say that Kerins had been amongst the assailants. Sixty-six exhibits were shown to the jury in an attempt to convince them that the man in the dock had either fired the shot that killed the detective or been a party to the ambush. The exhibits included the bicycle that was left behind, enlarged photos of the fingerprint left on the frame, and documents and ammunition that were found on the accused.[19]

The fear of giving evidence against the IRA may have been a factor for some witnesses who took the stand. Christopher Nolan, who worked for the ESB in the area, admitted seeing some men cycling but did not know how many or what they were wearing as he was 'not observant'. The same man also admitted to making a pact with ESB workers at the time to say that they had not seen anything. He said they had done this 'for no particular reason', although he denied being afraid, merely 'mixed-up'. When it was put to him that he had said shortly after the murder, 'Dinny O'Brien stopped a bullet and I don't want one', he refuted this. Unsurprisingly, when asked to identify the culprits at an identity parade he insisted that he could not. The guesthouse owner who had identified a photograph as that of Kerins in 1942 also withdrew his evidence, stating, 'I don't remember a thing about it now.' He also said that the man in the dock did not look anything like the boarder who had stayed with him. His wife similarly refused to identify the prisoner as the man who had been boarding in her house.[20]

The prosecution conceded that there was no direct identification of the accused at the scene of the crime but insisted that he had the means, the motive and the opportunity to commit the crime. They argued that the Thompson machine gun ammunition found in Kerins' room was similar to that used on Dinny O'Brien, while the fingerprint on the bicycle abandoned near the scene was also that of the right ring finger of the suspect. A witness had also testified that Kerins left the lodgings uncharacteristically early at 7.30 a.m. on the morning of the shooting on a bicycle, giving him ample time to reach the scene of the ambush before Denis O'Brien.[21]

It was also asserted that the man in the dock was the chief of staff of the IRA, the organisation that had masterminded the callous attack. Letters in his possession were addressed 'A Cathaill', the Irish for Charles, and appeared to refer to his important position in the organisation.[22] His membership of the IRA would be motive enough for the crime, the prosecution maintained. They also read aloud several letters purporting to be from Kerins in which he seemed to discuss the IRA's attitude to Fianna Fáil and the upcoming election. Other letters mentioned a grenade factory, Michael Quille's trial and what the IRA could do to ensure he was not sentenced to death.[23]

Kerins' defence gave no evidence, but many of the prosecution's witnesses did not give the evidence as expected. Mrs O'Brien also failed to identify Kerins in an identity parade, saying afterwards that she had been upset and made a mistake. The Special Criminal Court announced nevertheless that 'evidence of the state would seem to implicate the accused', despite the highly circumstantial nature of the evidence against him, and thus that a *prima facie* case had been proven against the suspect.[24] As the prisoner, who was facing the death penalty, had chosen not to give evidence, the court opted to adjourn for two days to give Kerins an opportunity to appoint counsel or defend himself against the accusation. He did neither. Returning at 11 a.m. on 9 October, Kerins was asked if he had made up his mind to make an application to the court. Kerins answered, 'You could have adjourned it for six years as far as I am concerned as my attitude towards the court will always be the same.' He was then asked if he wanted to call witnesses, make a statement or give any evidence. He replied, 'No.' The court once again adjourned but returned at 2.30 p.m., the president stating that the case against the prisoner had been proven and it was beyond reasonable doubt that he had been one of the ambush party that had killed Detective Dinny O'Brien. He thus announced that Charles Kerins was guilty of murder before asking if there was any reason that sentence should not be passed on him.[25]

At this point Kerins chose to speak at length for the first time.

All I can say is that if the Free State authorities are satisfied that I got a fair trial here, I hope their consciences are clear on that point. If this is an example of de Valera's justice, freedom and democracy, then I would like to know what dictatorship and militarism are. That is about all I have to say.

Finally, before being brought down, Kerins was asked if he had any application to make, to which he replied, 'Personally I do not think I am capable of making my application.' Charles Kerins was sentenced to death for the morning of 31 October 1944. He then spoke briefly to his sister, who had been present throughout the trial, before being escorted to the condemned cell. On the face of it, the fingerprint on the bicycle left at the scene was the main difference between Kerins' case and Quille's and possibly the difference between a hanging and an acquittal.

An appeal would be sought for Kerins, with Seán MacBride again choosing to defend the condemned IRA volunteer. MacBride appealed on seven grounds, including that inadmissible evidence had been heard and that the Special Criminal Court had misdirected itself in law. He stated that an attempt had been made to form an association between Kerins and Quille, who could also not be proven to have been in Rathfarnham at the time the shots were fired. It was mentioned that evidence which had helped Quille in his bid to be acquitted had been left out of Kerins' trial. A certificate of leave to appeal the sentence to the Supreme Court was refused by the three judges presiding, who stated that 'no valid reason had been brought in support of the application', and the evidence presented 'was amply sufficient in law to justify the verdict'.[26]

MacBride and Kerins' desperate last roll of the dice was a memorandum that they submitted to the Attorney-General Kevin Dixon, pleading that an appeal of the case should be heard in the Supreme Court. Pleas were made from numerous sources to commute Kerins' death sentence. TDs from several opposition parties and even from the government itself put forward an urgent appeal in the Dáil to the government, imploring them to reprieve Kerins. Kerry TD Dan Spring, who was known to Kerins, remarked that 'in view of the country's peace, the execution would serve no purpose. We feel the young man got no fair trial.'[27] A petition for a commutation of the death sentence, allegedly signed by 77,000 citizens, also arrived on the government's desk.

The Fianna Fáil government of the time clearly felt that a heavy-handed response was required, particularly as some members of the IRA were still attempting to collaborate with the Nazi regime and were thus a threat to Ireland's neutrality. Censorship of attempts to secure mercy for Kerins was widespread. Posters advocating a reprieve for the condemned prisoner were seized while a woman collecting signatures for a petition to commute the sentence was arrested. Cars with loudspeakers announcing the petition were impeded and attempts to bring up the matter in the Dáil were ignored. Although petitions were a common feature of Irish life where the death penalty was concerned, any effort to secure public signatures was blocked in this instance.[28]

It is therefore unsurprising that pleas for clemency from Kerry County Council and many others did not persuade the government. The Farmers' Party TD Dominic Cafferky reflected the feeling of many Irish people when pleading that Fianna Fáil might show leniency as 'they had preached these ideas to men at one time'. The government party remained unmoved, announcing that they 'would not be justified in advising the president to exercise the prerogative of mercy'.[29]

Charles Kerins, in his last letter, said, 'I do not mind what happens to me as long as the ideals for which I am dying are held sacred by my comrades'.[30] In a further insult to republicans, Kerins was hanged like a criminal rather than shot like a soldier. The hanging was at the hand of executioner Thomas Pierrepoint at 8 a.m. on the morning of Friday, 1 December 1944. Former governor of Mountjoy, Seán Kavanagh, who had overseen multiple executions over the previous two decades, had been friendly with Dinny O'Brien, having fought side by side with him in the War of Independence. Despite this, he described Charles Kerins as the 'bravest man I ever saw die by hanging'.[31]

The government would eventually have their say after the execution. The Minister for Justice, Gerald Boland, whose brother Harry was shot dead by Free State forces under dubious circumstances, insisted that the execution had been the right thing to do. Boland claimed that those attempting to secure a reprieve visited the widow of Detective O'Brien and 'persecuted that lady for hours' in an attempt to bully her into signing the petition. He also maintained that large numbers of the names on the petition were forged and added that he had no apology to make for the execution. On the contrary, he suggested that, 'If I have any apology to make to the Dáil it is that we have not been able to get the whole of the group that murdered the unfortunate man.'[32] Éamon de Valera, a former anti-Treaty IRA volunteer and now the Taoiseach, had at one time been reprieved when under sentence of death. Nevertheless, when speaking to the Dáil he insisted that the government 'would be failing in their duty if they failed to have the sentence carried out'. He mentioned the prohibited meetings, remarking that, 'We think that citizens themselves are very badly advised when they lend themselves to public demonstrations in matters of this sort.' He added that the IRA was an unelected organisation fighting against the freely elected government of the people and begged the population to understand that the hanging of Kerins would save lives in the long run.[33]

Ironically, IRA men executed in other jurisdictions would secure more sympathy from the Irish government of the day. In 1939 Peter Barnes and James McCormack were convicted of aiding in the planting of a bomb in a busy Coventry street. Five civilians died and the two Irishmen were convicted and sentenced to death by the Crown. Before their hanging, the Fianna Fáil government made numerous overtures to the British, imploring them to commute the men's sentences. They were unsuccessful and both men were hanged in February 1940. Tom Williams, executed in Belfast in September 1942 for being part of a group of IRA men who shot a RUC policeman, would also receive unsuccessful intercession from de Valera and the government, who asked their northern counterparts to reconsider.

On the instructions of Minister for Justice Seán MacEoin, the bodies of the IRA men executed during the war were released to their families after the Emergency. Charles Kerins was reinterred to his final resting place at the republican plot of Rath Graveyard on 19 September 1948 in 'one of the largest funerals seen in Tralee for years'. In his book, famous IRA rebel Harry White would give the names of the other members of the ambush party that shot Detective O'Brien as Ciarán O'Kelly and Archie Doyle. The latter was apparently also one of the assassins of government minister Kevin O'Higgins in 1927.[34]

Kerins was the last of six IRA volunteers executed by the Free State during the Emergency. The conflict came to an end less than a year after his death but by that point the Gardaí had effectively wiped out the upper echelons of the organisation by using mass internment. Flogging and executions were also employed as methods of halting the IRA's campaign of bank robberies, as well as its efforts to liaise with the Germans. The morale of the IRA was broken. Over 80 per cent of internees left the organisation after 1945.[35] The war ended, but the bitterness felt by many republicans at what they saw as a grave injustice lived on. Hundreds of republicans had been interned, dozens were flogged, three had been killed in fire-fights with Gardaí, one man was hanged and five others had met their death in front of a firing squad. Kerins' death aroused particular anger; the IRA had already been defeated by then and it was felt that it had been a pointless act of revenge. He would be remembered by his comrades; a song about his life, 'The Boy from Tralee', was penned, and his local Gaelic football team was renamed Kerins O'Rahilly's in his honour.

No one else was ever brought to justice for the shooting of Dinny O'Brien, whose name was placed upon the Roll of Honour of An Garda Síochána. His family were eventually awarded £3,641 compensation for the death of their husband and father.[36]

14

DETECTIVE
MICHAEL WALSH

'The detectives are coming.'

By 1942 the number of indictable crimes in Ireland had doubled from
that of three years before. Petty criminality had become rife, while
the IRA also involved themselves in numerous illegal activities. The
conflict between the organisation and the Garda Special Branch had
intensified still further by this point. With the full encouragement of
the Fianna Fáil government, who now viewed the IRA as a dangerous
menace, the Special Branch had clamped down mercilessly on the
organisation since the beginning of the decade. Emergency legislation, which had been bitterly opposed by Fianna Fáil ten years before,
was now their main weapon in targeting the IRA.

The legislation greatly aided the Special Branch, which had phe-
nomenal success in its fight against subversives between 1940 and
1942. The IRA soon found its number of active volunteers tum-
bling to just hundreds. This was due to a combination of factors:
imprisonments, infiltration by informers and even executions. Bank
raids, a tactic not used widely by the movement since the 1920s,

were again employed by the organisation in a desperate attempt to keep their finances healthy enough to support their campaign. These robberies led to further major conflicts between the security services and active volunteers. Indeed, it was the attempts to catch a suspected bank robber that ensured that Garda Michael Walsh's path crossed that of Patrick Dermody, with fatal consequences for both men.

Michael Walsh was born on 14 March 1901 in Barnfield, a townland lying on Lough Conn, 5 miles south of Ballina in County Mayo. He served in the IRA between 1919 and 1922. He took a pro-Treaty stance and enlisted in the National Army, reaching the rank of lieutenant. Numbers in the army were cut rapidly after the conclusion of the Civil War and in 1924 Walsh applied for a position in An Garda Síochána and was quickly accepted. He proved adept in his new role and was promoted to detective at an early stage. Deployed in the midlands towns of Athlone and Tullamore initially, Walsh was transferred to the station in Cavan Town in around 1930. By 1942 he had been in the area for twelve years and was well integrated into the community. Married with two children, the noted rider was also a well-known member of the Cavan Hunt Club.[1]

The year 1942 was a troubled time for the Gardaí, who found themselves embroiled in their greatest struggle with the IRA since the end of the Civil War. Detective O'Brien was just three weeks dead at this point and the Gardaí, despite strenuous efforts, were no closer to finding any of the gunmen. The border was another area where the IRA was particularly active, using their local knowledge to successfully smuggle arms and other goods from one jurisdiction to the other. The organisation was also able to count on the support of some sections of the local community and a network of safe houses. Walsh was one of the officers given the difficult task of maintaining order in a district within touching distance of the border of Northern Ireland.

In October 1942, the Cavan Gardaí found themselves on the lookout for Patrick Dermody. Dermody was a 22-year-old farmer's son and a native of Hilltown, near Castlepollard in County

Westmeath. His mother had died in the 1920s, leaving her husband to raise eight young children in poor circumstances. From a young age Paddy had been involved in republicanism and had been well known to the Gardaí for some time. There was a pig market in the country town of Castlepollard on 9 June 1941. At 11 a.m., a Meath-registered car pulled up outside the Hibernian Bank in the town and four men jumped out. They stormed the building, ordering all the officials to line up against the wall. One man covered them with a revolver while another stood at the door of the bank. The other two men took all the money they could find, eventually emerging with £600 in the daring daytime raid. Although the Gardaí arrived on the scene within ten minutes and gave chase, they missed their quarry. The car was found abandoned in nearby Oldcastle.

Patrick Dermody was suspected of being involved. He was also being sought for 'other activities connected with his membership of an unlawful organisation'.[2] He was cornered by a sergeant in Castlepollard on one occasion but managed to disarm him and escape. Dermody would have been well aware that over 1,100 IRA operatives had been interned during the Emergency, often in unspeakably harsh conditions or in solitary confinement. Consequently, he chose to go on the run rather than suffer this fate.[3] During his two years on the run from Gardaí, Patrick Dermody had taken the time to write to several newspapers, claiming to be innocent of crimes that the Gardaí suspected him of. According to his fellow IRA volunteer, Harry White, Dermody had been the O/C of the IRA's eastern command during his time on the run. He was mainly responsible for carrying arms across the border along with Charles Kerins (see Chapter 13) and Archie Doyle. Gardaí were aware that Jane Dermody, the wanted man's sister, had her wedding scheduled for 30 September 1942. Feeling that there was a chance that Patrick would show up to the ceremony, they decided to send a group of detectives to scope out the area.

Dermody and his fellow IRA man Harry White had been in Dundalk in a safe house belonging to the Gaughrans on the morning of the wedding but needed to get to Mount Nugent, County

Cavan, where another safe house awaited them. Cars in Ireland were at a premium throughout the 1930s and became even less common during the Emergency when Seán Lemass, Minister for Supplies, had introduced strict rationing of petrol. For that reason, the men were forced to travel the 40 miles by bicycle on what was a bleak and misty day. Harry White later recalled that both believed they had seen a ghost on the journey.[4]

Dermody had not told his republican colleague of his sister's wedding, but once in Mount Nugent he got himself cleaned up and insisted on going to the wedding party. Several people, including White, warned him that an occasion like that was sure to attract Gardaí. Dermody assured his compatriots that local men were watching the road for Gardaí and that, as the house was at the end of a long country boreen, they would be safe. White thus reluctantly agreed to accompany his companion and the pair departed, cycling to Joseph Fox's home in the townland of Lismacanican, between Ballyjamesduff and Mount Nugent at the southern end of County Cavan. The men abandoned their bicycles in a nearby field and went into the house well after midnight. It was crowded and a fiddler and accordion player were entertaining the guests.

At around 1.30 a.m. on the morning of Thursday, 1 October, the Gardaí decided to strike at the home of the newlyweds.[5] Aware of the presence of a large crowd and the potential danger of the mission, the large force of Gardaí included a number of armed detectives. As the policemen were approaching, a dog started to bark. The Gardaí then saw a man running from the gate to Fox's house. They followed him, quickly reaching the kitchen of the house and opening the door. They found that the party, complete with the accordion and fiddle, was still ongoing and that the room was crowded with dancing men and women. There appeared to be up to forty people in the noisy room and the lighting was bad. A detective sergeant said loudly on entering, 'We are police officers; No panic; stop the music.'[6]

The music did not stop, however, and after talking with his superior, Detective Officer Walsh approached the musicians on the fiddle and the accordion and insisted that they desist. A superintendent was standing in the middle of the room when suddenly a man appeared out of a door on the right-hand side of the kitchen. Another Garda, suspecting correctly that it was Dermody, moved in his direction. Dermody also moved forward, before producing a revolver and shooting at the Garda from a range of about 6ft. The bullet narrowly missed its target, flying past the policeman at chest height and striking the wall. A second bullet was then fired, which struck the superintendent in the chest. The fiddler, a man named Finnegan, was also shot in the leg.

Several of the Gardaí, including Michael Walsh, returned fire in the crowded room, but missed, and a number of women got between the gunmen while others dived for cover behind furniture. Dermody fired again and this time the bullet flew to the left of the same Garda officer. In the general panic a number of other shots were fired. Dermody quickly backed into the room from which he had come. One Garda assumed that he was trying to escape out a window and ran outside, taking the injured superintendent with him. He pulled the door closed behind him, shouting, 'Watch the window in front'. He heard a crash as he came around the gable, the sound of glass shattering. He turned to go towards the sound and ran into a man coming the other way. It was not Dermody but a man named Matthew Caffrey escaping the shooting.[7]

At this point most of the Gardaí had taken cover from the hail of bullets outside the house, apart from Michael Walsh and a colleague who were nowhere to be seen. Soon after this incident, colleagues saw Walsh stumbling out of the house with his hand on his side. He gasped, 'I am shot, sergeant'. Two figures then rushed out of the house and more bullets were fired. The silhouette of another man was spotted in a crouching position, making his way towards the haggard. He escaped, despite several shots being fired after him and the best efforts of the Gardaí to catch him on that dark night. Four shots were then fired into the air by the Gardaí and the people from the party were ordered to come out of the house. Detectives entered the house and discovered Dermody lying in a bedroom off the kitchen. He had also sustained bullet wounds in the crossfire.[8]

An ambulance was summoned for the injured men. Detective Walsh remained conscious in the aftermath of the shooting and gave a statement in which he said he thought he had shot Dermody in the house but the bullets that had penetrated him had come from the gun of another man who then escaped. He was quickly conveyed to Cavan hospital where Dr McInerney treated him. McInerney described how Walsh had been admitted at 3 a.m., suffering bullet wounds in the hypochondrium (upper abdomen) and the left wrist. One of the bullets 'had traversed the upper part of the abdomen and lodged alongside the spine'.[9] The Garda was suffering from shock and had lost a large quantity of blood. A blood transfusion was given the following day and an operation successfully removed the bullet from his spine. He seemed to make an improvement on the following day but it would ultimately be to no avail. Walsh received the last sacraments with his wife at his bedside and died at 8.30 p.m. the night after the shooting. The cause of death was attributed to shock and internal haemorrhaging.

Dermody had been brought to the same hospital, where he was pronounced dead on arrival. He had been shot beneath the right shoulder blade and the bullet had lodged beneath the skin about 2in above the nipple on the left side. He was suffering severely from shock and had lost a lot of blood. Dermody died shortly after being shot, the cause of death haemorrhage caused by the wound.[10] He was buried in Fore, County Westmeath, in front of a large crowd, which included a number of Gardaí and members of the army, presumably anticipating some trouble. His coffin was covered in a tricolour, and it was lowered into the ground as the crowd said a decade of the rosary in Irish.

A large congregation also gathered for Detective Walsh's funeral, which was removed from Cavan to Durrow, near Tullamore, where he was buried in his wife's hometown with full Garda honours. The cortège was met by 'moving gestures of sympathy' in several towns along the way to Offaly. As usual, the commissioner, the Minister for Justice and large numbers of Gardaí paid their respects as the coffin made its way into the ground. Taoiseach Éamon de

Valera also paid tribute to the fallen Garda, sending a telegraph to his widow, describing how her husband had 'left an example of fearless devotion to duty'.[11]

The inquest finally took place in November 1942. Several Garda witnesses described their approach to the house and the 'general panic' as shots rang out inside the house. Dermody and a companion (probably Harry White, who had escaped through the haggard) and several Gardaí were all firing in a room full of terrified onlookers.[12] The other Garda who was shot on the night described hearing Walsh say that a bullet had struck him. He had then helped take his colleague outside. Most of the civilians who had been present on the night either could not or would not give evidence, although many said that due to the general confusion on that evening they did not know what had happened. It was thought that Walsh had shot Dermody and one of Dermody's companions had fired the fatal volley into the Garda.

John Dermody, father of Patrick, did agree to appear on the stand and give evidence. He was present at the Fox household on the night, his daughter having married a member of that family the previous day. He described how his son had just arrived and the men went into the room off the kitchen where they drank tea. At that point, another son ran in, shouting, 'the detectives are coming'. John Dermody said that his son was shot shortly afterwards but refuted the evidence of the Gardaí, insisting that he not been killed in the general confusion but had been deliberately shot through the window by Gardaí. He admitted that he had not seen a bullet come through the glass, however. The judge dismissed this evidence, reminding him that they needed 'facts, not supposition'. That night's raid would leave two injured men and two fatalities; the inquest found that Walsh had died 'in the execution of his duty' while Dermody met his end 'trying to escape'.[13]

On 20 December 1942, Mrs Susan Walsh was awarded £650 compensation for the death of her husband while her two children were given the sums of £350 and £150.[14] In August 1945, however, the President of the High Court reviewed the compensation awarded to six Gardaí killed during the Emergency, and decided to increase the amount in all cases. The paltry sum awarded to Mrs Walsh was increased to £2,727.

Harry White, another IRA volunteer, was present on the night and wrote a memoir over forty years later in which he gave his version of events. 'We could not have been there three minutes when Gardaí burst in the door: bullets flew.'[15] He claimed that he ran after Dermody into the small candlelit room, shouting at him to turn off the light. At that moment a shot came through the window from the yard, striking his comrade. White then crashed through the window into the yard. He somehow managed to dodge the gunfire and went around to the back of the house. He then 'ran wildly between buildings, across a small paddock, smashed through a hedge and lay in a clump of whins, half a mile from the house'.[16] He had been shot twice in the leg. He spent twenty-four hours in the field, not daring to move. He told a story of a Free State soldier named Reilly helping him into a loft and bringing him food before giving him a bicycle and sending him on his way to Dublin. Whether or not this story was true, it would not be the last the Gardaí saw of White, nor would Michael Walsh be the last detective shot down in that turbulent month.

DETECTIVE GEORGE MORDAUNT

'He looked terribly wild and excited.'

The authorities continued to pursue the IRA relentlessly on both sides of the border and shoot-outs between the organisation and the Gardaí had once again become common. Many IRA men, similar to Patrick Dermody (see Chapter 14), found themselves in hiding for long periods of time in an attempt to avoid being arrested. When these fugitives from justice were eventually found by the Gardaí, they rarely went down without a fight. The ensuing struggles had fatal consequences on several occasions, both for the Gardaí and for the IRA men themselves. Detective Officer George Mordaunt was a victim of one such conflict and was the third member of the force, after detectives Michael Walsh and Dinny O'Brien, to be shot dead in just over six weeks.

George Mordaunt was born on 24 September 1897 on St John's Street in the Blackpitts, an area situated in the Liberties on the south side of Dublin City, although he spent much of his youth in Ballycanew, County Wexford. He had been a railway worker, but had also served in the IRA during the war, where he had been in the D Company of the 2nd Battalion of the Dublin Brigade from 1918. He sided with the pro-Treaty forces and enlisted in the National Army in March 1922, attaining the rank of sergeant.[1] Mordaunt was demobilised and enlisted as a Garda in early 1925. His initial posting was to Sneem, County Kerry, but afterwards his time in the force was mainly spent in the Dublin area. By 1942 he had seventeen years' service under his belt and had attained the rank of detective. Mordaunt, who lived in Fairview and was married with a son and a daughter, was stationed in the Special Branch in Dublin Castle by this point. It was a dangerous time to be a Garda.

Mrs P. Kelly owned a guesthouse on 14 Holly Road, Donnycarney, about 3 miles north of Dublin. On 19 October 1942, two men called to the door seeking lodgings. They introduced themselves as John Boyle and Maurice O'Connor. Both men paid their dues promptly, but strangely Boyle did not leave the house at any stage during his six-day stay. On the evening of 24 October, at approximately 8.45 p.m., a girl arrived at the house. She asked to speak to the two men and was shown in. The landlady recognised the woman as she had called to the house to visit the two lodgers before. She was evidently expected, as before she arrived Mrs Kelly had heard Boyle say to O'Connor, 'She's late.'

The two lodgers were playing cards. The caller, a woman named Maggie O'Halloran, was a courier for the IRA. Out of earshot of the landlady, she whispered to the men that their safe house had been compromised and that they needed to leave immediately. The men hurriedly prepared to depart. Bicycles belonging to both lodgers were kept in the garden and they wasted no time in going to retrieve them. Mr Kelly, who had kindly lent 'Boyle' a coat a short time before, then went to open the garden gate at the back to allow them out. The gate was somewhat difficult to manoeuvre and Kelly intended to help the pair by opening it.[2] At the same time Miss O'Halloran was being shown to the front door by Mrs Kelly. As the landlady was passing Boyle she caught sight of the handle of a gun sticking out from under his coat.

At 8 p.m., almost two hours before, a group of Gardaí had made their way to Holly Road. Unbeknownst to the occupants of No. 14, they had taken up positions convenient for watching the comings and goings from the house. 'Boyle' and 'O'Connor' were considered dangerous IRA operatives and were to be arrested immediately.[3] The mysterious lodgers were in fact named Harry White and Maurice O'Neill. The former had recently been released from internment and had been present when Detective Walsh was shot three weeks before. He was also wanted in connection with the murder of Detective Dinny O'Brien and there was a hefty £5,000 reward on his head. He would later become Chief of Staff of the subversive organisation. O'Neill was less well known, although he was the O/C of the Caherciveen Company of the IRA and had been in Dublin on IRA business for several months.

Two Gardaí waited at the back of the house while several others placed themselves at the front. Two Gardaí were situated on either side of the front door of No. 14. As soon as Mrs Kelly opened the door, the Gardaí grabbed both her and Miss O'Halloran. They took the two ladies with them and rushed into the living room. They were surprised to find no one present, the others having just exited out the back seconds before. Detective Mordaunt was part of the raiding party and he continued out through the back door after the men. His colleague returned to the other officers at the front to inform them of the situation. It was at this exact moment that O'Neill and White and their two bicycles were being led out of the back gate.

Shortly after Mordaunt left through the back door, the detectives inside heard what sounded like a number of shots coming from around the back of the house. They also saw a terrified Mr Kelly running up the garden. He had turned around to run back to the house when the first shots were fired, but ducked into the shed when he saw the Gardaí. The exact occurrences in those few moments are shrouded in confusion. Gardaí stationed at the end of the passage behind the house said that they heard a shot and found themselves face to face with the two men who had exited the back of No. 14. Mordaunt may also have been in the lane at this stage, although he was not seen alive by any of his colleagues again.

According to the testimony of the Gardaí, White and O'Neill had little intention of giving themselves up. They quickly fired a volley of shots after realising what was happening. Some of the bullets hit the fence just in front of the Gardaí. The Gardaí would later say that they only fired one bullet back at White and O'Neill, before they took cover around the corner of the fence. The men replied with two shots. Some of the bullets fired passed so close to the Gardaí that their escape was described as 'almost miraculous'.[4]

Maurice O'Neill, 'the tall man', later said that he could have escaped at this point but after hearing a groan turned around to help Harry White. O'Neill had lost sight of him, so he walked gingerly towards the corner of the passage. He quickly realised that he would not be able to get out that way alive, so he turned and attempted to enter another garden.[5] Failing in this endeavour, O'Neill fired a couple more bullets before running back through the gate of 14 Holly Road and into the house to reload his gun. He was unaware that the heavily armed Gardaí who had been at the front of the house were at this point waiting in the kitchen.

Maurice O'Neill thus ran in holding his long .45 Webley revolver only to be met by several guns pointed in his direction. He was immediately ordered to put up his hands. He reluctantly threw his gun on the table. 'He looked terribly wild and excited … and appeared to be in a very bad temper. A chief superintendent had to tie [his] hands behind his back.'[6] When searched, O'Neill was found to have a map of Dublin, a ration book with his name and an address in Caherciveen, and twelve rounds of ammunition in his possession.

His comrade Harry White had by now realised that there was little chance of making it around the corner unharmed. So, to avoid the heavy police presence, he jumped into the garden at No. 3 Oak Road, before continuing on into the back garden of No. 5. He barged in through the back door of that house and into the dining room of the house, where he came face to face with a family inside. They screamed. White implored them to be quiet, telling them that he was just passing through and would not harm them. He ran out the other door, coming out again onto Oak Road at the front of the house. It was in the garden of this house that the dead body of D.O. Mordaunt was discovered hours later.

White was quickly spotted by another of the Gardaí at this stage. The Garda described him as 'a bare-headed man, wearing a rain-coat'. He fired at the armed man, but White managed to evade his bullet by jumping headlong into a garden. He then succeeded in returning a burst of machine-gun fire. The Garda did not continue the fire fight as by that stage a young girl had started to scream and a number of women and children had run out onto the road, obscuring his view of the wanted man.[7]

This delay allowed White precious time to jump a fence. From there he was able to cross over onto the Malahide Road and into Clontarf Golf Club. A Garda could see his hand over the hedge moving along a railing and the fugitive vaulting over the obstacle. He fired a shot at White but it missed. At this point, White discarded the overcoat that had been lent to him by Mr Kelly and fled. His gun was found three-quarters of a mile up that road but Mr White himself would remain on the run for four years. This was his second incredible escape from Gardaí in just three weeks.

It was some hours later that a Garda went to look for a lost fountain pen in a garden close to the scene of the shoot-out. The absence of Detective Officer George Mordaunt had not been noted due to the lack of a roll call. After some minutes searching, the Garda stumbled across the body of his colleague lying facedown in the garden of No. 5 Oak Road.[8] He had been shot in the fire-fight. He was swiftly brought to Jervis Street Hospital but was pronounced dead on arrival. Dr John McGrath, the state pathologist, performed a post-mortem examination on the deceased policeman some time later. The detective's face had been covered in blood, which had mixed with mud and grass due to the prolonged period he had spent lying on the ground. The pathologist ascertained that Mordaunt had been shot once in the forehead, an inch above the right eyebrow. The shot had come from someone standing in front of him and the bullet had penetrated the brain and fractured the skull. His death was due to shock and laceration of the brain.[9]

Detective Mordaunt's funeral was reminiscent of the many seen before. His coffin, followed by a large party of Special Branch detectives, was removed to the church in Marino and onward to Mount Jerome Cemetery. A large congregation, amongst them Éamon de Valera and several members of his cabinet, bid their final farewell to the slain Garda.

A rigorous search had been conducted in the area in the aftermath of O'Neill's arrest and a Parabellum automatic firearm, as well as cartridges, was discovered discarded on the Malahide Road. With no means of catching Harry White, the person who was alleged to have fired the shot, the man arrested at the scene would enter the witness box alone to answer the murder charge. Maurice O'Neill was a native of Caherciveen, a picturesque town situated in South Kerry. Aged 25 years, O'Neill was a farmer's son from a staunchly republican family. He had been a volunteer in the IRA for several years before 1942 but had only been in Dublin for the past few months, having been summoned from the south-west to the capital to help run the operation. The IRA had suffered a huge number of losses through incarceration and execution and needed men like Maurice O'Neill to come and fill the leadership roles.

O'Neill appeared before the Military Court at Collins' Barracks on 2 November, barely a week after George Mordaunt's death. He pleaded not guilty to the charge, despite being aware that the government at the time showed little mercy to IRA men. A volunteer named Richard Goss had even been put to death the previous year for shooting a Garda in Longford and inflicting a non-fatal wound. Although in this case O'Neill had not fired the shot, the prospects were grim for any armed IRA member who had been involved in a fire-fight resulting in the death of a Garda.

Mr McCarthy outlined the state's case. He told those present that it did not matter whether O'Neill had himself fired the fatal shot; if he had been a party to the shooting, then he was equally culpable.

The prosecutor also assured the court that it would be proven that O'Neill had fired his gun five times and attempted to fire the last bullet, but it had misfired. The men 'fully armed and carrying spare ammunition … were determined to escape from the net of the law which was closing around them' and, according to the state, were willing to kill anyone who got in their way.[10]

The Gardaí admitted that they had fired twenty revolver shots, as well as eight rounds of Thompson machine-gun ammunition. Detective Mordaunt's revolver had also been fired once before he was killed. It was put to a detective in the dock that Mordaunt may have been in the laneway as they were firing indiscriminately. The Garda giving evidence admitted that it was possible but said that he was sure that Mordaunt had not been either of the two men whom he had seen in front of him in the passage. He would not entertain the possibility that his colleague had been shot as a result of a bullet from a Garda's gun.

Mr Patrick Kelly, the owner of No. 14 who had witnessed much of the fire fight, was also called to give evidence. He told the court that after he had let his lodgers out the back gate he heard 'loud voices and gunfire'. He immediately 'ran back to his own door'. His wife described how she was letting the girl out when 'two Garda officers walked in [and] everything was confused after that'.[11]

On Wednesday, the third day of the trial, O'Neill himself took the stand. He was more forthcoming with his evidence than many IRA prisoners in the dock, perhaps mindful that it was his only hope of avoiding the death penalty. He told the court that he was on his way to the North and had the gun with him for training purposes. When asked what he was training for, O'Neill replied simply, 'To go to the North.'[12] He explained that he had brought the gun with him on the night in question as he would not be returning to Holly Road due to an early departure the following morning. The accused man asserted that he did not know if his gun was loaded, or whether the other man in the house had slept with a loaded gun at night. He did admit that he had been practising speed-loading the weapon over the last few days but did not elaborate on the reasons to this.

O'Neill then outlined his version of events. He told the court that he had only gone 10 or 12ft from the back gate when he heard gunshots ringing out. He had abandoned his bicycle and thrown himself onto the ground. The shots kept coming, although he shouted 'Don't shoot' or 'Stop shooting'. He then said:

> Something struck me in the arm: I felt a pain and thought I was hit. I drew my gun then. I had it in the inside pocket of my inner coat. The shots were still coming and I fired in the general direction from which they came; although I could not see anybody. I did not want to be shot without making an attempt to save my life. That was the only motive I had in shooting.

He maintained that at no time had the Gardaí revealed their identity.[13]

Under cross-examination, O'Neill refused to tell the court where he had bought the bicycle he was riding on the night or any information about White, stating, 'I don't propose to make any statement in court regarding my friend. I won't give any information about him.' When asked about the shooting of Detective Sergeant O'Brien, O'Neill admitted he had seen it in the papers but refused to answer when asked if he knew that some of his associates were suspected of his assassination.

Seán MacBride was appointed as counsel, as he was with every major IRA prisoner during the 1940s. The barrister had become very familiar with the workings of the Military Court by that stage. He declared, 'Everyone deeply regrets the tragedy that resulted in Detective Mordaunt's death and everyone prays that we will be spared similar tragedies.'[14] He continued, however, to argue that the young Kerryman's only aim had been self-preservation and that anyone who found himself in the same position would take a similar course of action. His client had not fired first and the shot that killed Detective Mordaunt had not been fired by the accused; a ballistics expert declared that the bullet could not have come from O'Neill's gun. MacBride went on to say that the prisoner did not know that the men firing had been police and there was no evidence that any Garda at any time declared himself as such. As they had never identified themselves, MacBride argued that this was a clear case of killing in self-defence. He added that the bullet holes found near the Gardaí had been fired by a smaller gun than his client's, and that at times listening to the cross-examination it felt as if O'Neill was being sought for 'this and other tragedies', presumably referring to the as yet unsolved murder of Dinny O'Brien.[15]

It was a typically spirited defence from the talented MacBride but yet again it would be to no avail. On the fourth day of his trial, Maurice O'Neill was found guilty of shooting at three Garda officers with the intention of resisting arrest. Although it was never suggested that he had fired the bullet that killed Detective Mordaunt, the penalty for such a crime in the Special Criminal Court was death.

It came as no surprise that the government refused to overturn Maurice O'Neill's death sentence, although the news was greeted with widespread anger, particularly in his native County Kerry. In a letter to his brother before his death, O'Neill lamented the last game of cards he had played in Holly Road, saying that if they hadn't started it they would have had time to make good their escape. In the last letter he sent, O'Neill added that he was pleased he was not being reprieved as the thought of the horror that would have awaited him in Portlaoise Prison was worse than death.

The sentence of death was duly carried out early on the morning of 12 November 1942 when Maurice O'Neill stood in front of a firing squad and was shot dead.

Meanwhile, Harry White, alias Anderson, had managed to cross over the border. He stayed off the Gardaí's radar for four years after absconding that night, but in a swoop co-ordinated by both the Gardaí and the RUC he was captured in a house in Derry in 1946. The arrest proved controversial; it was argued that it was unlawful for the RUC to take him from Derry into the jurisdiction of the south and hand him over to the Gardaí.[16] White was tried in October of the same year for the shooting of Detective Officer George Mordaunt.

Despite admitting to being in the vicinity, White's defence team insisted that he had not shot Mordaunt. MacBride claimed that the detective had run out the back door and was in the laneway with O'Neill and White and could therefore have been shot by a member of his own team. They also complained that the Gardaí refused to give them access to certain records, including details of the weapons and ammunition used on the night.

The prisoner was initially found guilty and sentenced to death for the crime. Fortunately for White, the Emergency was over and the government were less eager to execute IRA men, even ones accused of killing a Garda. Seán MacBride's inspired defence came to the fore again. He argued that as the Gardaí did not know White was in the house, they had no lawful right to arrest him. For that reason, White had, in killing the Garda, been resisting unlawful arrest, making this a crime of manslaughter.[17] Harry White's conviction was downgraded to manslaughter on appeal and he was sentenced to twelve years' penal servitude. He would go on to serve just two years in jail. He was released along with Tomás Mac Curtain on 9 March 1948.

Maurice O'Neill's body was initially buried in the prison grounds but after much pressure his body was released to his family on 19 September 1948, the same day as Charles Kerins'. O'Neill was reinterred at Keelovarnogue in his native county and was carried to his final resting place on the shoulders of his six brothers.[18] Years afterwards, in an act of commemoration, the bridge to Valentia Island in Kerry was named the Maurice O'Neill Bridge.

Gerald Boland, the uncompromising Minister for Defence, later spoke of 1942, a year when three Gardaí were shot down in the course of their duty. 'We have again lost three gallant members of the force this year. I believe that thanks to the work of the Garda Síochána we are getting near the end.'[19] He pleaded for the public's assistance and support in any further dealings with subversives. The Emergency had taken a heavy toll on the Gardaí: six Gardaí had been killed by the IRA, with a similar number sustaining serious injury. The IRA too would be decimated by the conflict.

On 20 December 1943, the deceased detective's wife, Catherine, was awarded compensation of £550 while her daughters received £320 for the death of their father. This award was eventually increased to just over £2,000.[20] Meanwhile Detective George Mordaunt, registration number 6712, will forever be commemorated on the Garda Roll of Honour.

GARDA DENIS HARRINGTON

'Good God, lads, come in: something terrible has happened.'

Two Gardaí being killed in the line of duty on the same day was sadly not an isolated occurrence in the Irish Free State. However, two deaths in a Tipperary town in 1944 could be amongst the strangest and saddest of them all.

> A profound gloom was cast over Nenagh last Monday morning when the stunning news was confirmed that two highly esteemed members of the local Civic Guard had lost their lives as a result of a shooting affair in the storeroom of the local Garda Station, at about 10:30 that morning.[1]

So read the edition of the *Nenagh Guardian* after the deaths of Gardaí James Lynch and Denis Harrington on a spring morning in 1944.

Denis Harrington was born in 1900 in the rural townland of Mweenalaa, situated 3 miles to the west of Castleisland, County Kerry. He was the eldest of six children and the son of a farmer.[2] Harrington served as a volunteer for several years preceding the outbreak of the War of Independence and subsequently joined the Civic Guard in March 1923 as the Civil War raged on. Described as being good-humoured and quiet of disposition, the teetotaller had an excellent record in the force and had passed the written section of his sergeant's exam. He was a man of splendid physique who had won a Limerick County Championship in Gaelic football with Limerick Commercials. He was also heavily involved with the Irish language. The Kerryman had served in several stations in the Munster area, including Tournafulla, County Limerick, and Mullinahone in County Tipperary.

He had been stationed in Ballyneety for three years, eventually marrying local woman, Eileen McNamara. By 1944, however, Harrington was serving in the large Tipperary market town of Nenagh. He was 44 years of age at this point and had spent nine years in the area. Harrington lived at 52A Connolly Street in the town with his wife and four children aged between 3 and 13 years old. He acted as School Attendance Officer in the town and had done crime-detection courses, making him the station's resident expert on fingerprinting. His bravery had also been commended, it being noted that during his time in County Limerick he had once disarmed a dangerous gun-wielding wanted criminal. Recently, he had been given a job as assistant clerk in the station, allowing him to work from 9 a.m. to 6 p.m. daily.

James Lynch knew Harrington well. He was the third son of widowed mother Catherine and a native of Shanbally, Monkstown, County Cork. Aged 40 and married with one 8-year-old son, Lynch was equally well regarded within the Gardaí and his brother was also a member of the force. Like Harrington, he had enlisted in 1923 and had later been transferred to Nenagh. He had served in the town for an even longer spell than his fellow Garda, 1944 being his thirteenth year. Lynch was School Attendance Officer for the rural hinterland of Nenagh. This was an important job as school attendance for children up to the age of 14 had only been made compulsory in 1926. On top of this, he was a member of the Society of Prevention of Cruelty to Animals. Garda Lynch was held in such high regard that he was recommended for promotion in 1944. He was due to sit his sergeant's exam in April of the same year and was apparently studying very hard for this. Lynch's life appeared normal and happy from the outside. He was described as having 'a ready smile and breezy humour which gained the regard of all'. All was not well with him, however.[3]

Both men were rostered for work on the morning of Monday, 16 April 1944. Everything appeared normal and the day was shaping up to be a typically quiet Monday. Harrington arrived in for the 9 a.m. shift. At 10 a.m., Sergeant Foley and Garda Lynch met at the entrance door to the station. They conversed about Lynch's impending exam and discussed how he would be travelling up to the capital the following morning. Lynch appeared normal in every way. The conversation over, Foley walked into the day room but as he was doing so he spotted Denis Harrington coming down the stairs from the offices above. Harrington stopped and talked to Lynch. The sergeant could hear the men talking but could not make out what they were saying, although none of the exchanges seemed sharp or angry. Some moments later, both Gardaí went into the storeroom on the left and the sergeant went about his business.

Another sergeant, McLoughlin, walked into the same storeroom at about 10.10 a.m. The two Gardaí were still there. Harrington was sitting on the edge of a table near the front window while Lynch was some yards away, standing and talking. The conversation ceased as McLoughlin came in. He asked the men if there was any sign of his bicycle and one of the men pointed to the corner of the room, saying that there were a few bicycles present. Satisfied, McLoughlin exited the room. It was the last time either Garda would be seen alive.

Between five and ten minutes later, two sharp retorts were heard throughout the Garda station. There was about a three- or four-second gap between the sounds. Sergeant Foley heard the loud noise and assumed it must have been a lorry backfiring on the street in front of the station. He dispatched his colleague, Sergeant Quinlan, to go outside and investigate. Quinlan came back within seconds, reporting that there was no car or lorry in the street and that it must have gone.[4]

Some minutes later, Sergeant McLoughlin sent Garda Greally into the storeroom to tell Garda Harrington that he was wanted in the day room. Greally opened the door and saw Harrington lying on his back on the ground in a pool of blood. He immediately shouted, 'Good God, lads, come in: something terrible has happened.' All the Gardaí in the station rushed to the scene and discovered that Garda Lynch was also lying prostrate on the floor. A large amount of blood was oozing from a head wound. A long Webley revolver lay some 9in from his outstretched right hand. Garda Harrington was lying 3 or 4 yards away. He was just inside the door and also had blood flowing from an open wound on his head. The sergeant quickly examined the revolver, and discovered that five of its six chambers were loaded. There were three live and also two spent cartridges. At that point a doctor and priest were summoned to the scene. The former, Dr Mary Ryan, arrived after 11 a.m. She noted that Garda Harrington had a bullet wound beneath his left eye. His body was warm, but life was extinct. Lynch's wound was above his right ear and blood and brain matter had seeped out onto the floor. Both men were immediately pronounced dead and their bodies were brought to the morgue at Nenagh Hospital.

A seven-man jury was convened in the hospital and the inquest was held that very evening. Dr Courtney, the Nenagh coroner, summed up the case succinctly when he remarked at the outset, 'We are assembled to inquire into the deaths of two members of the Civic Guard who were found shot dead this morning. Nobody had witnessed the occurrence and nobody could give any reason why it should have taken place.'[5] Garda Harrington had been shot under the left eye but the trajectory of the bullet had been downward and it had exited at the centre of the neck, which appeared to be broken. Death was due to laceration of the spinal cord. It appeared that

Lynch had then shot himself in the right ear, the bullet coming out the other side of the skull. His death was caused by laceration of the brain. The gun itself had been issued to Nenagh Garda Station and should have been kept in a locked press in the barracks.

The coroner was well known to Lynch and gave evidence of his dealings with him. The Garda had been ill between 11 and 31 March and was examined by Dr Courtney. The doctor was treating a large carbuncle, or infected boil, over Lynch's right hip. While receiving attention, Lynch divulged to the doctor that he felt depressed and had not been sleeping well lately. The doctor described Lynch as 'excitable' and said that he would be particularly so after a fit of depression when he might have the tendency to become unbalanced. His wife had also been in hospital in the weeks coming up to the shooting, although she was discharged on the Saturday before the tragedy. On top of this, the Garda had been studying for the rigorous sergeant's exam, which had been due to take place the day after the murder. Harrington, prior to his death, had been in perfect health. The coroner described the event as a 'fit, a sudden impulse or burst of temper. A meaningless tragedy.'[6]

Both the coroner and the Gardaí present at the enquiry asserted that the two colleagues had always had a good relationship and other Gardaí considered the pair friendly. All parties expressed extreme shock and sorrow at the tragic incident. The jury returned a murder-suicide verdict, adding that the bullets were fired by Garda Lynch but they could not ascertain why, 'there being no evidence to show the state of his mind at the time of the occurrence'.

Both men's funerals were large affairs. Denis Harrington's last journey brought him to his hometown of Castleisland, where the church was packed to capacity. His coffin was lowered into the ground in Ardcrone Cemetery near his home. His colleague, James Lynch, was buried in his adopted home town of Nenagh in Lisboney Cemetery the following day, where a large congregation also gathered.

Mental health was a phrase which did not exist in the Ireland of the 1940s. Perhaps James Lynch was merely depressed, which caused him to commit the unthinkable act of killing his colleague and friend and ultimately himself. No one ever mentioned any animosity between the two men – we will never know what exactly their last conversation was about. Either way, it left two young families to mourn 'their sad irreparable loss'.[7] However, a motive emerged in the months after the shootings.

Garda Harrington's wife Eileen applied for compensation in January, following her husband's tragic death. Mrs Harrington, who had moved back to her native Ballyneety after Denis' death, insisted in court that her husband had 'died from injuries maliciously inflicted on him in the performance of his duties'. In applying for compensation, she divulged that she and her husband had an argument with the Lynchs in the weeks before the shooting and had been on bad terms with them since.[8]

Under cross-examination, Mrs Eileen Harrington admitted that she had been out walking with her husband on the afternoon of the 15 April, the day before the shooting. When they were on the Dublin Road, they met the Lynchs coming in the other direction. Eileen admitted that the two couples had not been on good terms coming up to that date but denied making a comment designed to anger the pair. She did admit that her husband had said, 'I can tell you anything you want to know', to Mrs Lynch. This was an apparent reference to a secret Garda Harrington knew about Garda Lynch that his wife was not aware of and that her husband was anxious to keep from her.

It would later transpire that Lynch had found himself in some trouble at work involving a local woman named Bourke. The nature of the problem was never mentioned in the media, but it was so serious that action was to be taken against the Garda, which would include his compulsory transfer out of Nenagh. There had been no major story involving the name Bourke in the newspapers for the Nenagh area in the preceding months. We can presume that since Garda Lynch's wife was not aware of it, it had been kept quiet.

On the evening of 15 April, Lynch was back at work as station orderly. He relieved Garda Greally to go on his break. When Greally returned, Lynch started a conversation by saying angrily, 'Mrs

Harrington threw the dirt about the Bourke case at my wife. My wife got excited and I had difficulty holding her.' Greally told him that he did not want to hear anything about his domestic affairs, at which point Lynch discontinued the conversation.

As relief station orderly, Lynch would have had access to the keys to the locked cupboard containing the station's gun and at some point later that evening he took the firearm without permission.[9] The following morning, Lynch was rostered to work early. He made similar comments about Harrington and the Bourke case to Sergeant Foley, who sympathetically told him not to take any notice. He also met Greally again, who mentioned Lynch's impending sergeant's exam and jokingly said, 'Don't come back on this occasion without the stripes.'

We may never know what happened, and why it caused Lynch to kill a man with whom he had been on good terms for many years before. Lynch appeared to have planned the attack, judging by the fact that he had the gun on his person when he went to the storeroom, and Harrington was obviously well aware of his colleague's secret. However, Harrington could not have known that Lynch was willing to kill to ensure that it never saw the light of day.

The claim for compensation was ultimately rejected as the judge felt that the shooting was more related to domestic than Garda matters. He thus insisted that it didn't come within the parameters of the Garda Compensation Act.[10]

Harrington was the first Garda deliberately killed by a colleague. However, seven years earlier, in January 1937, former IRA volunteer-turned-detective Thomas Carass was in Leech's Pub in Dolphin's Barn when he turned to his Special Branch colleague Patrick Kirwan and said, 'I hate you. You CID, you rat, you murderer.' Kirwan had been pro-Treaty during the Civil War. Kirwan ignored the provocation, leaving the premises. His colleague followed him and fired six shots in his direction, putting 'three holes in his overcoat'.[11] Amazingly, Kirwan was uninjured. Carass, who claimed to have been attacked before he fired the shots, was sentenced to eighteen months' hard labour.[12]

GARDA JAMES BYRNE

'Will I be hanged or get five years in jail?'

Incidences of Gardaí shooting and killing criminals are rarer in Ireland than in most countries, partly because the Gardaí are generally unarmed. There were a number of exceptions to this rule during the lifespan of the Free State, however. In 1929 Garda John Fitzpatrick shot Edmond Rohan. The Garda claimed he caught Rohan poaching in the Owenmore River near Castlegregory, County Kerry, and tried to shoot over the poacher's head as he ran away. Rohan was struck by a bullet into the back and died within hours. He was found near the river the following morning. Fitzpatrick was acquitted, despite the fact that he was not supposed to have been carrying firearms in the course of his duty.[1] Five years later, three detectives were responsible for opening fire on a boisterous crowd of 2,000 on Copley Street in Cork City in 1934. One man, Michael Lynch, was killed. Yet again, the offending officers would escape punishment.[2] Garda Daniel Duff was not so fortunate eleven years later. He discharged his firearm while on protection duty of a rural farm in County Limerick, but he shot and killed a fellow Garda named James Byrne.

James Byrne was born into a large farming family in December 1907. The Byrnes lived at Coolballintaggart in Askanagap, a mountainous area in the south of County Wicklow.[3] Byrne left the family home aged 20 to undergo training for the Gardaí in 1928. He was deployed to Wexford, Cork and Kerry before eventually being transferred from Farranfore in Kerry to Pallasgreen, County Limerick. His new station had a sergeant and seven Gardaí. Byrne worked the dayshift in the village until November 1944, after which Superintendent John Dunning rostered him for night patrol. Byrne was 39 years old, unmarried and content to work these unsociable hours. The Garda, who was 6ft 1in but weighed just 11 stone, devoted his free time to training and racing greyhounds and night duty would leave part of his day free to practise his hobby.[4]

The night patrol involved protection of disputed land belonging to the O'Kennedy family. In 1936 Mr Richard J. O'Kennedy, a prosperous farmer, had purchased a farm in Pallasgreen. O'Kennedy was a breeder of bloodstock thoroughbreds and had bred horses that had won major races in Ireland and further afield. The 16 acres of Mount Catherine were situated on land three quarters of a mile outside the village and seemed ideal. The large house and much of its contents had previously been burned to the ground in 1921 by the Black and Tans in a reprisal for the Dromkeen Ambush.[5] Afterwards the farmer had bought the land from the Land Commission, which had been set up to compulsorily buy and break up the large estates of landlords. This land was then redistributed amongst local families. The redistribution was not always fair or popular, however, and this particular farm was subject to a serious dispute. O'Kennedy was subjected to several threats from disgruntled locals and he also received intimidating letters, purporting to be from the IRA, the last of which arrived as late as Christmas 1945. O'Kennedy applied for overnight protection. The Gardaí granted his request and two members of the force were stationed nightly at the property on and off for the two years up until 1946.[6]

In November 1944, Kildare native Daniel Joseph Duff arrived at Pallasgreen Garda Station directly from the Garda depot. Duff was a native of Askinraw in Suncroft and was the third eldest of seven sons. At school he was considered a brilliant student and after leaving Newbridge College he joined the Defence Forces for a year and a half, where his conduct was described as excellent. On leaving the army, Duff enlisted in An Garda Síochána in June 1944. Pallasgreen was his first assignment, and after a year's daytime duty he was sent out to O'Kennedy's farm to join Garda Byrne on the night shift in June 1945. After two months, he was re-allocated to orderly duty. He would resume night duty on 11 December, when he again found himself in close quarters with Byrne.

Byrne and Duff worked from 11 p.m. to 6 a.m. each night, with longer hours in the summer. Both guards were armed with a Webley .45 calibre revolver and twenty-four rounds of ammunition on this particular duty, due to its isolated location and potential for confrontation. The two men initially got on well but the huge amount of time spent in each other's company meant that relations between them were occasionally strained. The only visitor they ever had to the lonely farm was their superintendent, who sporadically came to inspect his charges. When he was asked later about the relationship between Duff and Byrne, he said, 'They seemed alright. I did not notice anything wrong.' Other Gardaí said that the two men were very friendly sometimes but had not been on speaking terms at all in early September 1946. When pressed by another Garda as to what had caused the argument, Duff replied that it was over duty. On another occasion, Duff took Byrne's bicycle without permission, which resulted in Byrne refusing to speak to his colleague for three days. After this argument, Byrne had arrived back from annual leave and pointedly greeted everyone personally in the day room except Duff, whom he ignored.

Daniel Duff spent nine months on night duty out in Mount Catherine, most of them in the company of James Byrne. The young Garda later described how the long period of nocturnal labour left him tired, depressed and irritable. He worked seven days a week for ten continuous months, including Sundays and Christmas Day, only requesting one day off in that period. He had to sleep during daylight hours in the busy Garda station and found himself constantly being woken up when he tried to rest. The night duty itself was uneventful and repetitive, with no major incident occurring while the two men were stationed there.

To relieve the tedium of the long nights, Duff and Byrne did not always adhere strictly to the job's conditions. Sometimes both men would leave the premises. Duff would occasionally desert his duty and visit a local family in the townland of Nicker. Byrne too would depart the estate and go off on his own. Duff said afterwards that Byrne's attitude was that 'he wanted me to be at the farm when he wasn't but he wanted me to stay with him when he was there'.[7] It all culminated in August 1946, when the two men had a serious argument. Byrne insulted his younger colleague. Duff responded by threatening that if Byrne called him names again he would hit him. Byrne allegedly took out his gun and replied that if anyone ever hit him, he would 'blow his brains out'. Duff would later say that he believed the older Garda would carry out this threat because during a previous row he had also drawn his revolver and waved it under Duff's nose. He described Byrne as 'hot-tempered [and] reckless with a gun'.

But the argument blew over and the two men became friendly again. Byrne would often regale his younger colleague about his experiences during his seventeen years in the Gardaí. The superintendent again visited the two men on night duty on 23 September. All seemed normal and neither man mentioned their recent dispute. They worked together the following night and were on very friendly terms.

On 25 September, Duff visited Coffey's pub in the afternoon and drank several pints, also spending half an hour talking to a girl over the Garda station fence. He then ate dinner with Byrne before returning to the pub. When closing time was called, Duff went back towards the station, stopping to help the sergeant's children with their homework. Garda Byrne meanwhile was supposed to have gone to work at 10 p.m. but decided instead to drive out to Limerick Junction, a nearby village. Duff knew a girl out there and asked his colleague to tell her he was asking for her. Byrne arrived back in Pallasgreen shortly before 11 p.m. He met Duff and the two men walked out to duty. Both were under the influence of alcohol. Duff had consumed five pints in the village throughout the day and Byrne had also been drinking.

They were on good terms, laughing at a joke Byrne told as they left the station. They met two people on the road before entering the farm. The first was Bridget Kennedy. They did not speak to her, although one of them flashed a light in her face. Next they encountered local thatcher Jeremiah Coffey, who was known to both men. The trio stood and conversed for several minutes. Coffey later described the men as 'very friendly to one another and quite sober'.[8] That would be the last time James Byrne would be seen alive by anyone other than his colleague.

The night was dark and dry, with a slight breeze. When the men arrived at O'Kennedy's, they patrolled the farm. As they walked up towards the pear tree, they discussed Duff's impending transfer. He was finally being moved off night duty to the daytime shift in the station in Murroe, a village 12 miles to the north. Byrne was discussing a sergeant he had in a previous station who had made his night duty difficult. Duff responded that he wouldn't mind doing night duty again as it was alright once you got used to it. Byrne replied, 'You seem to be a very long time getting used to doing it here.' Duff retorted that he could say the same about Byrne, except 'you need not care because you have the superintendent on your side'.[9]

Garda Byrne said to his colleague that he seemed to expect the same treatment as men longer on the job. The pair traded accusations, Duff accusing his fellow Garda of having told the superintendent about rows between the two men and times he had left duty without permission. He also complained that Byrne deserted the farm whenever he wanted but if Duff did likewise he would get into trouble. Byrne countered that Duff had threatened to tell the superintendent that he was keeping greyhounds without his superior officer's knowledge.

The argument escalated to the point that both men were cursing and shouting at each other loudly, only lowering their voices when they walked past the farmhouse to avoid alerting the homeowners. Byrne was grinding his teeth. He said he was going to go up to the loft to sleep and that Duff could fuck off home if he liked. Duff told Byrne that he was thirsty and was going to get a pear from a tree in the orchard, about 100 yards from the rear of the house. He walked in that direction, but instead of going to the loft as he had said, Byrne followed his colleague, saying, 'That is right, be fucking contrary.' Duff answered, 'How is going for a pear being contrary?'[10]

When they got to the pear tree, Duff testified that the men again started swearing at one another. Byrne called his younger colleague a string of names and accused of him of always being contrary. He then roared into his face, 'You young pup. You must have only been dragged up. I will give you a slap on the mouth which you are looking for for a long time.' Duff laughed at his fellow Garda and answered that if there was slapping done, Byrne may not come off the better of it. He added that if he did not stop calling him names he would give Byrne the hiding of his life.

'I told you before, if you ever attempted to hit me I would blow your brains out,' shouted Byrne. At this point Byrne, according to Duff, made a quick movement of his hand towards his right pocket. This sudden movement made Duff panic. 'I drew quickest … I had my thumb on my gun in my pocket. I pulled out my gun and fired at him. I am not sure when the second shot was fired, because I lost my head.' Duff had fired one shot at Byrne, before taking a step forward and firing a second. Both bullets went through Byrne's heart. Duff later testified that his anger dissipated after the second shot. He saw Byrne toppling over backwards and jerking on the ground for a few seconds. He then lay still. Duff knelt down, asking, 'Jim, are you all right? Can you hear me?' Byrne was dead.

Duff whispered an act of contrition in his fatally injured colleague's ear before running to the farmhouse. The O'Kennedys were woken just before midnight by frantic shouts coming from outside their window. It was Garda Duff bellowing, 'Get up, get up. This is me, Duff. Byrne is shot. Come quickly.'[11]

The two O'Kennedys were originally supposed to be in Dublin for a horse fair that night but had decided to delay their journey by two days. They had just retired to bed at around 11.30 p.m. As they were climbing the stairs, they had heard what they thought was a stable door banging when the shots were fired. The couple then heard running steps and Duff's loud cries. They rushed downstairs and opened the hall door only for Duff to jump inside the house. He had his revolver in his right hand and he repeated, 'I shot Jim Byrne. He is dead. I had an awful row with him.'[12]

Mr O'Kennedy picked up a torch and accompanied Duff to the orchard, where they saw Garda Byrne. He was lying on his back with his mouth open and his legs facing the trunk of the tree. They did not touch the body, although they examined it carefully and confirmed that the Garda was dead. His walking cane, torch and cap lay a couple of yards away on the ground. The two men went back towards the house, where they met Mrs Ellen O'Kennedy. She suggested that they go back and say an act of contrition, but Duff replied that he already had. She then led the men to the kitchen, where Duff smoked several cigarettes and asked for brandy or whiskey. Richard O'Kennedy, suspecting that Duff had been drinking earlier in the day, did not grant his request. Duff continued nonetheless, 'We had an awful row. He was savage. He went for his gun – it was him or me. It is a dirty story. It will all come out now.' He added that he had lost his temper, that Byrne was very wicked and that the pair had fought all the way up the road. Duff still had a revolver in his hand at this point, which he put in his overcoat pocket after being requested to do so by Mrs O'Kennedy.

A pale and panicky Duff asked the shaken couple if they would go with him to the station. They agreed. On the way Duff mentioned the row with his colleague about three times, saying, 'It was either him or me' and also 'What will happen me now? Will I be hanged or get five years in jail?' Mrs O'Kennedy comforted him by saying, 'Well Duff, you did not mean to murder him.' Duff agreed, saying that it had all happened in the heat of the moment. The trio arrived at the station at 12.10 a.m. and Duff knocked on the door. The orderly answered the knock and Duff blurted out that, 'A terrible thing is after happening. I shot Guard Byrne.' He was arrested immediately.[13]

Meanwhile Mrs O'Kennedy had gone to a superintendent's house nearby. He arrived quickly after hearing the story. By this point, Duff was slumped in a chair with his head buried in his hands. He stood to attention when he saw his superior, however, saying, 'I am sorry sir, I could not help it.' The superintendent told him not to say anymore. Duff then handed over his gun to a colleague, urging him not to be afraid and telling him that he would not shoot him. He began to pace up and down the station while talking animatedly. Next, a statement was taken. In it, Duff admitted to shooting James Byrne but insisted he had done so in self-defence and that it was unplanned. A Garda colleague that was present answered that he would believe that it was an accident had it not been for the second shot.

After this the superintendent, another Guard and a priest went out to the orchard and found the body of the fatally injured James Byrne lying on the ground. His walking stick and torch lay close by, while his fully loaded revolver was in his right hip pocket. He was dead. A bullet, which appeared to have passed through his body, was found embedded on the ground 1½in behind him. The pathologist, on arriving at the scene, opined that Byrne had died a second or two after the first bullet had struck his heart and was dead by the time the second bullet had hit him. The paths of the two bullets had crossed. Byrne's body was removed to the barracks on the back of a farm cart. An inquest was held in the day room of Pallasgreen Station under the light of two small oil lamps and the evidence of Byrne's violent death was relayed.

A Garda being killed on duty would always make the newspaper headlines but the fact that his colleague was on trial made this a unique case. Pallasgreen itself, meanwhile, was described as being 'plunged into gloom ... Garda Byrne was very popular in the district and exceedingly well liked by everybody'.[14] Byrne's body was removed to the church in Pallasgreen the day after his death and a large crowd mourned his passing. He was ultimately buried in his native Askanagap on 29 September.

Duff was duly charged with murder. He responded by saying, 'I admit shooting him alright but there was no malice aforethought.' The case was brought to trial in the Central Criminal Court, Dublin, commencing on 19 November 1946. When the jury was selected, one potential juror was excused after admitting to having a conscientious objection to capital punishment.[15] It was a relevant point, the death penalty being a distinct possibility in this case and still widely used at that point. Daniel Duff pleaded not guilty to the charge of murder. The story was widely followed and the press were present every day to cover each detail of the scandalous affair.

There were no eyewitnesses to the fatal confrontation except the accused, but twenty-one witnesses did appear for the prosecution, most outlining the events of the day and discussing the turbulent relationship between Duff and Byrne. There was only one witness for the defence: Duff himself. Although one local man, James O'Donnell, had heard the two fatal shots, Duff was the only man alive who could know the truth of what had taken place on the night of Byrne's death.

He appeared in the witness box, looking 'pale and very tired with dark shadows under his eyes'.[16] He outlined his version of events, reiterating that he had shot Byrne in self-defence. Duff had been extensively trained in gun use in both the Defence Forces and the Gardaí and was asked several tough questions by prosecutor, Mr Murnaghan.

Murnaghan: You knew that firing at his chest was going to kill him?
Duff: I never thought of that.
Murnaghan: Was there anything to prevent you grappling with him to prevent him using his gun?
Duff: I didn't consider that, it entered my head immediately to use my gun. I just fired two shots at him. I fired at his chest alright.
Murnaghan: Were you taught only to use a revolver as a last resort?
Duff: No, I was never taught that.[17]

When it was put to the accused that Byrne's gun was in his left pocket, despite Duff saying he had reached for his right pocket during the stand-off, Duff replied that he could not explain that. Byrne had also been holding a walking cane and a torch in his hand. When the prosecution enquired of Duff how his colleague could have quickly drawn a gun with those two items in his hand, the accused did not answer the question. The prosecution insisted that to have shot Byrne through the heart twice on that dark night he must have been at close range and that he had not needed to discharge the bullet 'except if he wanted to kill Guard Byrne'. They added that even if Byrne had reached for his gun, Duff should have tried to 'grapple with the man, or run away into the darkness'.

Duff came across poorly in the courtroom, seeming unable to answer the simplest of questions. He did, however, assert that he had no hatred or ill will towards Byrne and that, 'I think I should say that I had no intention whatsoever of killing or harming in any way the dead Guard. The whole thing was a result of a savage quarrel and I only fired in self-defence.'[18]

The defence put it to the jury that the accused had been impaired by a chronic lack of sleep for the last nine months, as had the victim. A sergeant had recommended that Duff go on sick leave shortly before the tragedy as he looked pale and gaunt. He had promised that he would but had continued with the arduous night duty instead. Duff was, according to Mr Healy, 'by no means of the criminal class, strained by lack of sleep for nine months. [This was] A killing done in anger by two men equally armed.' When the judge was summing up, he rhetorically asked the jury 'would a reasonable man, faced with precisely the same position as the accused, have taken the step of firing a deadly weapon twice with the range not more than 6 or 7ft?'[19]

The jury clearly thought not. They had the option of acquittal for self-defence and manslaughter. They picked neither. The three-day trial ended with ninety minutes of deliberation, which was enough for the jury to find Guard Daniel Duff guilty of murder, with a unanimous recommendation to mercy. Judge Overend announced that he agreed with the verdict. He asked Duff if he had anything to say in response to the verdict. Duff, who had been listening carefully, showed no emotion and answered in a clear voice, 'I have nothing further to say now, my Lord.' Overend then donned the black cap, and sentenced the tall, dark-haired, young Garda to be executed on 11 December. He was then taken to a condemned cell in Mountjoy Prison.[20]

Five days before that date, the government announced that the sentence would be commuted to one of penal servitude for life.[21] Duff's version of events seemed unlikely and he proved to be a poor witness in his own defence. Still, there must have been a certain amount of sympathy for the talented young Garda who seemed to have been working under unbearable conditions. On top of this, there is little doubt that it would have been a national scandal to put to death a so-called guardian of the peace working to maintain law and order in the country. Perhaps for this reason, Duff avoided becoming the only member of An Garda Síochána to be executed for murder. He went on to serve five years and four months in custody and was granted early release in November 1951.

CHIEF SUPERINTENDENT SEÁN GANTLY

'There is something wrong there, come quickly.'

Seán Gantly was born in 1899 on Main Street, Roscrea, County Tipperary, into a family steeped in republican patriotism. His great-granduncle was the famous rebel of 1798, William Orr. He was also related to Michael Larkin, one of the Manchester Martyrs who was put to death by the British government in 1867. Gantly's father, Joseph, continued the legacy, playing a prominent role in Irish politics during the days of the Land League. It is therefore unsurprising that Seán joined the IRA after he had come to live in Dublin in 1917. The teenager managed to juggle his work as a commercial officer with being an active member of the B Company of the Dublin Brigade. The young volunteer took part in many engagements against the Black and Tans and after the truce was announced he wasted no time in enlisting in the National Army.

At the culmination of the Civil War in 1923, Gantly joined the Gardaí, a force of which three of his younger brothers were also members. He rose quickly through the ranks, securing the coveted post of superintendent within just two years, all the while captaining the Garda hurling team. After stints in the depot in Dublin, he served in Cork and Donegal. He also spent some years in Kerry, leading the investigation into the Rathmore murder of Ellen O'Sullivan, a gruesome crime for which her neighbour David O'Shea was convicted and subsequently executed. It was one of the most notorious murder cases in Irish history. Gantly was admitted to the Special Branch in 1934. After successfully re-organising the Detective Branch in Dublin Castle, the Tipperary native was next promoted to the lofty rank of chief superintendent in 1941. He masterminded several raids against the IRA throughout the difficult years of the Emergency and even secured the capture of the Nazi's top-ranked Irish spy, Hermann Gortz. The IRA made a particular effort to identify members of the Special Branch and Gantly would have been well known to them, being amongst its most prominent members. He soon became a target for republicans, to the point that his house was under permanent armed guard during the Emergency.[1]

Gantly witnessed the deaths of several of his colleagues, killed in battles with the IRA, and would even give evidence against Harry White regarding the shooting of George Mordaunt, having been a member of the raiding party on that fateful night. By 1948, the major threat of the Emergency years appeared to have passed. Although Fianna Fáil had initially had reservations about the force, the governing party and the Gardaí worked closely during the Emergency. Gantly was congratulated for his contribution to the safety of the country by none other than the hard-line Minister for Justice, Gerald Boland. The chief superintendent had six children by that stage. He had been married almost twenty years and was living in Clontarf. The danger of working in the Special Branch was ever-present, however, and this was tragically illustrated by a sequence of events on a winter's day in 1948, which resulted in Gantly becoming the last Garda killed in the Irish Free State.

Although the rate of violent crime in Ireland remained low throughout the 1940s, instances of petty larcenies and house-breaking had spiralled during the Emergency and continued their upward trend at the war's end. In 1946 the number of larcenies in the country was more than 12,000, over 62 per cent of which occurred in the capital city.[2] A number of gangs were known to roam the city, conducting robberies and raids on unsuspecting members of the public. William Laverty and James Nolan were amongst their number.

Laverty and Nolan were a pair of hardened felons; both men had spent several years involved in petty criminality and by 1947 they were detained in Mountjoy Prison after being found guilty of conducting a smash-and-grab raid on a jewellers on Parnell Street. Nearly £1,800 worth of property was stolen in the robbery. Somehow both men managed to break out of the prison on Christmas Eve 1947 while awaiting trial. After their escape they withdrew to a flat in a basement on Mount Street in Dublin, where they stayed with Andrew Nugent, a fellow ex-soldier and petty crook. The men, conscious of the extensive Garda operation to re-arrest them, did not leave the flat in daylight at any stage over the Christmas period.

Nolan (24) was an ex-British commando while Laverty (29) was a petty criminal with a string of convictions. He was a member of the Spider Gang, a criminal organisation with a long history of house-breaking in the Dublin area. Both were known to be highly dangerous individuals. They were suspected in a number of other crimes before their incarceration. The Gardaí were also aware that they were in possession of firearms, making their re-arrest particularly hazardous. Although the men did not leave the house, the Gardaí eventually received intelligence regarding their whereabouts.[3]

Acting on this information, Gardaí raided the basement of a house on Mount Street at 8.30 a.m. on the morning of 21 January 1948. They were heavily armed with revolvers and machine guns, due to the likelihood of the escaped prisoners having firearms in their possession. The Gardaí smashed in through the door only to discover that it was the wrong house. The two men, along with Andrew Nugent, were in fact hidden in the basement of an adjoining building and on hearing the commotion managed to run upstairs, although all were only half-dressed and Nolan was wearing no shoes. All three managed to make it onto the roof of the building before Gardaí could apprehend them.

All the while a huge crowd, who had gathered in the heavily populated area after witnessing the spectacle, watched from below in amazement. What followed was described as a scene reminiscent of the Sydney Street Siege in London in 1911 when the British police and army had a fatal shoot-out with members of a Latvian criminal gang.[4] The men scattered quickly, Laverty running in the opposite direction to his two comrades. He quickly sustained a bullet wound to the shoulder. Despite being badly injured, William Laverty continued running. More bullets were fired in his direction and he threw himself onto some sloping slates on another roof below, managing to crawl through a window in the neighbouring Kelvin Hotel. A young law student and the son of a former senator, Liam Westropp-Bennet, happened to be in the room that Laverty entered. The criminal told the startled occupant his name and that the police were after him. He then took a towel to staunch the blood, before producing a bundle of notes and offering them in return for the young man's jacket. The student refused. He comforted the fugitive, telling him he was safe before leaving the room only to be met by several detectives. They stormed in and overpowered the suspect, firing one shot, which tore a hole in the wall. Laverty was then taken without further resistance.[5]

Meanwhile Nugent and Nolan had managed to slide and scramble their way across the roof towards a small tenement named Power's Court. One of the men made a desperate attempt to get through the window of Hayes' pub to evade the Gardaí. The proprietor happened to spot him and made a grab for his shoulder, forcing the intruder to flee along the roof again. As the men continued to run, one of them fired a revolver over his shoulder. He held up his trousers with his other hand, having left his belt behind in the rush from his hideout. Eventually Nugent and Nolan managed to reach the house of Mrs O'Hanrahan, who lived at No. 35 Power's Court. Nugent flopped exhausted into a chair. Within seconds Gardaí had burst through the door and asked him his name. He replied 'Nugent,' and allowed himself to be arrested.[6]

Nolan did not come so easily. He jumped out the window of No. 35, landing on the courtyard 10ft below, where he continued into a neighbouring house belonging to Mrs Hannigan. He failed to find the staircase so he quickly exited again, the startled locals watching him escape over rooftops with Gardaí giving chase. Three shots were fired in Nolan's direction. None of them hit their target, however, and Nolan escaped his pursuers. Further searches revealed nothing and the Gardaí's trail ran cold.

A cordon was quickly thrown around the area and the Gardaí were confident that their quarry could not have escaped from the confines of Mount Street and the surrounding maze of avenues. The rooms that the fugitives had been staying in were also searched. They were said to be in complete disarray and a revolver, wireless sets and stolen property were discovered.

At 12.30 p.m., a number of detectives, led by Chief Superintendent Gantly, arrived at Sir Patrick Dun's Hospital. It was felt that Nolan may have been wounded in his neck and the Gardaí thought it was possible that he had admitted himself to the hospital for treatment. They asked the staff if anyone matching Nolan's description had been seen.[7] Gardaí were then told by several locals that a man matching the description of Nolan had been spotted several times between Lower Mount Street and the South Quays. On foot of this information, the Gardaí went to Grattan Street, where workers from the Hammond Lane Foundry told them of a stranger who had been spotted in the area. The Gardaí wasted no time. Two squad cars containing eight Gardaí, led by a plain-clothed Chief Superintendent Gantly, arrived at the foundry and conducted a search. Gantly himself led the way, going off in the direction of the stores shed. He was unarmed, having left his gun in the office.

The officers made a careful search of a loft over the main entrance shed but found nothing of note. They then returned downstairs. Detective Daniel Slattery, who was coming down the stairs behind Gantly, saw his colleague suddenly crouching down. When asked what he was doing, Gantly answered, 'There is something wrong there, come quickly.' Suddenly a tall man in an overcoat, of about 5ft 10in, appeared and seemed to pull something out of his breast pocket. A Garda behind Slattery shouted, 'There he is, get him.' The passageway was narrow and smoky due to a tar boiler nearby and confusion reigned. Slattery, who was to the left of Gantly, thought that the man had fired a shot in their direction. He pulled out his revolver and fired a shot towards the shadowy figure. The shot missed its target, however, and the suspect quickly disappeared out the door.[8]

Meanwhile, the other detectives had heard the gunshots and converged on the small hallway where they were met by the sight of a body lying on the ground. It was Superintendent Gantly, who had suffered a bullet wound to the heart. He was rushed by fire brigade ambulance to Sir Patrick Dun's Hospital, where he had been just minutes before making enquiries about the suspects. He was pronounced dead on arrival.

Immediately after the shooting, lorry-loads of armed soldiers arrived and closed all the entrances into the foundry before throwing a cordon as far as the South Quays area. Several hundred workers were forbidden to leave. Each house in the vicinity was searched and the doors were smashed open if no reply was received. The passengers on the boats from Dún Laoghaire were scrutinised and the border with Northern Ireland was watched, while Radio Éireann advised people in the area to check their homes carefully to make sure the fugitive was not hidden within. In No. 53 Lower Mount Street, Gardaí discovered an array of stolen goods, including fountain pens, stamps and more than £200. There was also a revolver and ammunition. There was no sign of the elusive Nolan though and the cordon around the area was withdrawn at dusk.

An inquest was convened, where it was quickly ascertained that Gantly had been shot by a bullet from a revolver belonging to his colleague, Detective Daniel Slattery. The inquest found that the bullet had struck him from behind and entered his body through the lung and the heart. He had died instantly, due to shock and haemorrhage. He would be the most senior Garda ever killed in the line of duty in what had been a tragic case of friendly fire.

Gantly was granted a state funeral, which was attended by such luminaries as the President, the Taoiseach and several government ministers, indicating the esteem in which the deceased officer was held. After his heroics during the Emergency, Gantly was even described as one of the best-known members of the Garda Síochána. Thousands of people lined the route to his final resting place in Glasnevin Cemetery. The Minister for Justice also paid tribute to Gantly, whom he had known well, describing his 'conspicuous courage, zeal and integrity'. In a letter to the chief superintendent's wife, he added that her husband 'has left behind an honoured memory and a fine example'.[9]

The coroner's jury met to discuss the case a month after the shooting. They came to the conclusion that Chief Superintendent Gantly had been shot by Detective Daniel Slattery, one of his own men, who had been behind him as he conducted the search. Slattery had been attempting to save the lives of his colleagues in the crowded hallway and was free from blame. He was exonerated, although he made a heartfelt apology for the bullet having come from his gun.

Nolan was eventually apprehended at a café in Talbot Street a week after the death of Chief Superintendent Gantly and was returned for trial with his partners in crime. The men's crime spree was outlined, including 17 October 1947 when they had committed three robberies in one night. A gunsmith pointed Nolan out in an identity parade as the man who had robbed his shop. The prisoner responded by hissing, 'I will get you', at the witness.[10] The men were not charged with Seán Gantly's death as it had already been proven that the fatal bullet did not come from a gun belonging to any of the defendants, who all denied vehemently having firearms in their possession during the chase.

Nolan pleaded to the judge for a five-year sentence, promising that he intended to turn his back on crime after his release. Laverty denied point-blank all of the serious charges laid against him, insisting he had merely been a visitor to the house in Mount Street on the day in question. When shown the stolen property, he replied, 'I don't know anything about that stuff.' The judge was not in a sympathetic frame of mind towards either of the prisoners. An unemployed Nugent, who when arrested had twenty-three ten-shilling notes on his person, claimed that the two men had been at his house for two weeks because 'somebody sent them down'.[11] He claimed that he did not know either of his housemates' names and that on the morning of the shooting they had threatened to shoot him if he did not run with them from the Gardaí. The judge described him as 'a cowardly participator in the crime', who had associated with criminals and handled stolen goods. Nugent received a seven-year sentence. Jail breakers and ring leaders Nolan and Laverty, meanwhile, were given a sentence of fifteen years' penal servitude. The judge remarked that 'the day of reckoning has come for you both. You are both young and you have ruined your lives.' That was far from the end of the story.[12]

Incredibly both men escaped from prison again on 5 June, barely a month into their sentence. Along with a third man, Nolan and Laverty sawed through the bars of their cell and climbed a drainpipe onto the wall of Mountjoy Prison before jumping 15ft down onto the soft grass margin on the other side. The men, who were barefoot, then quickly discarded their overcoats and ran. It was Laverty's third successful escape from the prison and his second time in the company of Nolan. On the first occasion he had taken part in a riot with 180 prisoners, which was estimated to have caused £3,000 worth of damage. This time the convicts, despite being dressed in prison garb, somehow managed to make their escape without attracting attention from local residents. Unsurprisingly the escape caused uproar and resulted in 'the most intensive manhunt ever carried out in this country'.[13] The entire Special Branch and every Garda car in the city was again mobilised in a desperate attempt to find the elusive pair.

On Sunday 20 June, Gardaí received word that there were strangers encamped in a rural field near the village of Finglas, north of Dublin City. A huge number of Gardaí put in place a cordon extending for 2 miles and closed in on their quarry. They quickly spotted Nolan, although he had grown a moustache and was described as well dressed. He was unarmed and made a run for it on spotting Gardaí but was quickly arrested.[14] It appeared that he had been living in the field for at least four days. The arrest did not unduly affect his mood and it was reported that the day after his re-arrest Nolan was 'whistling like a lark' on his way to court.

A further search of the field revealed that Nolan had been staying there with two companions, one of whom was believed to have been William Laverty. He did not return to the field after his colleague's arrest, however, and it was several months later, on 23 December 1949, that Laverty was surprised in bed in a house in Henrietta Street in the capital. Almost a year to the day since his first escape from Mountjoy, a group of officers burst into a bedroom in the house. Laverty again attempted to flee, going for the window but finding his way barred. He was carried struggling from the premises, finally telling Gardaí, 'I have only been out five times since I escaped and I did not intend to go out again.' Laverty, who had dyed his hair black and grown a moustache while on the run, was then interned in Portlaoise Prison, described in media reports as 'the prison from which nobody ever escapes'.[15]

The men featured in further court cases during their internment when they attempted to claim money in a post office account as their own. The application was rejected. Every court appearance involving Laverty and Nolan resulted in a noticeably heavy Garda presence, the authorities presumably mindful of the men's proven escape capabilities. The men served out their sentences in Portlaoise Prison. There was shock when the Minister for Justice exercised his power under the Courts of Justice Act in September 1953 to grant the men early release, stating that they had spent the equivalent of seven and a half years in prison. Nolan was released first and his compatriot Laverty was freed a week later, promising to leave Ireland for London.[16]

Five oil paintings in honour of the five members of the Special Branch who met their death due to an IRA bullet were unveiled in Dublin Castle Recreation Hall in September 1948. Gantly was amongst them. Although he was the highest-ranking officer to die in the line of duty, his name would not appear on the Garda Roll of Honour until almost sixty years after his death. After several years of pressure from his family and local community, Chief Superintendent Seán Gantly's name was finally included on the list in 2008, and a road was named in his honour in his home town in the same year. A fitting tribute for a man who, like so many others, had laid down his life in defence of the state.

AFTERWORD

After Seán Gantly's death, the Gardaí experienced a period of unprecedented calm. Between 1948 and 1970 no Garda was deliberately killed in the state, although there were accidental deaths of members of the force. In 1970 this peace was shattered when Richard Fallon was shot dead while attempting to foil a Dublin bank robbery. This ushered in a period during which the Troubles in Northern Ireland crossed the border – a time when the life of a Garda was in even more danger than in the early 1920s or during the Emergency; thirteen Gardaí were killed in just fifteen years between 1970 and 1985. Several of the perpetrators were sentenced to death for capital murder, although none of the executions were actually carried out. The violence of this period led to renewed calls from certain quarters to arm rank-and-file members of the police in this country, a call that was not acted upon. Although the years after 1985 would prove to be less bloody, some high-profile cases still occurred. Jerry McCabe was shot dead in Adare in 1996 in a cold-blooded assassination that shocked the country. His death would not be the last. Several Gardaí were murdered after the turn of the twenty-first century. At the time of writing, eighty-eight Gardaí have lost their lives in the line of duty. Although many have been accidental, dozens have been little more than murder. The era of the Free State was a dangerous one for ordinary Gardaí; the present day poses similar risks.

APPENDIX

Force	Rank	Name	Date	Birthplace	Location of Death	Assailant
Garda Síochána	Garda	Henry Phelan	14 November 1922	Mountrath, County Laois	Mullinahone, County Tipperary	Officially unknown (suspect named in court)
Garda Síochána	Sergeant	James Woods	3 December 1923	Doolin, County Clare	Scartaglen, County Kerry	Officially unknown (Michael Healy acquitted)
Garda Síochána	Garda	Patrick O'Halloran	28 January 1924	Gort, County Galway	Baltinglass, County Wicklow	Felix McMullen (Executed)
Dublin Metropolitan Police	Detective	Arthur Nolan	29 February 1924	Rathfarnham, County Dublin	Pearse Street, Dublin City	George Lane (declared insane)
Garda Síochána	Sergeant	Thomas Griffin	6 May 1924	Greenmount, Cork City	Cregg, County Tipperary	Unknown (suspect named as Sonny O'Dwyer)
Garda Síochána	Garda	John Murrin	6 May 1924	Bruckless, County Donegal	Cregg, County Tipperary	Unknown (suspect named as Sonny O'Dwyer)
Garda Síochána	Garda	Thomas Dowling	28 December 1925	Castlecomer, County Kilkenny	Fanore, County Clare	Unknown (John O'Connor and Patrick Conway acquitted)
Garda Síochána	Sergeant	James Fitzsimons	14 November 1926	Strangford, County Down	St Luke's, Cork City	Unknown (suspected IRA attack)

Force	Rank	Name	Date	Place	Place	Perpetrator
Garda Síochána	Garda	Hugh Ward	14 November 1926	Nobber, County Meath	Hollyford, County Tipperary	Unknown (James Ryan and Edward O'Reilly acquitted)
Garda Síochána	Detective	Timothy O'Sullivan	11 June 1929	Skibbereen, County Cork	Tullycrine, Cooraclare, County Clare	Unknown (suspected IRA attack)
Garda Síochána	Superintendent	John Curtin	20 March 1931	Meelin, County Cork	Dundrum, County Tipperary	Unknown (suspected IRA attack)
Garda Síochána	Detective	Patrick McGeehan	14 February 1932	Fintown, County Donegal	Fenagh, County Leitrim	Joseph Leddy (twelve-month sentence; manslaughter)
Garda Síochána	Detective	John Roche	3 January 1940	Abbeyfeale, County Limerick	Patrick Street, Cork City	Tomás Óg Mac Curtain (sentenced to death: reprieved)
Garda Síochána (Special Branch)	Detective	Richard Hyland	16 August 1940	Maynooth, County Kildare	Rathgar Road, Dublin	Patrick McGrath (executed), Thomas Harte (executed), Thomas Hunt (reprieved)
Garda Síochána (Special Branch)	Detective Sergeant	Patrick McKeown	16 August 1940	Keady, County Armagh	Rathgar Road, Dublin	Patrick McGrath (executed), Thomas Harte (executed), Thomas Hunt (reprieved)
Garda Síochána (Special Branch)	Detective Sergeant	Denis O'Brien	9 September 1942	Pim Street, Dublin	Ballyboden, County Dublin	Charles Kerins (executed)
Garda Síochána	Detective	Michael Walsh	1 October 1942	Barnhill, County Mayo	Mount Nugent, County Cavan	Patrick Dermody (shot dead)
Garda Síochána (Special Branch)	Detective	George Mordaunt	24 October 1942	Blackpitts, County Dublin	Donnycarney, County Dublin	Maurice O'Neill (executed) Harry White (served two years for manslaughter)

Garda Síochána	Garda	Denis Harrington	17 April 1944	Castleisland, County Kerry	Nenagh, County Tipperary	James Lynch (murder-suicide)
Garda Síochána	Garda	James Byrne	25 September 1946	Askanagap, County Wicklow	Pallasgreen, County Limerick	Garda Daniel Duff (Sentenced to death: reprieved)
Garda Síochána (Special Branch)	Chief Superintendent	Seán Gantly	21 January 1948	Roscrea, County Tipperary	Hammond Lane, Dublin	Shot accidentally by colleague Detective Daniel Slattery

NOTES

Abbreviations

NAI: National Archives of Ireland
UCD: University College Dublin
NLI: National Library of Ireland
CSO: Central Statistics Office
BMH: Bureau of Military History
CCA: Court of Criminal Appeal

Introduction

1   Leeson, D.M., *The Black and Tans*, p. 16.
2   Hopkinson, Michael, *The Irish War of Independence*, p. 56.
3   Macardle, Dorothy, *The Irish Republic*, p. 235.
4   Dáil Éireann Minutes, 10 April 1919.
5   Maguire, Martin, *The Civil Service and the Revolution in Ireland*, p. 1.
6   Brady, Conor, *Guardians of the Peace*, p. 37.
7   *Garda Review Annual*, 1929.
8   *The Irish Times*, 8 March 1922.
9   Lawlor, George, and Reddy, Tom, *The Murder File*, p. 5.
10 *Kildare Observer*, 24 June 1922.
11 NAI, Department of Justice, H Files 3058.
12 Corcoran, Donal P., *Freedom to Achieve Freedom*, p. 36.
13 *The Irish Times*, 15 April 1922.
14 *The Irish Times*, 14 April 1922.
15 *Freeman's Journal*, 18 November 1922.

16 McGarry, Fearghal, *Eoin O'Duffy: A Self-Made Hero*, p. 124.
17 NAI, Department of the Taoiseach S3058.
18 NAI, Department of the Taoiseach S6093A.

Chapter 1

1 NAI, Census 1911.
2 Hurley, Tom, *Henry Phelan, A Boy of Good Character*, radio documentary, Tipp FM.
3 *Kilkenny People*, 10 October 1997.
4 Hopkinson, Michael, *The Irish War of Independence*, p. 123.
5 *Freeman's Journal*, 20 April 1923.
6 *Kilkenny People*, 18 November 1922.
7 *Freeman's Journal*, 20 August 1924.
8 *Irish Examiner*, 21 August 1924.
9 *Kilkenny People*, 18 November 1922.
10 *Ibid.*
11 *Ibid.*
12 *Evening Herald*, 2 August 1924.
13 *Irish Examiner*, 23 November 1922.
14 Hurley, Tom, *Henry Phelan, A Boy of Good Character*, radio documentary, Tipp FM.
15 *Kilkenny People*, 17 May 2012.
16 Garvin, Tom, *1922: The Birth of Irish Democracy*, p. 117.
17 *Leinster Express*, 3 January 1998.

Chapter 2

1 *Ulster Herald*, 18 November 1922.
2 *Irish Independent*, 17 January 1923.
3 UCD Archives, Desmond and Mabel Fitzgerald Collection 80/725.
4 UCD Archives, Desmond and Mabel Fitzgerald Collection 80/726.
5 BMH, Witness Statement 1095.
6 NAI, 1911 Census.
7 Brady, Conor, *Guardians of the Peace*, p. 75.
8 *Freeman's Journal*, 5 December 1923.
9 *Irish Examiner*, 16 January 1925.
10 *The Irish Times*, 12 July 1924.
11 *Irish Examiner*, 23 January 1925.
12 *Irish Independent*, 9 July 1924.
13 *Tralee Star*, 6 December 1923.
14 *Freeman's Journal*, 7 December 1923.
15 Wallace, Colm, *Sentenced to Death: Saved from the Gallows*, p. 55.

16 *Freeman's Journal*, 12 December 1923.
17 *Irish Examiner*, 4 July 1924.

Chapter 3

1 Irish Statute Book, Public Safety (Emergency Powers) Act, 1923.
2 *Irish Independent*, 5 March 1924.
3 *Leinster Express*, 8 March 1924.
4 *Freeman's Journal*, 31 January 1924.
5 NAI, Census 1911.
6 *Connacht Tribune*, 28 October 1966.
7 *Kildare Observer*, 2 February.
8 *Connacht Tribune*, 9 February 1924.
9 *Irish Independent*, 1 February 1924.
10 *Freeman's Journal*, 18 February 1924.
11 *Irish Examiner*, 20 February 1924.
12 *Irish Independent*, 12 March 1924.
13 *Freeman's Journal*, 9 July 1924.
14 *Ibid.*
15 *Freeman's Journal*, 22 July 1924.
16 *Anglo-Celt*, 2 August 1924.
17 *Irish Independent*, 2 August 1924.
18 *Kildare Observer*, 2 August 1924.
19 Seán O'Mahony Papers, NLI, M/S 44, 076/8.
20 *Freeman's Journal*, 2 August 1924.

Chapter 4

1 *Irish Independent*, 19 September 1925.
2 Brady, Conor, *Guardians of the Peace*, p. 123.
3 *Irish Examiner*, 5 March 1925.
4 *Irish Independent*, 8 April 1925.
5 *Ibid.*, 12 March 1924.
6 *Irish Examiner*, 27 November 1922.
7 McMahon, Paul, *British Spies and Irish Rebels*, p. 34.
8 *The Irish Times*, 1 March 1924.
9 *Irish Independent*, 3 March 1924.
10 *Evening Herald*, 18 March 1924.
11 *The Irish Times*, 1 March 1924.
12 *Evening Herald*, 1 March 1924.
13 *Freeman's Journal*, 13 March 1924.
14 *Irish Independent*, 19 March 1924.
15 *Freeman's Journal*, 13 March 1924.

16 *Evening Herald*, 1 March 1924.

17 *Ibid.*

Chapter 5

1   *Evening Herald*, 20 October 1924.
2   NAI Census 1911.
3   *Kilkenny People*, 13 December 1924.
4   *Munster Express*, 23 June 1923.
5   Hopkinson, Michael, *Green Against Green*, p. 263.
6   NAI Census 1901.
7   *Evening Herald*, 9 May 1925.
8   *Ibid.*, 20 October 1924.
9   *Donegal News*, 25 October 1924.
10 *Kilkenny People*, 13 December 1924.
11 *The Irish Times*, 8 May 1924.
12 *Ibid.*, 9 May 1924.
13 *Irish Examiner*, 10 May 1924.
14 *The Irish Times*, 21 October 1924.
15 *Irish Examiner*, 17 May 1924.
16 NAI, Department of Justice, H Files 249/16.

Chapter 6

1   NAI Department of the Taoiseach S 3058.
2   *Munster Express*, 6 May 1922.
3   Central Statistics Office, Census 1926.
4   De Vere White, Terence, *Kevin O'Higgins*, p. 174.
5   *Irish Independent*, 24 March 1925.
6   NAI, Department of Justice, H Files 67/5.
7   *Kilkenny People*, 30 December 2016.
8   UCD Archives, Desmond and Mabel Fitzgerald Collection P80 726.
9   *The Irish Times*, 30 December 1925.
10 *Irish Independent*, 30 December 1925.
11 *The Irish Times*, 16 January 1926.
12 *Ibid.*, 10 February 1926.
13 *Ibid.*, 23 April 1926.
14 *Kilkenny People*, 21 May 1999.
15 *Ibid.*, 2 January 1926.
16 *The Irish Times*, 13 February 1926.
17 *Irish Examiner*, 24 March 1926.
18 *The Irish Times*, 26 January 1926.
19 *Ibid.*, 27 January 1926.

20 *Ibid.*
21 *Irish Independent*, 28 January 1926.
22 *Irish Examiner*, 24 March 1926.
23 *Irish Independent*, 10 February 1926.
24 *Evening Herald*, 22 April 1926.
25 *Evening Herald*, 23 April 1926.
26 *Irish Independent*, 23 April 1926.
27 NAI, Department of Justice, H Files 235/129/12.
28 NAI, Department of the Taoiseach 235/129/15.

Chapter 7

1 *Evening Herald*, 9 March 1927.
2 Hanley, Brian, *The IRA 1926–1936*, p. 11.
3 *Irish Examiner*, 9 November 1926.
4 *Meath Chronicle*, 13 January 1973.
5 *Irish Independent*, 19 November 1926.
6 Ó Duibhir, Liam, *Prisoners of War*, p. 315.
7 *The Irish Times*, 19 November 1926.
8 English, Richard, *Armed Struggle*, p. 46.
9 *Irish Examiner*, 16 November 1926.
10 *Evening Herald*, 16 November 1926.
11 *Irish Examiner*, 10 March 1927.
12 *Evening Herald*, 16 November 1926.
13 Breen, Dan: *My Fight for Irish Freedom*, p. 111.
14 *Sunday Independent*, 30 January 1927.
15 *Irish Independent*, 17 November 1926.
16 *Evening Herald*, 15 November 1926.
17 *Irish Independent*, 16 November 1926.
18 *Leinster Express*, 22 November 1926.
19 *Irish Examiner*, 16 November 1926.
20 *Ibid.*
21 *Nenagh Guardian*, 27 November 1926.
22 *Irish Independent*, 19 November 1926.
23 *Irish Examiner*, 17 November 1926.
24 McCullagh, David, *John A. Costello, The Reluctant Taoiseach*, p. 68.
25 *Irish Independent*, 19 November 1926.
26 *An Phoblacht*, 6 May 1927.
27 *Irish Independent*, 20 November 1926.
28 *Limerick Leader*, 20 November 1926.
29 *Nenagh Guardian*, 12 November 1927.
30 *Meath Chronicle*, 20 November 1926.
31 Gillogly, James, *Decoding the IRA*, p. 109.

32 UCD Archives, Kevin O'Higgins Collection 197/170.
33 NAI, Department of the Taoiseach S 5260.
34 UCD Archives, Kevin O'Higgins Collection P197/100.
35 UCD Archives, Kevin O'Higgins Collection P197/218.
36 *The Irish Times*, 17 November 1927.
37 NAI, Department of Justice, H Files 235/129/12.
38 *Meath Chronicle*, 5 July 2014.

Chapter 8

1   NAI, Department of the Taoiseach, S6093A.
2   BMH, Witness Statement 602.
3   *Garda Review*, October 1932.
4   *Ibid.*
5   *An Phoblacht*, 22 June 1929.
6   UCD Archives, Desmond and Mabel Fitzgerald Collection P80/857.
7   *The Irish Times*, 22 June 1929.
8   *Irish Independent*, 18 November 1926.
9   *Ibid.*, 14 June 1929.
10 *Southern Star*, 22 June 1929.
11 *Ibid.*, 29 June 1929.
12 *Irish Independent*, 15 June 1929.
13 *Southern Star*, 15 May 2010.
14 *Irish Examiner*, 20 June 1929.
15 *The Irish Times*, 14 June 1929.
16 Hanley, Brian, *The IRA 1926–1936*, p. 122.
17 Central Fund Bill – Dáil debate – 14 March 1929.
18 *Ballina Herald*, 15 June 1929.
19 NAI, Department of the Taoiseach S5997.
20 *Southern Star*, 8 September 2007.
21 *An Phoblacht*, 29 June 1929.
22 *Ibid.*
23 Coogan, Tim Pat, *De Valera*, p. 431.
24 UCD Archives, Eamon de Valera Collection 150/2149.
25 *Kerry Reporter*, 17 September 1932.
26 *Irish Independent*, 25 June.
27 NAI, Department of the Taoiseach S5997.
28 *Ibid.*

Chapter 9

1   *Irish Examiner*, 23 March 1931.
2   *The Irish Times*, 11 November 1927.

3   *Ibid.*, 27 June 1931.
4   *Irish Examiner*, 21 June 1930.
5   *Ibid.*, 23 March 1929.
6   Marnane, Denis G., *Tipperary Historical Journal* 1992.
7   UCD Archives, Desmond and Mabel Fitzgerald Collection P80/856.
8   *Nenagh Guardian*, 21 March 1931.
9   *The Irish Times*, 27 June 1931.
10 *Irish Examiner*, 23 March 1931.
11 *The Irish Times*, 28 March 1931.
12 *Irish Independent*, 23 April 1931.
13 *The Irish Times*, 28 March 1931.
14 *Donegal News*, 18 April 1931.
15 *Nenagh Guardian*, 28 March 1931.
16 *Irish Examiner*, 24 May 1931.
17 *An Phoblacht*, 28 March 1931.
18 Coogan, Tim Pat, *Ireland in the Twentieth Century*, p. 208.
19 *Evening Herald*, 5 May 1931.
20 *Nenagh Guardian*, 5 December 1931.
21 Irish Statute Book, Constitution Amendment No. 17, 1931.
22 NAI, Department of Justice, H Files 235/129/32.
23 UCD Archives, Desmond and Mabel Fitzgerald Collection P80/856.
24 *Ibid.*
25 UCD Archives, Desmond and Mabel Fitzgerald Collection P80/857.
26 NAI, Department of the Taoiseach S2207A.
27 Coogan, Tim Pat, *Ireland in the Twentieth Century*, p. 194.
28 *Strabane Chronicle*, 8 August 1931.

Chapter 10

1   NAI, Department of Justice, H Files 235/129/51.
2   *Strabane Chronicle*, 20 February 1932.
3   *The Irish Times*, 8 March 1932.
4   *Leitrim Observer*, 12 March 1932.
5   *Longford Leader*, 20 February 1932.
6   *Leitrim Observer*, 12 March 1932.
7   *Evening Herald*, 19 February 1932.
8   *Leitrim Observer*, 27 February 1932.
9   *Evening Herald*, 7 March 1932.
10 *Ibid.*
11 *Longford Leader*, 12 March 1932.
12 *Leitrim Observer*, 27 February 1932.
13 *Irish Examiner*, 16 February 1932.
14 *Fermanagh Herald*, 27 February 1932.
15 *Leitrim Observer*, 12 March 1932.

16 *The Irish Times*, 10 March 1932.
17 *Ibid.*, 10 March 1932.
18 *Fermanagh Herald*, 20 February 1932.
19 *Evening Herald*, 10 March 1932.
20 NAI, Department of Justice, 235/129/51.

Chapter 11

1 *Irish Press*, 2 February 1948.
2 Carroll, Joseph T., *Ireland in the War Years*, p. 15.
3 MacEoin, Uinseann, *Harry*, p. 74.
4 Seán O'Mahony Papers, NLI, M/S 44, 075/2.
5 *Irish War*, 13 July 1940.
6 *Irish Press*, 6 January 1940.
7 *The Irish Times*, 27 April 1935
8 NAI, Department of the Taoiseach S8209.
9 *Irish Press*, 24 March 1941.
10 *Evening Herald*, 22 March 1941.
11 *Donegal News*, 6 January 1940.
12 NAI, Department of the Taoiseach S11931.
13 *Irish Press*, 2 February 1940.
14 *Ibid.*
15 NAI, Department of the Taoiseach S11931.
16 *Irish Press*, 3 February 1940.
17 *Irish Independent*, 5 January 1940.
18 *Irish Press*, 4 January 1940.
19 Seán O'Mahony Papers, NLI, MS 44, 075/5.
20 *Irish Independent*, 8 January 1940.
21 NAI, Department of the Taoiseach S11931.
22 *Irish Press*, 13 January 1940.
23 Seán O'Mahony Papers, NLI, M/S 44, 075/5.
24 Maguire, John, *IRA Internments and the Irish Government*, p. 32.
25 *The Irish Times*, 15 June 1940.
26 *Irish Press*, 3 February 1940.
27 *Ibid.*, 12 June 1940.
28 *Ibid.*, 12 June 1940.
29 Seán O'Mahony Papers, NLI, MS 44, 075/5.
30 *Irish Press*, 13 June 1940.
31 MacBride, Seán, *That Day's Struggle*, p. 127.
32 NAI, Department of the Taoiseach S 11931.
33 MacBride, Seán, *That Day's Struggle*, p. 127.
34 *The Irish Times*, 21 May 1946.

35 *Irish Press*, 15 March 1948.
36 Garda Síochána Compensation Act – Dáil Debate – 1 February 1945.

Chapter 12

1   BMH, National Army Census 1922.
2   *Irish Press*, 17 August 1940.
3   Seán O'Mahony Papers, NLI, M/S 44, 076/10.
4   *The Irish Times*, 28 September 1940.
5   *Ibid.*
6   *Evening Herald*, 20 August 1940.
7   *Irish Examiner*, 21 August 1940.
8   *Irish Independent*, 21 August 1940.
9   *Kerryman*, 11 November 1939.
10 *New York Times*, 21 August 1940.
11 *The Irish Times*, 22 August 1940.
12 *Ibid.*, 27 August 1940.
13 *Irish Independent*, 27 August 1940.
14 *The Irish Times*, 27 August 1940.
15 *Ibid.*, 18 September 1940.
16 *Ibid.*, 28 September 1940.
17 *Irish Independent*, 22 November 1940.
18 *Irish Press*, 20 September 1948.

Chapter 13

1   *Irish Independent*, 10 September 1942.
2   BMH, Witness Statement 0805.
3   *Irish Press*, 10 September 1932.
4   UCD Archives, Éamon de Valera Collection 150/2133.
5   MacEoin, Uinseann, *Harry*, p. 105.
6   *Irish Independent*, 12 January 1943.
7   *Evening Herald*, 2 October 1942.
8   *Irish Examiner*, 10 September 1942.
9   *Irish Independent*, 12 September 1942.
10 *Irish Press*, 15 September 1942.
11 *Ibid.*, 11 September 1942.
12 *New York Times*, 10 September 1942.
13 *Irish Examiner*, 10 October 1942.
14 *Ibid.*, 16 January 1943.
15 *Evening Herald*, 2 October 1944.
16 Seán O'Mahony Papers, NLI, M/S 44, 076/8.
17 CCA Files, 94/1944.

18 *Irish Press*, 3 October 1944.
19 CCA Files, 94/1944.
20 *Irish Examiner*, 3 October 1944.
21 *Irish Press*, 6 October 1944.
22 *Evening Herald*, 5 October 1944.
23 *Irish Examiner*, 5 October 1944.
24 *Irish Press*, 7 October 1944.
25 CCA Files, 1944/44.
26 *Irish Press*, 16 November 1944.
27 *Ibid.*, 30 November 1944.
28 *Ibid.*, 2 December 1944.
29 *Evening Herald*, 2 November 1944.
30 Seán O'Mahony Papers NLI, M/S 44, 076/5.
31 Seán O'Mahony Papers, NLI, M/S 44, 076/8.
32 *The Irish Times*, 2 December 1944.
33 *Irish Press*, 2 December 1944.
34 *Kerryman*, 25 September 1948.
35 Maguire, John, *IRA Internments and the Irish Government*, p. 53.
36 *Irish Press*, 1 August 1945.

Chapter 14

1 *Irish Examiner*, 2 October 1942.
2 *Irish Independent*, 2 October 1942.
3 Maguire, John, *IRA Internments and the Irish Government*, p. 3.
4 MacEoin, Uinseann, *Harry*, p. 112.
5 *Westmeath Examiner*, 10 October 1942.
6 *Anglo-Celt*, 5 December 1942.
7 *Ibid.*
8 *Irish Press*, 30 November 1942.
9 *Meath Chronicle*, 10 October 1942.
10 *Irish Examiner*, 30 November 1942.
11 *Irish Press*, 5 October 1942.
12 *The Irish Times*, 30 November 1942.
13 *Irish Press*, 30 November 1942.
14 *Ibid.*, 21 December 1943.
15 *Anglo-Celt*, 30 May 1996.
16 MacEoin, Uinseann, *Harry*, p. 114.

Chapter 15

1 BMH, National Army Census 1922.
2 *Irish Examiner*, 3 May 1943.

3   MacEoin, Uinseann, *Harry*, p. 120.
4   *The Irish Times*, 3 November 1942.
5   *Irish Examiner*, 3 November 1942.
6   *Ibid.*
7   *The Irish Times*, 3 November 1942.
8   *Magill*, March 1999.
9   *Irish Independent*, 27 October 1942.
10 *The Irish Times*, 3 November 1942.
11 *Irish Examiner*, 3 November 1942.
12 *Irish Independent*, 5 November 1942.
13 *The Irish Times*, 5 November 1942.
14 *Irish Independent*, 7 February 1949.
15 *The Irish Times*, 6 November 1942.
16 NAI, Department of the Taoiseach S13975.
17 *Irish Press*, 3 November 1942.
18 *The Irish Times*, 3 November 1942.
19 Seán O'Mahony Papers, NLI, M/S 44, 076/5.
20 *Irish Press*, 1 August 1945.

Chapter 16

1   *Nenagh Guardian*, 22 April 1944.
2   NAI, Census 1911.
3   *Evening Herald*, 17 April 1944.
4   *The Irish Times*, 18 April 1944.
5   *Nenagh Guardian*, 22 April 1944.
6   *Irish Independent*, 18 April 1944.
7   *Nenagh Guardian*, 22 April 1944.
8   *Irish Press*, 26 January 1945.
9   *Nenagh Guardian*, 3 February 1945.
10 *Irish Press*, 31 July 1945.
11 *Irish Examiner*, 14 January 1937.
12 *Irish Press*, 11 March 1937.

Chapter 17

1   *Irish Independent*, 21 November 1929.
2   *The Irish Times*, 8 July 1937.
3   NAI, Census 1911.
4   *Evening Herald*, 21 November 1946.
5   *Limerick Leader*, 7 February 1921.
6   *The Irish Times*, 21 November 1946.
7   *Evening Herald*, 21 November 1946.

8   *Irish Examiner*, 20 November 1946.
9   *The Irish Times*, 21 November 1946.
10 *Irish Independent*, 21 November 1946.
11 *Irish Examiner*, 20 November 1946.
12 Wallace, Colm, *Sentenced to Death: Saved from the Gallows*, p. 150.
13 *Irish Independent*, 20 November 1946.
14 *Irish Examiner*, 27 September 1946.
15 *Ibid.*, 20 November 1946.
16 *Evening Herald*, 4 October 1946.
17 *Ibid.*, 19 November 1946.
18 *Irish Times*, 21 November 1946.
19 *Irish Examiner*, 22 November 1946.
20 *Irish Press*, 22 November 1946.
21 *The Irish Times*, 7 December 1946.

Chapter 18

1   *Irish Independent*, 16 September 2007.
2   *Ibid.*, 21 December 1946.
3   *The Irish Times*, 22 January 1948.
4   *Irish Independent*, 22 January 1948.
5   *Ibid.*
6   *The Irish Times*, 31 January 1948.
7   *Irish Examiner*, 22 January 1948.
8   *The Irish Times*, 28 February 1948.
9   *Irish Independent*, 22 January 1948.
10 *Ibid.*, 2 March 1948.
11 *Irish Press*, 10 March 1948.
12 *The Irish Times*, 7 June 1948.
13 *Ibid.*
14 *Irish Examiner*, 22 June 1948.
15 *Leitrim Observer*, 1 January 1949.
16 *Irish Independent*, 9 September 1953.

FURTHER READING

Abbot, Richard, *Police Casualties in Ireland 1919-1922* (Dublin; Mercier Press, 2000)

Allen, Gregory, *The Garda Síochána: Policing Independent Ireland 1922–1982* (Dublin; Gill and MacMillan, 1999)

Bew, Paul and Patterson, Henry, *Seán Lemass and the Making of Modern Ireland 1945–1966* (Dublin; Gill and MacMillan, 1982)

Brady, Conor, *Guardians of the Peace* (Dublin; Gill and MacMillan, 1974)

Breen, Dan, *My Fight for Irish Freedom* (Dublin; Talbot Press, 1924)

Carey, Tim, *Hanged for Murder* (Cork; Mercier Press, 2013)

Carroll, Joseph T., *Ireland in the War Years* (Dublin; David and Charles, 1975)

Coogan, Tim Pat, *Ireland in the Twentieth Century* (London; Hutchinson, 2003)

Coogan, Tim Pat, *De Valera: Long Fellow, Long Shadow* (London; Hutchinson, 1993)

Corcoran, Donal P., *Freedom to Achieve Freedom, The Irish Free State 1922–1932* (Dublin; Gill and MacMillan, 2013)

Costello, Peter, *Dublin Castle in the Life of the Irish Nation* (Dublin; Wolfhound Press, 1999)

De Vere White, Terence, *Kevin O'Higgins* (London; Halcyon Books, 1948)

Deale, Kenneth E.L., *Beyond Any Reasonable Doubt?* (Dublin; Gill and MacMillan, 1971)

English, Richard, *Armed Struggle: The History of the IRA* (Oxford; Oxford University Press, 2003)

Garvin, Tom, *1922: The Birth of Irish Democracy* (Dublin; Gill and MacMillan, 1996)

Girvan, Brian, *The Emergency: Neutral Ireland 1939–1945* (London; Pan, 2006)

Hanley, Brian, *The IRA 1926-1936* (Dublin; Four Courts Press, 2002)

Hopkinson, Michael, *Green Against Green: The Irish Civil War* (Dublin; Gill and MacMillan, 1988)

Hopkinson, Michael, *The Irish War of Independence* (Dublin; McGill-Queen's University Press, 2002)

Kelleher, Patrick, *One Mortal Night: A Miscarriage of Justice* (Bantry; Somerville Press, 2010)

Lawlor George and Reddy, Tom, *The Murder File: An Irish Detective's Casebook* (Dublin; Gill and MacMillan, 1991)

Leeson, D.M., *The Black and Tans: British Police and Auxiliaries in the Irish War of Independence* (Oxford; Oxford University Press, 2011)

Macardle, Dorothy, *The Irish Republic* (Dublin; Irish Press, 1937)

MacBride, Seán, *That Day's Struggle* (Dublin; Currach Press, 2005)

MacEoin, Uinseann, *Harry* (Dublin; Argenta Publications, 1986)

Maguire, John, *IRA Internments and the Irish Government: Subversives and the State 1939–1962* (Dublin; Academic Press, 2008)

Maguire, Michael, *The Civil Service and the Revolution in Ireland 1912–1938* (Manchester; Manchester University Press, 2008)

McCarthy, Brian, *The Civic Guard Mutiny* (Cork; Mercier Press, 2012)

McCullagh, David, *John A. Costello, the Reluctant Taoiseach* (Dublin; Mercier Press, 2010)

McGarry, Fearghal, *Eoin O'Duffy: A Self-Made Hero* (Oxford; Oxford University Press, 2005)

McVeigh, Joe, *Executed: The Life and Death of Tom Williams* (Belfast; Beyond the Pale, 1999)

O'Brien, Mark, *De Valera, Fianna Fáil and the Irish Press* (Dublin; Irish Academic Press, 2001)

Ó Duibhir, Liam, *Prisoners of War: Ballykinlar Internment Camp 1920–1921* (Dublin; Mercier Press, 2013)

O'Halpin, Eunan, *Defending Ireland: The Irish State and its Enemies since 1922* (Oxford; Oxford University Press, 1999)

Pierrepoint, Albert, *Executioner: Pierrepoint* (London; Harrap, 1974)

Regan, John M., *The Irish Counter-revolution 1921–1936: Treatyite Politics and Settlement in Independent Ireland* (New York; St Martin's Press, 1999)

Reynolds, John, *46 Men Dead: The Royal Irish Constabulary in County Tipperary 1919–1922* (Cork; Collins Press, 2016)

Ryan, Meda, *Liam Lynch, The Real Chief* (Dublin; Mercier Press, 2005)

Wallace, Colm, *Sentenced to Death: Saved from the Gallows* (Bantry; Somerville Press, 2016)

Walsh, Liz, *The Final Beat* (Dublin; Gill and MacMillan, 2001)

INDEX

Abwehr 142
Agrarian Violence 15, 74–5,
Aiken, Frank 45
Anglo-Irish Treaty 9–17, 23, 27–9,
    35, 45, 55, 73, 87–90, 156,
    169–171, 182, 186, 194, 211
Aran Islands 74
Arbour Hill Prison 164
Armstrong, Albert 112
Army Mutiny 46
Auxiliary Division 8–9

Ballykinlar Internment Camp 89
Ballyseedy Massacre 27
Baltinglass 37–50
Barnes, Peter 149, 182
Barry, Tom 104
Black and Tans, the 8, 9, 14, 43,
    81, 88, 214, 225
Blueshirts, the 114, 144, 171, 172
Bodenstown 113, 125
Boland, Gerald 181, 202, 226
Boland, Harry 181
Brosnan, Thomas 33–4
Broy Harriers 171
Brugha, Cathal 156

Casey, Con 97
Castlepollard 186–7
Clann na Poblachta 153

Collins, Michael 7, 12, 96
Collins' Barracks 150, 163, 164,
    177, 198
Connaught 15, 139
Connemara 74, 185
Cosgrave, W.T. 96, 97, 113, 114,
    135
Courts of Justice Act 233
Criminal Investigation
    Department (CID) 13, 51,
    54–5, 59–60, 105, 123, 133
Cumann na mBan 123, 169–70
Cumann na nGaedheal 111, 119,
    127, 129, 135, 138, 170, 171
Curragh Camp, the 18, 42

D'Arcy, Tony 150
de Valera, Éamon 8, 76, 101, 113,
    126, 134, 141, 145, 153, 156,
    161, 164, 171, 174, 179, 182
Death Penalty, the 50, 59, 82, 124,
    150, 163–8, 179, 181, 199, 201,
    221
Doyle, Archie 182, 187
Dromkeen Ambush 214
Dublin Castle 8, 17, 155–7, 171,
    194, 226, 234
Dublin Metropolitan Police
    (DMP) 10, 41, 44, 50, 53–9,
    105, 156

Duffy, Justice Gavan 165
Duggan, Éamon 9

Easter Rising 8, 43, 143, 160, 166, 169
Electricity Supply Board 170, 177, 178
Emergency, the 142, 144, 167, 172, 182, 183, 187, 188, 192, 202, 226, 227, 231, 235
Emergency Legislation 37, 96, 112, 119, 125, 143, 145, 161, 165, 185

Fallon, Richard 235
Famine, the 8
Fascism 171
Fianna Fáil 97, 101, 106, 11, 125–7, 134, 138, 141–5, 152–6, 164, 166, 170, 121, 178–82, 185, 226
Firing Squads 16, 166, 183, 201
Fitzgerald, Desmond 123
Fitzgerald-Kenney, James 113
Frongoch 166

'G' Division 55, 105
Gaelic Athletic Association (GAA) 97, 124
Gaffney, Jeremiah 33, 59
Garda Síochána Compensation Act 211
Garda Síochána Temporary Provision Act 16
Germany 142, 143, 183
Gilmore, George 114
Gortz, Hermann 226
Goss, Richard 198
Green Street Courthouse 46, 59, 135, 163
Gweedore 75

Hammam Hotel 156
Hayes, Stephen 177

Hunger Strike 149, 150, 161

Intoxicating Liquor Act 75
Irish Language, the 75, 206
Irish Republican Army (IRA) 7–37, 61–73, 87–127, 141–205
Irish Republican Police 9

Jerry McCabe 235

Kildare Mutiny 12, 13
Kilkee 15
Kilroy, Michael 97, 150
Kilrush 114
Kickham, Charles 19

Land Commission 214
Land War, the 8
Larkin, Michael 225
Leen, Denis 33
Lemass, Seán 171, 188
Lourdes 67

MacBride, Seán 150–3, 165–7, 175, 180, 200–2
Mac Curtain, Tomás (Snr) 143, 144, 149, 150
MacEoin, Seán 182
MacNeela, Seán 150
MacNeill, Eoin 9
Madden John, Dr 97
Manchester Martyrs 225
McAteer, Hugh 175–7
McCabe, Henry 89
McCarthy, Seán 97
McCormack, James 182
McGlade, Charlie 172
Mellows, Liam 170
Military Tribunals 124, 150, 171
Mountjoy Prison 60, 98, 135, 138, 161, 166, 167, 170, 181, 223, 227, 232, 233
Mulcahy, Richard 9
Munster 15, 206

Munster Republic 27

Neligan, David 113, 171
Newbridge Camp 170
Northern Ireland 87, 142, 153,
    156, 167, 182, 186, 199

O'Connor, Rory 14, 170
O'Duffy, Eoin 7, 12, 18, 19, 22,
    28, 33, 67, 75, 99, 100, 111,
    122, 124, 126, 171
O'Dwyer, Sonny 63–71
O'Higgins, Kevin 9, 34, 36, 54, 63,
    74, 99–101, 122, 183
O'Kelly, Ciarán 182
Offences Against the State Act
    145, 157, 161
Oriel House 13, 54, 105
Orr, William 225

Phoblacht, An 97, 112, 123, 124
Phoenix Park Depot 68, 143
Pierrepoint, Thomas 181
Portlaoise Prison 153, 201, 233
Poteen 74–85

Quille, Michael 175–80

Rathmore Murder, the 226
Rebellion of 1798 225
Rebellion of 1867 225
Reynolds, Mary 138
Rice, Liam 172
Royal Irish Constabulary (RIC)
    8–12, 18, 24, 29, 87, 93, 104,
    118, 130, 145
Royal Showgrounds 11
Royal Ulster Constabulary (RUC)
    142, 167, 182, 201
Russell, Seán 143
Ryan, TJ 112–14

Saor Éire 123
Scotland 143

Sheehy, John J. 97
Ship Street Barracks 17
Soloheadbeg Ambush 8, 118
Special Branch 105, 113, 120,
    126, 144, 155, 160, 171, 172,
    185, 194, 211, 226, 233
Staines, Michael 10, 12
Stephens, James 18
Sydney Street Siege 228

Treacy, Seán 93

United States of America 24, 75

Vice-Admiral Henry Somerville
    142

Wales 143
White, Harry 172, 175, 182, 187,
    188, 191–202, 226
Williams, Tom 182
Wolfe Tone 15
Wolfhill 45